DO YOU REALLY NEED A LAWYER?

Some say the practice of law is the oldest profession of all. A doctor, an attorney, and an engineer were having an argument as to which of their callings had been in existence the longest.

"Everyone knows," said the physician, "that the practice of medicine is the oldest profession. Why, when God created Eve from Adam's rib, He performed an act of surgery. So medicine is the oldest profession."

"Not so," protested the engineer. "Even before Adam, God created the earth and the heavens. And anybody can tell you that this act of creation was a feat of planning and engineering. So engineering is the oldest profession," he added proudly. "Why before that, there was nothing but chaos and confusion."

"Aha," beamed the lawyer, "but who caused the chaos and confusion!"

HOW TO AVOID LAWYERS

A Legal Guide for Laymen

NEWLY REVISED

by Edward Siegel, Attorney-At-Law

FAWCETT CREST • NEW YORK

TO HELEN
Whose encouragement
made this book possible

CONTENTS

Chapter 4: SO YOU THINK YOU WANT A DIVORCE

Chapter 5: SO YOU'RE WONDERING ABOUT A WILL

Chapter 6: SO YOU'RE GOING INTO BUSINESS

FOREWORD

I never cease to be amazed at the public unawareness of elementary legal procedures and techniques, and of the widespread suspicion and hesitation about going to a lawyer. Because of this, I felt a real need existed for this book.

I don't intend it to be a comprehensive "text" of the law, or a general treatise of legal concepts or abstract principles. Rather, I have attempted to cover the practical side of the law, as the average person might encounter it, in several basic areas, with down-to-earth suggestions and warnings.

I have tried to avoid being too technical. In many cases, this has required a superficial treatment of some complex problems. My purpose, though, was not to teach the reader to be a lawyer, but to show him how to avoid attorneys, when possible, and what to expect when he does need a lawyer's assistance.

In several situations, I refer to the great variation in state laws. Someday there may be more uniformity across the country. But until then, the reader should understand that he can't always rely on the "majority rule," unless he checks to see that his state fits into that category. Primarily because of this difference in state laws, you'll find that the advice given in a number of places in the book is general, rather than specific, since it's not practical to deal with every possible legal difficulty that might arise. I hope, though, that enough concrete illustrations are furnished so that the reader will know how to cope with a variety of legal problems, what steps to take, and some of the hazards.

The forms at the end of each chapter obviously can't cover every conceivable legal contingency. If they did, they'd be too detailed and cumbersome for use. Instead, I have tried to put in the most important, and most common provisions found in the usual case, with appropriate alternatives that can be adapted to fit other circumstances.

If you care to, you can read the book straight through, from cover to cover. Or you can jump from one part to another, since each chapter is a separate unit. But don't put the book aside. Keep it handy so that you can refer to it when a particular legal difficulty comes up.

We live in a hectic, troubled world. The law changes from day to day. Much of our law is archaic and perplexing. This book, obviously, isn't intended as a substitute for a good attorney, and sometimes, of course, you'll need a lawyer. I hope, though, that the following pages will help you to know when that time arises, and how to meet it.

EDWARD SIEGEL

CHAPTER 1

So You Were Hurt In An Accident

COURTROOMS ARE LIKE HOSPITALS; THEY'RE O.K. IF YOU DON'T have to go there. Unfortunately, if you drive an automobile, your chances of landing in one or both places increase every day.

Most lawyers will tell you that cases involving car accidents make up almost one-fourth of all the courtroom litigation in the United States. And whether you agree or not, most of these accidents don't "happen"; they're caused. More than five million people will be injured in one this year. It's not likely, though, that this will encourage you to walk, especially since pedestrians haven't learned to avoid automobiles.

So suppose you become one of that rapidly expanding species who have "been in an accident." What should you do? Should you see a lawyer right away? Is it best to try to handle it yourself? How do you start?

A. The Whiplash Injury

Let's assume you're happily driving the family limousine to work one morning, studiously observing the traffic signals. You carefully slow down for a red light, and come to a complete stop. A second later you hear the dreaded sound of brakes squealing, a loud crash behind you, and you are jolted forward. You've been rear-ended. Welcome to the growing army of "whiplash" injuries!

If you're typical of those hurt in such an accident—and the number increases every day—you may not even feel any pain or discomfort right away. The damage to the car may even be minor.

But don't fall into the trap.

The so-called "whiplash," or sprain of the cervical area, can be a serious and painful injury that often doesn't bother you until two or three days after the accident. X-rays will generally show nothing abnormal since the damage is to the "soft" tissue, and, typically, will not appear in the x-rays. The term "whiplash" describes the way the head is snapped back and then forward and down, and can involve a wrenching or tearing of the neck muscles. It can cause severe head pains, dizziness, numbness, nervousness, and a number of related symptoms.

B. The First Contact with the Adjuster

If the other driver had insurance, it's likely that the company adjuster will come bounding up your front porch that evening with a big smile and an offer of $25 for a release (unless you're in a state with the new "no-fault" insurance; more on this in Section D). *Don't sign anything!* In fact, the best advice at that point is don't even talk to him. Tell him politely, but firmly, that you're not ready to discuss the claim, and that you'll be in touch with him at some future time.

He probably won't give up that easily, and will want to take a statement from you. It's dangerous and foolhardy for you to give him one, at least at that time. Most adjusters are honest, but many have a charming, if unintentional, habit of slanting the story, at best, and putting down some of the information inaccurately, at worst.

"Oh," you say, "I'll correct any mistakes when I read it over." But all too often you won't catch the subtle slanting. Or you'll miss the mistake. Or you might not realize you've given him some incorrect item. Or you may not be sure of a "small" detail (such as speed or distance or time of day), which the adjuster will "prompt" you into estimating, often adversely to your claim.

So rule one: do not—(REPEAT!)—do not give any statement to the adjuster, at the beginning.

It's wise for you to write out your own version of the facts, for yourself, while the accident is still fresh in your mind; but giving the adjuster a statement without thinking it out—and without understanding the law involved—can be devastating to your claim.

The adjuster may agree to your "no statement" desire, but then start pumping you with questions, anyway. Often he'll have a tape recorder in his coat pocket. Don't discuss the claim with him. Again, tell him courteously that you'll contact him later.

He may even imply that you must have something to hide if you're "afraid" to talk to him. Don't be fooled. You have plenty of time to talk to him, at *your* convenience.

By not giving the adjuster a statement, you'll accomplish the following:

1. Save yourself from botching the claim at the very beginning.
2. Give the adjuster some worries, and put him on the defensive.

C. Should You See a Lawyer?

What's the next step? Should you see a lawyer?

For the so-called "bread-and-butter" type of injury—the typical rear-end case or the cuts-and-bruises situation—you can often handle it yourself with satisfactory results, if you know what you're doing, and where to begin.

But if your claim involves substantial and major injuries (long hospitalization, serious multiple fractures, or the probability of permanent disability), you'll generally be better off to turn the matter over to an attorney without delay, since these cases are too complicated to "do-it-yourself."

Even for the "major" injuries, though, there's one notable exception where you can get good results on your own: if you're certain that the other driver had only the minimum required amount of insurance coverage. This amount varies in each state (and should be checked), but the most common figure is $10,000 for injuries to one person. In such a situation, if your injuries are *clearly* worth more than the insurance coverage, you can probably get the adjuster to pay the full policy limit, or very close to it, without an attorney. But be *sure* you know the amount of insurance before you sign the release. Demand to see the policy, or a photocopy of it.

D. Where to Begin to "Do-It-Yourself"

To start with, you should understand that the law permits an injured person (if he's not at fault) to recover certain items of "damage" over and above out-of-pocket expenses. This means you're entitled to money for pain and suffering, for inability to do work or household chores, and for disfigurement. This is perfectly proper, and you shouldn't feel that you're doing anything wrong by asking to be reimbursed for such damages.

However, if your state has passed a "no-fault" insurance law, your right to collect these damages is greatly restricted. "No-fault" is a new concept which requires your own insurance company to pay you certain expenses—such as lost income and medical bills—regardless of fault. Sounds fine, so far. But in exchange, you give up your right to recover anything for your pain—unless you can show extraordinary injuries (for example, the statute might require permanent disability or $1,000 in medical bills before you can collect). So some of the comments in this chapter may not apply if your state has "no-fault" insurance of the type limiting your right to collect for pain and suffering.

Otherwise, as soon as you can, you should get a copy of the police report, which will be furnished to you, in most states, for a nominal charge, generally $1.00 to $3.00. Customarily, the report will show the names and addresses of the parties and witnesses (although the police often omit listing some key witnesses); name of the insurance company; the weather and road conditions; a diagram of the scene of the accident; and other pertinent details. A copy of a report used in Florida is shown at the end of the chapter.

If you can talk to the witnesses before the insurance adjuster speaks to them, you'll stand a good chance of getting them committed to your side of the case. Try to get them to write out what they saw, in their own words, but if they're not willing to do this, then jot down on a pad some notes of what they tell you, and have them sign the paper.

Some of the important points to cover are: (1) the name, address, age, and marital status of the witness. (2) where the witness was when the accident happened. (3) the directions the cars were going. (4) the speeds. (5) any traffic control. (6) weather and road conditions. (7) names of any other witnesses known to him. (8) any statements he heard the other driver make. (9) any evidence of intoxication. (10) place of impact. (11) any obstructions to view. (12) how the accident happened.

It many states, it is necessary to give the witness a copy of the statement, so be sure to have some carbon paper with you.

If you're physically or emotionally unable to hop around from witness to witness, or are not the "interviewing" type, and if there's a good chance that the insurance adjuster will claim you were at fault in the accident, then you should consider the advisability of consulting a lawyer to help you.

But in a surprisingly large number of cases, there will be no real dispute about the other driver being at fault. It may be a case where he's drunk (and arrested by the investigating officer), or went through a stop sign, or clearly violated some other law. If you can get one witness, in such a situation, to give you a statement, you will probably need no others.

Don't always count on the police report for help, though. Generally, the police report cannot be used as evidence in court; and in many states any statements to the officer are considered "privileged" and not admissible against the driver. On the other hand, if the police report indicates that the other driver is solely to blame, it's likely the insurance company won't fight too hard on the point. The adjuster may try to bluff you on the question of fault, but you'll have the stronger hand.

E. Your Doctor

If you have a family doctor, you should plan to have him examine you as soon as possible. Even if your aches are minor, don't try to treat them yourself. An aspirin and some rest may be all you really need, but it is just as likely that you have some injury you're not aware of. Just as important—from the standpoint of being paid for your damages—is the fact that your injuries will be worth much more, in the adjuster's eyes, if they warrant going to a doctor (even if the doctor can't find anything seriously wrong with you).

If you don't see a doctor, but you still try to claim you had cuts and bruises, or pains, and that you lost time from work, you won't get much of an offer for your injuries. But if you do see your doctor, and have him write a report (as explained later), the settlement value of your case improves tremendously.

When your injury is mild, your doctor will probably see you two to six times, on the average (occasionally more), without any complicated treatment. You can expect, in the typical situation, to be x-rayed, given some pills, told to rest for a few days, and possibly advised to take some heat therapy.

If the injury is more serious, you may have to wear a cervical collar (a neck brace) for a few weeks. This can be uncomfortable, and literally, a "pain in the neck," but it will help the value of the claim (and hopefully your recovery). Your doctor may also refer you to a specialist, such as an orthopedist (bone doctor) or a neurologist (specialist in nervous system disorders).

You should not consider trying to settle your case until the doctor discharges you. This could take only a few days, or several months. When he does discharge you, it doesn't necessarily mean that you're "cured"; it may mean that you've reached "maximum medical improvement," and that there's not much else the doctor can do for you, medically, even though you're still having discomfort.

At any rate, when the doctor discharges you, you should request that he send you a medical report. Specifically, you will want the report to outline his findings, treatment, diagnosis, and prognosis. The prognosis, or prediction of any future disability and pain, is the most important part of the report. You'll probably be relieved if it shows "no permanent disability," but such a report will kick a good sized hole in the value of your claim. If he says you'll keep having some pain or difficulties for a few more weeks, this is better than the "no-permanent-disability" letter, but not much.

Some physicians will routinely report that the prognosis is "guarded," or that you'll continue to suffer for an undetermined period of time in the future. This is really the fairest kind of report in a great many cases, since the doctor obviously has no crystal ball. This language considerably increases the settlement value of your case, but, unfortunately, most doctors will not write that kind of report.

The doctor may tell you, during the examination, that you will have some pain or discomfort for a few more months, and will learn "to live with it." However, when you get the report, you'll find no mention of this prognosis, but merely the optimistic conclusion of "no permanent disability." If this happens, don't hesitate to immediately call the doctor and remind him—tactfully—of what he had told you in his office. Ask him to revise the report and include the statement of future pain or discomfort, and his opinion that you'll learn to live with it. This one sentence, in his report, will substantially raise your settlement prospects.

If your injury will produce any kind of permanent scarring, even if minor, be sure the doctor includes this in the report. Any mention of a "permanent" condition will greatly enhance the value of the claim.

Incidentally, within the last few years, it's become common for many doctors to make a charge for writing a report. This can vary from $50 to as much as $150 for specialists. It's wise to get some idea, in advance, from the doctor's secretary, about the charge. Regardless of the cost, though, you should consider the report as indispensable to your claim, since you will generally only get a "nuisance" type of settlement (under $500) without the report.

One caution: don't sign any authorization for the doctor to release medical reports to the insurance adjuster. Let the report come to you first. If it's a fair report, then you can forward a copy to the adjuster. By coming through you, you'll have the opportunity of reviewing the report and getting it revised by the doctor, when appropriate. If it goes direct to the adjuster, without your looking it over beforehand, then it's too late to get any additions by the doctor. You may end up, in such a situation, with two strikes against you before you even submit the claim.

F. What about Photographs?

If your accident causes any injury that is visible (such as a burn, deep cuts, or large, discolored bruises), you should consider having some photographs taken immediately. Frequently, "home-made" pictures will be adequate, but if you can afford to pay a commercial photographer, let him take them for you. Usually, two photos are sufficient. In a particularly graphic or gory injury, you should have color photos. These are expensive, but can be quite dramatic, and can add to the settlement.

Give the pictures to the adjuster, but make sure you keep the negatives in case the originals get lost.

Sometimes it will help your claim to take a few shots of the damage to your car, especially if the damage is extensive. If the repairs are minor, forget about pictures.

G. Getting the Bills Together

You now have the doctor's medical report (and photographs, if appropriate). Your next step should be to make copies of all your bills, even the ones that may have been paid by Blue Cross or other insurance. These bills will include the medical expense, drug bills, car repair estimate (or bill), and car rental expense. Some adjusters will give you an argument on the car rental, but in most states it's proper if you rented a car while yours was being fixed.

If you lost any time from your job, try to get a statement from your employer, listing the days (or hours) missed and your pay scale. You should do this even in cases where you have no actual loss of money, as, for example, when your salary—or part of it—is paid by your own insurance, or by taking sick leave, or some other wage continuation plan of your employer. Under the law in many jurisdictions, these payments to you are said to come from a "collateral source," and can be claimed by you in determining your damages, even though you are paid.

There's nothing immoral or illegal about this, since the wrong-doer (the one causing the accident) and his insurance company are not entitled to reap the benefit of your sick leave or other plan that allows you to continue to draw your wages. So if you missed a month's work because of your injuries at, say, $1,000 a month, you're entitled to claim a $1,000 loss, even if you were paid for the lost time.

Don't expect the adjuster to give in gracefully on this. Very often he'll want to know whether you actually did lose any income. Since you have probably been charged with sick leave, it is not unfair to say that you have, indeed, suffered a financial loss. If he tells you you're not entitled to claim lost wages without an actual loss of salary, you should tell him that under the collateral source rule, it's perfectly legitimate. Surprisingly, most adjusters don't know this.

When you have all your bills and expenses together, list them on a piece of paper. It's also a good idea to throw in an estimate for transportation costs in going to and from the doctor. The adjuster generally won't complain if your figure is between $25 and $50. If it's more, you'll probably need to justify it.

If you haven't kept your drug receipts, but you know you've spent money on aspirin, sleeping pills, and other medication, you can get by with "estimating" drug expense. A figure of $25 to $50 will usually not be questioned too strenuously.

You should also add something for "future medical expense"—anywhere from $50 to $300, depending on your injury and what your doctor has reported.

H. Submitting the Claim

So now you're ready to submit the claim. Write out (or, better yet, type) a summary of how the accident happened and what your injuries were. Don't exaggerate, but point them out as forcefully as you can, emphasizing whatever discomfort you're still having. If you're continuing to have some problems sleeping at night, or digesting your food, or if you're jumpy and nervous, be sure to say so. And never say you're having "headaches." Everybody has headaches. Call them "head pains." A model form of a Statement of Claim is reproduced at the end of the chapter.

How much should you ask for, and how do you decide what your injuries are worth? This is tough even for experienced lawyers, since there's no accurate yardstick to measure pain and suffering. But there are certain guides or formulas that are helpful.

One such rule-of-thumb, used successfully by many insurance companies, is that a claim is worth three to four times the amount of the "out-of-pocket" expenses (sometimes spoken of as the "specials," meaning the special damages you've suffered). According to this approach, if you have $300 in expenses, your claim should be worth $900 to $1,200.

Don't believe it!

This so-called "rule" is strictly an insurance company gimmick. It's arbitrary and illogical, and shouldn't be used as a guide. In many cases, the amount of the "specials" has no reasonable relationship whatsoever to the pain and disability suffered. For example, an accident may cause the amputation of a foot, with medical bills of only a few hundred dollars. But certainly such a claim would be worth many thousands of dollars.

On the other hand, the value of a claim necessarily does have some relationship to the amount of your bills. Why? Because a claim with doctor bills of $500 will be worth more than a claim with bills of $50. The adjuster will normally reason that if you were hurt badly enough to run up $500 worth of medical expense, then your injuries must be fairly substantial. But if you only see a doctor once or twice, and your bills are about $50, then they figure you can't be hurt too seriously. This is one reason, incidentally, why you should go for treatment as often as the doctor recommends. You may be accused of padding the bill, or malingering, but it's an unfortunate fact of settlement negotiations that the more doctor visits, the higher the claim value.

Of course, this can be overdone. If you have a cut finger and you camp on the doctor's doorstep every day for a month, you're not going to get much sympathy from the adjuster. Or much money either.

The old cliché is also true that no two claims are alike. Many variables are involved besides the injuries. You'll always hear wild stories about the cousin of a neighbor's uncle on his sister's side who got $10,000 for the "same" injury. These stories are seldom true.

Some circumstances will add to the value of a claim; others will decrease it. Your claim will be helped, for example, when:

1. The defendant (the one causing the accident) is a large company or corporation (referred to as a "target defendant").

2. The accident took place in a big city (metropolitan juries consistently bring in higher verdicts).

3. You are under medical treatment for a long time (usually more than three months).

4. You are "clean-cut" and make a good impression.

5. The liability (negligence or fault of the defendant) is "open and shut."

6. You have not filed any claims in the past.

7. The injuries will produce some kind of permanent condition or disability.

Conversely, certain factors will cause a claim to be "downgraded." This can occur when:

1. The defendant is an individual, rather than a company. (This is important, since in most states the fact that there is insurance cannot be brought out or discussed before the jury.)

2. You are a member of a minority group or nationality. (This can still be true, unfortunately, for blacks in parts of the South, and other minorities elsewhere.)

3. You have been convicted of a crime. (The other side can bring this out in court to "impeach" your believability.)

4. You have filed more than one previous claim.
5. The liability is not clear.

All or some of these matters can have an important bearing on whether your claim is worth "top-dollar."

It's also a universal rule that insurance companies do not pay the amount you "ask for." If a company does, then you can bet you've asked for far too little. If this should happen to you, you should consider telling the adjuster that you want to wait a little longer to be sure you've recovered. Then come back with a higher demand later.

Since the company will ordinarily not pay your opening demand (even if it's reasonable), it's necessary to ask more than a claim is actually worth to give both sides some "bargaining" room. It's something like a poker game, with the better bluffer winning the pot even though he may not hold the stronger hand. And don't be afraid to bluff. You have a strong trump card: the threat of turning the case over to a lawyer for litigation. When this happens, it means new expense to the insurance company—for court costs, depositions, and legal fees—and they'd like to avoid that. If they think you mean business, they'll settle with you, if they can get out for a reasonable figure.

It would be nice if you could give a "take-it-or-leave-it" one-shot figure to the adjuster, and not have to haggle. Some people try to do this, but such a tactic will work only if you have positively decided to sue if the offer is turned down, or if your "demand" is really less than the actual fair value of your claim.

Most insurance companies will not give you their "top" offer the first time around. Occasionally an adjuster will do this, but it happens infrequently. When the initial offer is given to you, it's usually advisable to tell the adjuster politely that you're not willing to settle for that amount, but that to save litigation you might consider a little less than your first figure. At this point, he'll probably ask you what you'll "really take." Reduce your offer between 10 and 15 percent. Usually he'll offer more, or he'll re-submit your proposal to his supervisor and report to you later. It's very unlikely that a reputable adjuster will withdraw his offer, or tell you he can't pay as much as he originally proposed. If he tells you this, he'll generally be bluffing.

Listed at the end of the chapter are some suggested guidelines to use in settling your case. Remember, though, that these are "average'' situations and need to be adjusted to fit your own case, depending on the circumstances mentioned previously, on pages 10 and 11. The valuation will also vary depending on whether you have ''fully recovered'' or whether the doctor's report shows you'll have future problems.

I. When You Ask for "Too Much"

A great many adjusters, after receiving your demand, will tell you that you're asking so much, and you're so far ''out-of-line'' on your demand, that there's no use their even making an offer until you ''come down.'' This is a clever attempt to make you bid against yourself. The adjuster has a pretty good idea, of course, of the value of the claim, and there is no real reason why he can't submit an offer, regardless of how high your demand is. His tactic, though, is to have you immediately cut your asking price without his having to even make an offer.

You should handle such an approach in one of two ways. The best method is to stand firm, and to tell him that you feel your offer is fair, and that you are unwilling to ''cut'' your claim. He may try to ''out-bluff'' you and tell you that there is no use negotiating any further.

If the conference ends at this stage, it's usually advisable to let about two weeks pass, in the hope that he'll call you. If he doesn't, then you should write a ''final demand letter,'' telling him that you're turning it over to your attorney for suit, and pointing out that it is evident that the company is not willing to make any reasonable settlement offer. You should always do this in writing (not by telephone), and send a copy to the other driver. You should add, in your letter, that you will hold the claim another ten days on the chance that they may reconsider their position. Such a letter will put some pressure on the adjuster, since his file is being reviewed by a supervisor or claims manager. A form of suggested letter is shown at the end of this chapter.

The second method to use if the adjuster tries the ''you're-asking-too-much-I-can't-even-offer-you-anything'' approach is to cut your demand by between 10 to 15 percent. Tell him that you are not willing to accept less than that, and that you would like to know his offer. If he repeats the ''you're-asking-so-much'' routine, then you should terminate the discussion and proceed as previously outlined on page 12, eventually writing the "final demand letter."

If the final letter still gets no satisfactory results, then you will probably be better off turning it over to an attorney for filing suit, since you won't get a fair offer from the adjuster.

J. The Company Doctor

Very often the adjuster will tell you he wants you examined by one of their doctors before he can consider your demand. If your injury is an obvious one—a broken arm, fractured jaw, dislocated shoulder—with so-called "objective" symptoms (ones that a doctor can see), such an examination won't particularly hurt the claim. But if your injuries involve entirely "subjective" symptoms (those that you "feel" but are not visible to the doctor), such as head pains or back pains, it's usually not good strategy to allow yourself to be examined by the company doctor (or one selected by them). Why? Because most of the time their doctors will find nothing wrong with you; or, in polite terminology, they will see "no objective basis" for your complaints. At best, they'll say you'll be fully recovered in a short time—usually three to six weeks (almost always much shorter than the estimate given by your own doctor).

These doctors are not dishonest. But they've seen enough exaggerated injuries that they tend to be suspicious of even legitimate claims. In addition, they haven't had the benefit of seeing you over an extended period of time, as your own doctor has. Also, they're paid by the insurance company, so it's natural that they will lean toward the company (perhaps subconsciously) if there is any doubt about your condition.

So, as a general rule, be wary of a request that you see a doctor picked by the insurance company. If your refusal causes the negotiations to break down, and the adjuster coolly informs you that they can't settle with you, or if he offers some ridiculously small amount, it is advisable to write the "final demand letter" mentioned previously (unless you are willing to gamble and risk the examination by the company doctor).

K. What to Do About the Car Damage

Should you do anything special about your damaged car? If you have collision insurance (the so-called "$100 deductible"), you have the right to make a claim against your own company for the car damage, after paying the deductible amount. Your company will have you sign a "subrogation agreement," allowing them to be reimbursed or "subrogated," when you settle your claim with the other driver's insurance company.

Sometimes, though, this doesn't work out too well. A few companies are notorious for cancelling policies when such claims are made, particularly if you're partly at fault in the accident. Recent legislation in some states has attempted to overcome this type of cancellation, but the problem still exists. A few of the larger companies are now offering non-cancellable policies, which may one day be adopted by all companies.

If the accident is not your fault—so that your own company will get its money back—there would seem to be no logical reason that this should "go against you," or cause your cancellation. To be on the safe side, talk to your agent and try to find out whether there's any chance of cancellation in your case if you make the claim.

The ideal situation would be to have the other driver's insurance company pay for the car repairs right away (thereby saving you the risk of making claim against your own company), and then at a later date presenting your claim for bodily injuries. In most cases, this is wishful thinking. The "splitting" of damage claims (that is, settling your car damage now, and your injury claim later) is not permitted by the overwhelming majority of insurance carriers. Their reasoning is that since they might end up in court later, anyway, there's no advantage to them in settling the car damage separately.

Recently, a number of companies have announced that they'll relax this rule when they feel their insured is entirely at fault. In those situations, they'll pay the car damage ahead of the injuries. But except for those few companies, the only time you can get the other driver's insurer to pay the car repairs, is when you settle the personal injuries.

Do you have to get two or more estimates for the car damage? Most insurance companies will try to insist on it, but if you have one estimate from a reputable repair shop, you can usually get by with it. Don't let the insurance adjuster bully you on this.

If you do decide to make a claim under your $100 deductible

policy, your company will give notice to the other insurance carrier of its subrogation claim. They'll get paid when your injury claim is settled. Sometimes the two companies will submit the car damage to arbitration if the liability is not clear.

Be careful about signing a release when you finally settle your injury claim. Be sure there's a provision that excludes any claim of your insurance company for the car bill (if you've collected under your $100 deductible). Otherwise, you may get stuck paying back your own insurance company for the car repairs. A suggested clause, to add to the release, is:

> *"This release excludes the subrogation claim of _____ Insurance Company, for property damage."*

L. How to Handle Medical Payments Coverage

You should check your automobile policy to see if you carry "medical payments" coverage. This is a separate part of your policy, and you pay extra for it. But it's worth it for the small premium. Since you're shelling out money for this "med-pay" coverage, you should take advantage of it.

Med-pay generally pays you and your passengers up to a certain amount (usually $1,000, but sometimes as high as $5,000) for medical expenses incurred within a year of the accident.

The company will pay regardless of who's at fault. Some policies, in recent years, have included a subrogation clause, permitting the company to get back its medical payments the same as it does for the car repairs under the $100 deductible. Look over your policy to be certain, or talk to your agent. If there's no subrogation provision, then go ahead and make a claim. They won't cancel you for this unless you've been abusing the privilege by making claims every year for the last three or four years.

If your policy does have a subrogation on the med-pay, you should probably still consider filing a claim under it, so that you can get the doctors paid. Otherwise, they might have to wait a long time for their bills—until you settle your injury claim. If the doctors are willing to wait, or if you have the money to pay them as you go, then you can pass up the medical payments provision when there's subrogation. If no subrogation, then make the claim. You'll get paid by your own company, and again by the other driver's company. Don't feel there's anything improper about this; remember, you're *paying* for the med-pay coverage.

The adjuster for the other driver may ask you whether you've collected under medical payments coverage. This is the same ploy used in regard to claimed lost wages (see page 8). You should tell him you feel it doesn't have any bearing on the settlement. Unfortunately, he'll cut down the amount of his offer when he knows you've already been paid your medical bills.

M. What to Do When There's No Insurance

Suppose the other driver has no insurance. Don't give up. Many states now require your own company to include an "uninsured motorist" clause in your policy. This means if you're injured by a driver with no insurance, your own company has to pay off (usually up to $10,000, although lately more companies are offering policies that will pay considerably more).

You're entitled to claim everything (except property damage) that you could if the other car had insurance. This includes lost time from work, pain, suffering, and medical expense.

Some insurance carriers call this "family protection" coverage, but it's still the same thing. If you don't have it, ask your agent about it and try to have it added to your policy.

One possible drawback is that if you and the company can't agree on the amount of your damages, you usually have to "arbitrate," rather than sue and let a jury decide the case. The arbitration hearing is informal, and is usually conducted under rules set up by the American Arbitration Association. Some of the larger companies, though, don't follow this procedure; instead, they require you and the insurance carrier to each pick an arbitrator, and the two arbitrators pick a third one.

The arbitration proceeding sounds good in theory, but sometimes it's slow and can include some unfair conditions—such as making you pay half the expense, even if you win. The costs can run fairly high in some cases, particularly if you have to bring in a doctor to testify. In a few states, the arbitration provisions have been declared invalid by the courts, and the policy-holder is given the right to present his case to a jury.

If there's no insurance, and you don't have uninsured motorist coverage, you're probably going to have difficulty collecting anything. You might try writing to the other driver and telling him how much you think he should pay. In Florida and some other states, if an uninsured driver has an accident, he must get a signed release from the other car owner or his license will be suspended. This will sometimes be a sufficient amount of pressure to force him into paying you something, since he'll need you to sign a release for him. But most of the time, if there's no insurance, then anything you can get will be like found money.

N. Signing the Release

Mention was made previously, about adding certain language to a release to cover the subrogation for the car damage (page 15). You should also remember that once you sign a release, it's final and you won't be able to get any more money later, even if your injuries turn out to be worse than you thought. There are some rare exceptions to this rule that a lawyer might help you on, but it's quite difficult to have the release set aside. So be sure you don't sign if you have any doubts about the future, or the amount of money you should have.

O. The Lawyer's Charges

What if you've done everything suggested here and the insurance adjuster still tells you your $10,000 claim is worth only a hundred bucks, and that's all he'll pay? Unless you feel that's all the claim is really worth, you should go ahead and turn it over to a lawyer.

Most lawyers can do a competent job handling your accident claim. There are also "accident specialists," or negligence lawyers, who spend the bulk of their time handling automobile cases. The majority of them will handle your case on a contingent fee basis; that is, the fee is "contingent," or dependent, upon how much they can get for you. The rates have become fairly uniform, although they might vary slightly, depending on what state you're in.

You can expect the fee to be approximately 33⅓% if settled without suit, 40% if the case goes to court, and as high as 50% if an appeal is taken. Some states, though, have now limited the percentage that can be charged. A typical contingent fee agreement

("Authority to Represent") is shown at the end of the chapter. If you've already had a modest offer from the adjuster—which you've rejected—and you now plan to see an attorney, you should try to work out a fee arrangement which will take into account your own efforts and the previous offer. Try to limit the fee to a percentage of any amounts collected over what you've already been offered. So, if you've been offered $1,000 already, by your own efforts, don't let the lawyer charge you a fee on that. The lawyer may feel he should have a higher percentage of what he gets for you if this arrangement is used (some will ask for half of all amounts over what you've been offered). Generally, though, they'll go along with the usual contingent fee percentage, especially if your case is a good one, and you protest gently. So you should end up paying the contingent fee only on the amounts he gets for you over the amount you were offered through your own negotiations.

If you're not the type to protest the fee, then you probably shouldn't try to handle your own case in the first place. But it's worth the effort.

SAMPLE COPY

1 ☐ LAW ENFORCEMENT SHORT FORM REPORT
2 ☐ DRIVER'S REPORT OF TRAFFIC ACCIDENT

DATE OF ACCIDENT Day 07 / 11 / 88 Year	TIME OF ACCIDENT 8:00 PM	DATE OF REPORT 07 / 11 / 88	INVEST AGENCY REPORT NUMBER		HSMV ACCIDENT REPORT NUMBER 809670458		

LOCATION OF ACCIDENT-City or Town (Check if in City or Town) ☐   NEW   JACKSONVILLE   COUNTY   DUVAL

Feet or 2 Miles N.E.W.S of JACKSONVILLE

NEXT NODE NO   STREET ROAD OR HIGHWAY   MOTOR BLVD   AT OR NEAR INTERSECTION OF   HIGHWAY RD.

Section 1 — Motor Vehicle/Bicyclist/Pedestrian

YEAR 87	MAKE FORD	TYPE 2-DR.	VEHICLE LICENSE TAG NO 2-11111	STATE FL	YEAR 88	VEHICLE IDENTIFICATION NUMBER ABF326681

INSURANCE COMPANY (LIABILITY OR PIP) ACE INSURANCE CO   POLICY NO BLR627-321

OWNER'S FULL NAME (Check if Same as Driver) JOHN DOE   ADDRESS 123 SPEEDY ST.   CITY AND STATE JACKSONVILLE, FL   ZIP CODE 32201

DRIVER SAME

DRIVER'S LICENSE NUMBER 324798   STATE FL   LIC TYPE OP   DATE OF BIRTH 01/15/31   Race W   Sex M   EST AMOUNT OF DAMAGE $1,000

DRIVER/PEDESTRIAN BUSINESS PHONE NONE   HOME PHONE 904-211-1234

PASSENGER'S NAME NONE

Section 2 — Motor Vehicle/Bicyclist/Pedestrian

YEAR 86	MAKE CHEV	TYPE 4-DR.	VEHICLE LICENSE TAG NO 2-11112	STATE FL	YEAR 88	VEHICLE IDENTIFICATION NUMBER RXV 27911

INSURANCE COMPANY (LIABILITY OR PIP) ATOMIC INSURANCE CO   POLICY NO OK 37264

OWNER'S FULL NAME (Check if Same as Driver) JAMES ROE   ADDRESS 41 RACER ST.   CITY AND STATE JACKSONVILLE, FL   ZIP CODE 32299

DRIVER SAME

DRIVER'S LICENSE NUMBER 0061328   STATE FL   LIC TYPE OP   DATE OF BIRTH 02/24/34   Race W   Sex M   EST AMOUNT OF DAMAGE $1,200

DRIVER/PEDESTRIAN BUSINESS PHONE NONE   HOME PHONE 904-211-4321

PASSENGER'S NAME NONE

Section 3 — Motor Vehicle/Bicyclist/Pedestrian

(blank)

PROPERTY DAMAGED - Other than vehicles NONE   EST AMOUNT of DAMAGE   OWNER-Name

WITNESSES other than PASSENGERS   NAME NONE

RANK AND SIGNATURE OF RESPONDING/INVESTIGATING OFFICER L. M. Lockout, Sgt.   ID/BADGE NO 9999   DEPARTMENT SHERIFF'S OFFICE

☐ YOU MUST READ AND COMPLY WITH THE INSTRUCTIONS ON THE BACK OF THIS FORM
☐ NO FURTHER ACTION REQUIRED BY YOU. REPORT COMPLETED BY LAW ENFORCEMENT AGENCY

45 HSMV 90006 (REV 1/86)S

DIAGRAM

INDICATE NORTH WITH ARROW (↑)

POINT OF IMPACT

VEHICLE #1 WAS STOPPED IN A LINE OF TRAFFIC
WHEN VEHICLE #2 RAN INTO THE REAR OF
VEHICLE #2

CONTRIBUTING CAUSES–DRIVER/PED

	1	2	3
01 Inattentive Driving	01	02	
02 Careless Driving			
03 Failed to Yield Right-of-Way			
04 Improper Backing			
05 Improper Lane Change			
06 Improper Turn			
07 Alcohol-Under Influence			
08 Drugs-Under Influence			
09 Alcohol & Drugs-Under Influence			
10 Followed Too Closely			
11 Disregarded Traffic Signal			
12 Exceeded Safe Speed Limit			
13 Disregarded Stop Sign			
14 Failed to Maintain Equip./Vehicle			
15 Improper Passing			
16 Drove Left of Center			
17 Exceeded Stated Speed Limit			
18 Obstructing Traffic			
19 Improper Load			
20 Disregarded Other Traffic Control			
Driving Wrong Side/Way			
77 All Other			
88 (same as Running)			

CONTRIBUTING CAUSES–VEHICLE

	1	2	3
01 No Defects			
02 Def. Brakes	01	01	
03 Worn/Smooth Tires			
04 Defective/Improper Lights			
05 Puncture/Blowout			
06 Steering Mechanism			
07 Mechanical Wipers			
08 Equipment/Vehicle Defect			
77 All Other			
88 (same as Running)			

VEHICLE MODIFIED

	1	2	3
01 Yes 88 No, Unknown	02	02	
02 No 03 Not Applicable			

VEHICLE MOVEMENT

	1	2	3
01 Straight Ahead	01	01	
02 Slowing/Stopped/Stalled			
03 Making Left Turn			
04 Backing			
05 Making Right Turn			
06 Changing Lanes			
07 Interchanges or Parking Spaces			
08 Improperly Parked			
10 Making U-Turn			
11 Passing			
12 Driverless or Runaway Veh			
77 All Other			
88 (same as Running)			

LOCATION ON ROADWAY

	1	2	3
01 On Road	01	01	
02 Not On Road			
03 Shoulder			
04 Median			
05 Turn Lane/Safety Zone			

PEDESTRIAN ACTION

	1	2	3
01 Crossing Not at Intersection			
02 Crossing at Intersection			
03 Walking Along Road With Traffic			
04 Walking Along Road Against Traffic			
05 Pushing/Working on Vehicle in Road			
06 Other Working in Road			
77 All Other			

VEHICLE FUNCTION

	1	2	3
01 None	01	01	
02 Parking, Same-frame			
03 Pulling Other Veh			
04 Transport Business			
05 Pulling House Trailer			
06 Pulling Farm Trailer			
07 Pulling House Trailer			
08 Pulling Small Trailer			
09 Van Being Towed/Pushed			
10 Pulling Pole Trailer			
11 Pulling			
77 All Other			
88 Unknown		-1	

FIRST/SUBSEQUENT HARMFUL EVENT

F □ S □

01 Collision With MV in Transport Rear-end
02 Collision With MV in Transport Head-on
03 Collision With MV in Transport Left Turn
04 Collision With Parked Car
05 Collision With Guardrail Cable
06 Collision With MV in Transport (Sideswipe)
07 Collision With MV in Transport (Sideswipe)
08 MV Hit Other Fixed Object
09 MV Hit Utility Pole/Light Pole
10 Collision With MV in Transport (Backed)
11 Collision With Pedestrian
12 Collision With Moped
13 MV Hit Tree/Shrubbery
14 Collision With Bicycle

15 Collision With Bicycle (Bike Lane)
16 Collision With Bicycle
17 Ran Off Road/Into Water
18 Overturned
19 MV Hit Ditch/Culvert
20 Collision With MV on Other Roadway
21 MV Hit Sign/Sign Post
22 MV Hit Guardrail
23 Collision With Fixed Object Above Road
24 Fire
25 Explosion
26 Collision With Moveable Object On Road

27 MV Hit Concrete Barrier Wall
28 MV Hit Bridge Pier/Abutment/Rail
29 Occupant Fell From Vehicle
30 Collision With ...
31 Collision With Construction Barricade/Sign in Road
32 Collision With Traffic Gate
33 Collision With Crash Attenuators
34 Collision With Train
77 All Other Explain

CONTRIBUTING CAUSES-ROAD
01 No Defects
02 Obstruction With/Without Warning
03 Road Under Repair/Construction
04 Loose Surface Materials
05 Shoulders-Soft/Low/High
06 Holes/Ruts/Uneven Paved Edge
07 Standing Water
08 Worn/Polished Road Surface
77 All Other Explain — **01**

CONTRIBUTING CAUSES-ENVIRONMENT
01 Vision Not Obscured
02 Inclement Weather
03 Parked/Stopped Vehicle
04 Trees/Crops/Bushes
05 Load on Vehicle
06 Buildings/Fixed Object
07 Signs/Billboards
08 Fog
09 Smoke
10 Glare
77 All Other Explain — **01**

TRAFFIC CONTROL
01 No Control
02 Speed Control Zone
03 Traffic Signal
04 Stop Sign
05 Yield Sign
06 Flashing Light
07 Railroad Signal
08 Officer/Guard/Flagman
09 Posted No U-Turn
77 All Other Explain — **01**

ROAD SYSTEM IDENTIFIER
01 Interstate
02 U.S.
03 State
04 County
05 Local
06 Turnpike
07 Other Toll Control
08 Arterial
77 All Other Explain — **05**

ROAD SURFACE CONDITION
01 Dry
02 Wet
03 Slippery
04 Icy
77 All Other Explain — **01**

WEATHER
01 Clear
02 Cloudy
03 Rain
04 Fog
77 All Other Explain — **01**

SITE LOCATION
01 Not At Intersection/RR Xing/Bridge
02 At Intersection
03 Influenced By Intersection
04 Driveway Access
05 Railroad Crossing
06 Bridge
07 Entrance Ramp
08 Exit Ramp
09 Parking Lot-Public
10 Parking Lot-Private
11 Private Property
77 All Other Explain — **01**

LIGHTING CONDITION
01 Daylight
02 Dusk
03 Dawn
04 Dark Street Light
05 Dark No Street Light
88 Unknown — **01**

ROAD SURFACE TYPE
01 Slag/Gravel/Stone
02 Blacktop
03 Brick/Block
04 Concrete
05 Dirt
77 All Other Explain — **02**

TRAFFICWAY CHARACTER
01 Straight-Level
02 Straight-Upgrade/Hillcrest
03 Curve-Level
04 Curve-Upgrade/Downgrade — **01**

TYPE SHOULDER
01 Paved
02 Unpaved — **01**

WITNESS-NAME — NONE

ADDRESS   CITY & STATE   ZIP

VIOLATOR	FL STATUTE NUMBER	NAME	CHARGE	CITATION NUMBER
2	FS 622	JAMES ROE	FAILURE TO CONTROL VEHICLE	162

Page 2 of 2 Pages

STATEMENT OF CLAIM
(For Settlement Purposes Only)

XYZ Insurance Company
    100 Main Street
    New York, New York
RE: John Doe vs. Richard Roe
DATE AND PLACE OF ACCIDENT: Sept. 30, 1988, at Oak Street and
    Walnut Street.
SUMMARY OF FACTS: I was driving my 1985 Chevrolet south on Oak
Street at about 5:30 P.M. when I slowed down in a line of traffic near
the corner of Walnut Street. As I stopped, my car was struck in the rear,
with great impact, by Mr. Roe's car. I was knocked forward about 20
feet. I hurt my neck and back, and had a deep cut on my finger. I went
to Dr. William Weirdo for treatment. I saw him over the next two months,
as I continued to have constant head pains and soreness in my lower
back. I have also been extremely edgy and nervous. I missed five days
of work from my job at Sunup Service Station. I'm still having head
pains, some difficulty sleeping, and am still jumpy and tense. I was in
good physical condition before the accident and never had any unusual
back or head pains.

My car was damaged and repaired at Gouger's Garage. I paid $100
under my deductible insurance and my company (ABC Insurance) paid
the rest.

DAMAGES:

Dr. William Weirdo (8 visits)	$ 240.00
Dr. C. D. Films (X-rays)	80.00
Miscellaneous drugs (estimate)	50.00
Transportation to and from doctor	50.00
Future medical expense (estimate)	150.00
Lost wages (5 days at $60 per day)	300.00
Car damage ($100 deductible)	100.00
	$ 970.00
Pain and suffering	5,000.00
TOTAL CLAIM (if settled without suit)	$5,970.00

(Signed)
JOHN DOE

SUGGESTED "AVERAGE" GUIDES FOR SETTLEMENT

Injury	Amount of bills (not including car damage)	What to Ask for	Expected Settlement Range
1. Neck (whip-lash) or lower back (no long-term or perma-nent disability)	$ 25 to $ 50 50 to 100 100 to 200 200 to 300 300 to 500	$ 750 1,000 1,500 2,000 3,000	$ 250 to $ 500 350 to 850 500 to 1,000 750 to 1,200 1,200 to 2,000
2. Neck or lower back (with long-term dis-ability)	100 to 200 200 to 300 300 to 500	2,500 3,000 4,000	1,000 to 1,800 1,200 to 2,000 1,500 to 2,500
3. Vertebrae	50 to 100 100 to 200 200 to 400	1,500 2,000 3,000	750 to 1,000 1,000 to 1,500 1,200 to 2,000
4. Concussion (no brain damage)	50 to 100 100 to 200 200 to 400	2,000 2,500 3,500	750 to 1,200 1,200 to 1,800 1,500 to 2,500
5. Cuts and bruises (stitches)	50 to 100 100 to 200 200 to 400	1,500 2,000 2,500	750 to 1,000 1,000 to 1,500 1,200 to 1,800
6. Cuts and bruises (no stitches)	25 to 50 50 to 100	750 1,000	150 to 500 350 to 750
7. Broken nose	200 to 400 400 to 600	3,500 5,000	1,500 to 2,500 2,500 to 3,500
8. Loss of tooth	100 to 200 200 to 400	2,500 3,500	1,200 to 1,800 1,500 to 2,000
9. Broken leg or arm	200 to 400 400 to 500 500 to 750	4,000 4,500 5,000	1,800 to 2,500 2,000 to 3,000 2,500 to 3,500
10. Hip fracture	200 to 500 500 to 750	5,000 6,000	2,000 to 3,000 2,500 to 4,000

FORM OF "FINAL DEMAND LETTER"

16 Squirrel Street
New York, N. Y.
Date: _____

XYZ Insurance Company
100 Main Street
New York, N. Y.

Attn: Mr. _____, Adjuster

Re: John Doe vs. Richard Roe

Dear Sir:

Since I haven't heard further from you regarding my offer to settle my accident claim of September 30th, I am turning the case over to my attorneys for suit.

I felt that my proposal for settlement was fair and not "out-of-line," in view of my injuries and expenses, and the fact that I am still having discomfort. However, it is evident to me that your company isn't willing to make any reasonable offer.

I will plan to hold the claim another ten days, on the chance that you may yet reconsider your position, and make an effort to settle the case on an equitable basis.

If I have not heard from you by December 20th, I will assume you have no desire to settle the claim.

Sincerely yours,
(Signed)
John Doe

cc: Mr. Richard Roe

AUTHORITY TO REPRESENT

I, the undersigned client, hereby retain and employ _____ as my attorney to represent me in my claim for damages against _____ or any other person, firm or corporation liable therefor, resulting from an accident that occurred on the _____day of _____ 19_____.

As compensation for said services, I agree to pay for the costs of investigation and court costs, if necessary, and to pay my attorney from the proceeds of recovery, the following fee:

    33-⅓% if settled without suit
    40%   if suit is filed
    50%   if an appeal is taken by either side

It is agreed that this employment is on a contingent fee basis, so that if no recovery is made, I will not owe my attorney any amount for attorney's fees.

Dated this _____day of _____ 19_____.

_____(SEAL)
Client

I hereby accept the above employment.

_____(SEAL)
Attorney

CHAPTER 2

So You're Going To Buy A House

PROBABLY THE LARGEST SINGLE PURCHASE YOU'LL EVER MAKE IS the buying of a house. Yet millions of people enter into such transactions virtually blindfolded and generally ignorant of what to look for, what to do, and what traps lie in their paths. They often discover—too late—that ignorance is indeed not bliss.

If you're looking for a house, you'll usually have some idea of what you want and how much you can afford. But if you're a typical buyer, you'll have little or no understanding of the mysterious language of the world of real estate: discounts, title insurance, abstracts, equities, closing costs, escrows, prorations.

Let's start right after you've finally found the little dreamhouse you've been searching for. You've checked the heating system, crawled up in the attic, and looked for cracks in the ceiling. But what do you do next and what should you sign? Do you give a deposit?

A. How Important Is the Contract?

You should understand, to begin with, that next to picking the right house, the one most important part of your purchase is the sales contract. Whether it's written on the back of an envelope (as some are), or is a printed agreement prepared by a realtor, you're going to be bound by what it says—and more significantly—by what it *doesn't* say. So before you sign on the "dotted line," you should have a pretty good idea of what you're entitled to and what you should expect.

It's likely that thousands of homes are sold each year without any "formal" contract. The parties will draw up a homemade agreement, often on a slip of paper, or on the side of a check, with nothing more elaborate than something like this:

> "Received from John Jones $100.00 as a deposit on our house at 123 Main Street. Balance $1,000, and take over payments on mortgage."

Legal? Maybe. But in many situations (such as in cases when a family's homestead is offered for sale), sometimes two witnesses are required for a binding contract. Also, an informal agreement like this one leaves out far too much. Who pays the costs—documentary stamps, transfer fees, and recording? What happens if the title isn't clear? What furniture or personal property goes with the house? When will the sale be completed? And dozens of other legal points.

The typical real estate agreement should have at least the following:

1. The date.
2. The names of the parties.
3. The "legal description" of the property.
4. The selling price and the terms of payment.
5. The type of deed to be given.
6. Rights of the parties in case somebody backs out.
7. What property or furnishings go with the house.
8. When possession will be turned over.
9. Who pays the costs.
10. What items—such as taxes and insurance—are divided ("prorated") between the parties.

A good portion of the terms of the contract will be based on old-fashioned "horse-trading," rather than what the law requires. For instance, in most states, there's no "law" about who pays for transfer fees and documentary stamps on a deed. These items will have to be paid, but the question of who does the paying is a matter ripe for bargaining. From your viewpoint, as buyer, you'll naturally try to get the seller to pay as many of the costs as you can. And in many areas of the country, where houses are plentiful, you can occasionally find that the seller will pay *all* the costs. But this will vary, depending on the market and the city.

There are certain key points you should try to have in the contract. If you're buying a house that's more than a few years old, you should insist on a provision for termite inspection, requiring the seller to furnish you proof, from a licensed local exterminator, that the house is free from termites. Too many purchasers have bought houses that appeared clean and well-built, only to be met later with a horde of termites and several hundred dollars of expense.

In addition, if the house has seen better days, it's wise to make the sale subject to a roof inspection, calling for the roof and eaves to be in good repair and water-tight. Other matters, such as plumbing, heating and wiring, are sometimes mentioned, too. If you're in a good bargaining position, you can also try for a clause requiring all appliances, equipment, wiring, and plumbing to be in good working order and free from defects at closing, and for 30 days afterwards. This provision isn't too common, though, and don't be disappointed if the seller doesn't go for it.

You can expect that the seller will ask you for a deposit. In some states this is called "earnest money" (to show you mean business), or a "binder," to "bind" the deal while the deed is being prepared and the title is checked. This money is generally forfeited if you back out. The seller will often want five to ten per cent of the purchase price as a deposit, but you should try to get by with as little as possible. Why? Even though the deposit will be credited on the purchase price, it's always possible that some unforeseen problem will arise to force you to change your mind (sickness, loss of job, death in the family), and the smaller the deposit, the less you forfeit. Technically, the seller could elect to sue you for breach of contract or to force you to perform, if you back out, but as a practical matter—in the overwhelming majority of cases—he usually just keeps the deposit, gripes a little, and then tries to find another buyer.

So a binder of anywhere from $100 to $500 is the ideal range from the buyer's standpoint.

If the seller demands a higher deposit, it's usually smart to ask that the binder money be held by a reputable third party in escrow or trust. This can be a bank, a real estate agent, or a lawyer. But be sure you find out if there will be a fee for the escrow-holder. If a realtor is handling the sale, he usually won't charge for his escrow services. And sometimes your bank will do it and make no charge. But don't assume this is true without checking.

The seller may be offended if you ask that the money be held in escrow. But unless you know his financial picture, you run a risk of his moving away, spending the money, or dying, and you'd have difficulty recovering your down payment.

The contract should also show the correct legal description of the property, as well as the street address. If the description is long, paste it on an extra sheet and attach it to the contract. If you can't do this, then at least have the contract refer to the book and page where the deed is recorded in the county public records (this will be shown someplace on the seller's original deed). If it's not practical to get the legal description or the book and page number, you might be able to get by with just the street address, but this should be done only as a last resort.

If any equipment or furnishings go with the house, see that they're listed in the contract. These would include stove, drapes, venetian blinds, carpeting, window air conditioner, etc. There's a possible exception to this advice: see Chapter Three, regarding a requirement of the Federal Housing Administration. It's generally not necessary to list "built-in" items—called fixtures—such as commodes, sinks, light fixtures, since these are considered a part of the house. But there's sometimes an argument over what's a "fixture," so it's best to list the item if there's any doubt at all that it might be removed.

If the house is owned by a married couple, be sure both of them sign the contract. In fact, in some states, even if one spouse, alone, owns the property, the other spouse still must sign the papers (the wife signs to release what is called "dower" rights; and in several places, a deed executed by a married woman is void unless her husband joins in). So it's safer to insist that both spouses sign the contract unless you're certain your state doesn't require it.

What about witnesses? They're not necessary in all cases, but there are too many exceptions. Plan to have two friends or neighbors sign as witnesses. The real estate agent, if you're using one, can be one of the witnesses, but don't let your wife act as a witness. Usually the contract doesn't need to be notarized, unless you want to record it (but this isn't customarily done).

If at all possible, you should specify that the seller furnish you an up-to-date survey. Most owners will have an old survey around, but if there are any fences or recent buildings erected, or if you can't locate the corner markers or stakes, you should have the property rechecked by the surveyor. In subdivisions, this can cost around $175. You can consider passing up the survey if the seller has a fairly recent one (within a year or so), or if there have been no recent additions or fences on or near the property, or if the amount of money you're paying is too small to warrant the cost. For instance, it's generally not practical to ask for a new survey when you're paying only $500 and taking over the mortgage payments on a house (this was common a few years ago on houses sold with loans insured by the Federal Housing Administration, or guaranteed by the Veterans Administration).

If you're planning to "refinance the house" (see Section B, this chapter), or will be getting a new mortgage, it's essential that you put in the sales contract a provision substantially as follows:

> "This agreement is contingent upon the Buyer qualifying for a mortgage loan (F.H.A., V.A., conventional) in the amount of $............................, and if Buyer is not approved for such mortgage within 30 days after the date of this agreement [NOTE: Or you can agree on some other reasonable period], this agreement shall be void and the deposit shall be returned to the Buyer."

This will protect you if you're disapproved for the mortgage. Otherwise, without such a clause, you'd forfeit the deposit. The seller will often add a provision—which is not unfair—requiring you to apply for and proceed with the loan with reasonable diligence.

If there are to be any other special conditions or contigencies—such as your having to be in the house by a certain date; or certain repairs or improvement to be made by the seller—then be sure that these are in the contract. If they're not, you probably won't be able to enforce them.

What happens if the house burns down or is seriously damaged by storm between the signing of the contract and the closing of the sale? Not all laws are the same on this, although many states place the loss on the buyer, and you could be legally compelled to complete the sale (or forfeit the deposit). So you should put in a provision placing such risk of loss on the seller, and giving you the option of cancelling the agreement if such event happens and the house isn't repaired.

Sometimes you'll be buying a house that's being rented to a third party. Watch your step here. Be positive he's out before you turn over the balance of the purchase price; otherwise, you may have some trouble, and you could end up spending money to evict him.

Occasionally you'll have a situation where the seller himself wants to stay in the house for a few weeks, or even months, after the closing. This isn't an ideal arrangement; but if you're agreeable, you should specify, in the contract, that he'll pay you rent (you'll need to decide on an amount), and that he'll keep the house in good condition. You better be certain, though, that the fire insurance is changed to your name, or buy a new policy. If you're able to, try to hold back part of the purchase price as sort of a "security deposit" in case there's damage while he's living there. If he's only talking about staying in the house for a couple of days or so, then it's generally not worth making a big to-do about it.

It's customary, in the contract, to have a sentence "prorating" taxes. This means that the seller pays you—or gives you a credit on the purchase price—for part of the current year's taxes, which haven't come due yet. This proration is based on what portion of the tax year has passed. For example, if taxes aren't due until next January 1st, and the sale is closed on July 1st, you should receive credit, or payment from the seller, for half the year's taxes. If you're uncertain how to prorate, or don't know when the taxes are due, you can usually call the local tax collector for this information. Be careful, though, about using "last year's taxes" as a basis for proration if there's any likelihood that the tax rate or assessment will be raised. It's not unusual for the contract to require an adjustment of the tax proration when the actual tax bill is issued.

On houses with an existing F.H.A. or V.A. mortgage, the tax proration often works out automatically, without calculating it. This is because the mortgage companies, in such cases, usually collect a monthly deposit, called an "escrow," to cover future tax payments (see page 37). When you buy a house with such an existing mortgage (usually spoken of as "buying an equity"), the escrow account is transferred to your name by the mortgage company. Sometimes the seller will want you to reimburse him for this escrow deposit, since it's technically his money (see discussion in Chapter 3).

There are other prorations that are frequently mentioned in the contract. These include insurance (if the existing policy is being continued), rentals, and sometimes interest payments. In case you're paying part cash for the property, and giving a note or other deferred payments for the balance, you should make it clear whether any prorations will be credited against the cash being paid (this is more common), or against the deferred payments. This really depends on what the parties agree on, but it should be in the contract to save arguments later.

The contract should also state what kind of deed the seller will give you. You should normally get a general warranty deed, which is a "guarantee" or warranty that the title is good. This sounds great, in theory, but really only means something if the seller is financially responsible. In other words, you wouldn't have any worries if you were buying from General Motors or Standard Oil. But suppose the seller is an individual that you've never seen before. He could leave town, or be heavily in debt. The point is that if the title turned out to be defective, how could you get your money back? As protection, you should consider another type of guarantee known as title insurance (see the discussion in Section E, this chapter).

If you're not familiar with real estate, you might be offered a different type of deed called a "quit-claim deed." This is merely a transfer of all the seller's right or interest in the property, without warranting the title. Ordinarily, you shouldn't accept this kind of deed (see page 42). It's often a sign that there could be some flaw in the title (although it's sometimes used in special situations).

Even though the seller agrees to give you a warranty deed, it's advisable that the contract require a "good and marketable" title, not just an "insurable" title. Some title companies will insure a deed even if there are some minor defects in the title. This would technically make it "insurable." But you still might run into objections from a buyer when you resell the property later. On the other hand, if it's required to be "good and marketable," you'll be protected against this danger.

Most subdivisions or developed areas have "restrictions" on record, or are zoned in certain ways so as to limit the use of the property. These restrictions are usually beneficial and common to the neighborhood, and prevent you from having a commercial business on the property, or from putting up an outhouse. The contract will often have a clause specifying that the property is being sold subject to such recorded restrictions, zoning regulations, and easements. This is ordinarily not objectionable, but every once in a while, you can get smacked in the face with some burdensome, out-dated limitations. To avoid taking a chance, it's better to add this language to the contract: *"Provided, the restrictions, regulations, and easements have not been violated or encroached by the existing improvements, and do not render the title unmarketable or subject to forfeiture."*

Forms of suggested contracts of sale (or "binder agreements") are reproduced at the end of this chapter. Form 1 is for use in buying an "equity," when you're assuming or taking over an existing mortgage. Form 2 is to be used when you will refinance and make a new mortgage. Form 3 is applicable when the seller himself takes back a mortgage from you and finances the property. In the rare but happy situation when all cash is being paid and no mortgages are involved, the contract can be modified accordingly.

Very often the contract will be prepared either by a realtor (usually a printed form with some blanks filled in), or by a lawyer for the seller. Some contracts used by realtors have been carefully worked out and cover most of the necessary provisions. Form 4, at the end of this chapter, is such a contract, reprinted with the permission of the Jacksonville Board of Realtors, Inc. But even in these contracts there can be confusing "small print," or paragraphs that are unfair to you as the buyer. Merely because the contract is printed or mimeographed and is represented by a realtor as being "standard," don't rush to sign it. Look it over carefully. Don't put your name on it unless it covers all the matters and contingencies needed for your protection. If there's anything that's not perfectly clear to you, make sure you find out what it means, or that the realtor explains it to your satisfaction.

But if the real estate broker or agent tries to tell you what the *law* is, be on your guard. It's true that many brokers do know a great deal about such matters, but too many of them only know part of the law, sometimes the wrong part. If you're really in doubt, you'll be better off calling a lawyer. In the cases where the realtor *does* give you an explanation or interpretation of some provision in the contract, have him put it in writing. If he refuses, then you better tread cautiously.

When there's something in the contract that you don't agree to, see that it's deleted. Crossing out any inappropriate language, or adding any phrases, is permissible, but everybody should initial the changes, so that there's no disagreement afterwards. Don't, under any circumstances, allow the seller or the realtor to tell you "not to worry" about certain language that you disagree with. The time to settle the matter is before you sign the papers; if you're told that the objectionable part won't apply, or doesn't really mean what it seems to say, then take it out.

If the contract is prepared by the seller's attorney, it may or may not have some provisions in it that lean too much in the seller's favor. Don't be afraid or ashamed to insist on necessary changes or explanations.

In several sections of the country, the bar associations have adopted uniform sales contracts that are generally fair to both sides. But they still contain plenty of legal terms that you'll have difficulty deciphering. If you're in doubt as to the meaning of anything, find out before you sign—not later. If it's all Greek to you even *with* an explanation, then it'll probably pay you to have a lawyer help you.

B. What About Financing?

If you're paying all cash, you won't have to worry about financing. But if you plan to take over someone's existing mortgage, you may be faced with a "due-on-sale" clause in the mortgage (more on this in Section D).

But in most situations you'll need to borrow the money for the purchase price. Where do you get it and how do you start?

Sometimes the owner will finance the balance owing. In other words, if the house costs $50,000 and you pay $5,000 cash, the seller may agree to accept the balance by having you sign a promissory note and a mortgage, and pay him monthly. This is not usual, though, and it will generally be your responsibility, as buyer, to borrow the money from some other source.

The vast majority of home loans are financed through the Federal Housing Administration (F.H.A.), the Veterans Administration (V.A.), or through "conventional" mortgages (insurance companies, savings and loan associations, mortgage companies, and other private lenders).

The F.H.A. was created in 1934 as part of the National Housing Act. Contrary to common belief, the F.H.A. does not, itself, lend you any money. It merely insures the loan for a private lending institution if the loan complies with certain rules and regulations. You'd normally begin the process by applying to such an institution (not to the F.H.A.), telling them how much you need to borrow, and showing the contract, if you've already signed it. They'll take a detailed financial statement from you, and arrange for an inspection and appraisal of the house by the F.H.A. In many cases, the seller will have already obtained the appraisal.

Although the interest rate on F.H.A. loans is set nationally, it can change from time to time, depending on the availability of money. For many years, the F.H.A. rate has been somewhat lower than conventional loans. In addition, your required down-payment is low (in early 1988, for example, it was three percent of the first $27,000 of the appraised value, and then five percent of the excess over $27,000, but you could still borrow 97% if the loan was under $50,000.) This means that on a $60,000 house, for example, you could get an F.H.A.-insured mortgage for $57,540. Another advantage is that the term of the loan can be stretched to 30 or 35 years, which can provide you with low monthly payments. F.H.A. has, in the past, also granted mortgage subsidies to low-income buyers, and has an optional "graduated" payment plan, with smaller payments at the beginning, and larger payments after a few years. (Some savings associations also offer such terms.)

Then how come everybody doesn't get an F.H.A. loan? In the first place, many older homes won't pass the F.H.A. inspection. The house must be in fairly good shape (no termites, no major maintenance needed). The F.H.A. can require a seller to spend several hundred dollars to meet the government's standards, before it'll approve the loan. Although for a buyer this is fine, and can protect you considerably, it discourages many owners from selling through the F.H.A.

In addition, the lender often charges a "discount" or "bonus" of anywhere from a couple of hundred dollars to as high as a thousand dollars for an F.H.A. loan (more on this in Chapter 3, Section D). There's also a maximum amount you can borrow under F.H.A. (it varies around the country).

The main disadvantage to you, as the buyer, is that there's a certain amount of red tape connected with the loan, and in many areas you may have to wait several weeks while the mortgage is being processed.

There are also restrictions on "secondary financing," meaning there are limitations on your right to borrow money from any other source to make the down payment, and the rules are a little tricky and complicated. If a relative gives the money to you, this is permissible, but you can't have any understanding that you'll pay it back.

Despite these minor drawbacks to you, as the buyer, if you don't have a large amount of cash to put into a house, and if the owner is willing to finance under F.H.A., it's usually your best method of financing a moderately-priced home.

Veterans Administration loans, which are "guaranteed" by the V.A., are available only to certain eligible veterans. These loans were originally established through the Servicemen's Readjustment Act of 1944 and have several advantages if you qualify. The interest rate is lower than most other mortgages, and you can often borrow the full purchase price of the house, without having to make any down payment at all (although you usually have to pay for some miscellaneous expenses, such as fire insurance). On mobile homes, the maximum loan is slightly less than 100%.

A V.A. mortgage is usually hard to find, though, and you need to be careful when you resell the house later (see page 51).

The third most common mortgage is the "conventional" loan. This is generally the fastest to process, with less red tape than the others, and is often the easiest to obtain.

But there are disadvantages. The interest rate is often one or two percent higher than the F.H.A. or V.A. loans, and the down payment, or amount of cash you have to put into the purchase price, is generally higher. Most conventional loans require a down payment of 10% to 20% of the price (although some savings and loan associations advertise loans calling for only a 5% down payment).

The repayment period for conventional loans is customarily shorter then F.H.A.-V.A. loans, and is typically 15 to 25 years, although occasionally it's more.

Surprisingly, not all conventional lenders have the identical requirements. Even in the same community, it pays to shop around, and to call on some of the insurance companies, savings and loan associations, and other commercial lenders. You'll often find one or two with lower interest rates than the others, or a longer repayment period.

It's also a good idea to call different *types* of conventional lenders. For example, in some places, all the federal savings and loan associations may charge a "service" fee or "origination" fee of one or two percent of the loan, while in the same city an insurance company might make the same loan without such a charge.

And just because the realtor, or the seller, "recommends" a particular bank or mortgage company, don't accept it blindly. You should do some checking on your own. The savings can be substantial. If the realtor tells you all the mortgage companies are the same, don't believe it. In some cases, he'll be getting a one percent "finder's fee" for steering your loan to a particular lender. And you can't expect him to broadcast this to you. So if he appears overly anxious for you to do business with the company that he seems to be pushing, take it easy, and do some telephoning to the other lenders in town.

C. What to Look for in the Mortgage

When you're finally approved for a loan, a "closing" will be arranged, usually at the office of the lender or its attorney. You'll have to sign a promissory note agreeing to repay the money, generally in monthly installments. You'll also sign a mortgage, which is the document pledging the new house and property, as security for the loan. If you don't pay, the lender can foreclose the mortgage. In some parts of the country, other names are used for mortgages, such as "deed to secure debt," "deed of trust," or "mortgage deed," but they're essentially the same thing.

The F.H.A. and V.A. have standard form mortgage instruments, specially prepared for each state. So even though you may not like all the "whereases" and "wherefores," you won't be able to make any changes. The actual form of the conventional mortgage, on the other hand, varies even from lender to lender, but generally will have provisions similar to the F.H.A. and V.A. instruments. All of them require you, of course, to make the payments, as agreed, although you usually have a grace period of from 10 to 31 days. F.H.A. loans, for example, have a one-month grace period. You should always know, in advance, how long a grace period you have in your particular mortgage.

The mortgage will also customarily provide for a late charge of from two to five percent of the payment if you don't make your payment on time. Normally, this charge is assessed if the payment is 15 days late.

There will also be clauses preventing you from committing "waste" on the property, meaning you can't damage the house or tear it down. The mortgage will also require you to pay taxes as they come due, and to carry adequate insurance against fire and other hazards.

On F.H.A. and V.A. loans, and on some conventional mortgages, the lender will collect from you each month a sum to cover one-twelfth of the estimated taxes and insurance. This charge goes in an escrow account that the mortgage company keeps for you (see pages 30 and 82). At the end of the year, they then pay the taxes and insurance for you from this escrow. You might feel you should be able to handle these tax and insurance payments yourself, but it's not likely that you'll be allowed to do it.

If the taxes are raised or lowered in a given year, you can expect that your monthly escrow payment will be adjusted, and you'll be notified to send in more (or less) in the future.

Many mortgages contain a "prepayment penalty." This means if you decide to pay off the mortgage in advance, you have to pay an additional charge. On F.H.A. mortgages, the amount can be up to 30 days' interest, but on some conventional loans, the penalty is higher. The V.A. at present has no prepayment penalty.

If you're planning to get a conventional loan, and you think you might pay if off in a few years, it'll be wise for you to inquire about the prepayment penalty while you're shopping around for the loan, since the requirements aren't uniform.

D. The Second Mortgage

One other type of financing you may run into is the "second mortgage." This comes up most frequently when you're buying an equity and taking over a mortgage. You find, though, that you don't have enough money to pay the full amount of the seller's equity. So the owner may agree to take your promissory note and a mortgage, and have you pay him over a period of time—usually a few months to five years (see Chapter 3).

Occasionally, the seller may have previously borrowed some money himself, and may already have a second mortgage on the house. It's not unusual for the buyer to take over both mortgages. Just be certain you know about the second loan, from checking the abstract or title insurance (Section E), and then get a status letter from the mortgage-holder (see Section H), certifying the correct balance and payments.

If you're planning to take over a house with an existing mortgage—particularly one with a second mortgage—you should see a copy of it, and the promissory note, before you sign the contract for sale. Particularly dangerous in some mortgages are "balloon" payments, requiring a large lump sum at the end of the regular payment period. Even worse is a provision which has become increasingly popular, called a "due-on-sale" clause, requiring payment in full of the entire balance if the property is transferred by the seller—which means you could be made to come up with the full amount owing.

If the seller agrees to hold the second mortgage himself, insist on having a prepayment clause giving you the right to pay off the loan without a penalty.

In any case—but especially with second mortgages—look carefully at the interest rate, the monthly payments, the grace period, the provisions for late charges, and the "due-on-sale" provisions.

E. Should You Have Title Insurance?

No matter how familiar you are with an owner or the piece of property he's selling, there's always the possibility that the title isn't clear. This can come about in several ways: through past typographical errors in legal descriptions, through failure of a prior owner to properly sign a deed, or by not having a deed witnessed, by liens being filed against the property, and even through previous forgeries and impersonations.

Sound improbable? Thousands of property owners lose their title to land each year through just such events. How, then, can you protect yourself? In recent years, title insurance has become increasingly popular. This is a type of insurance policy issued by certain companies specializing in checking land records. For a specified premium, paid once only, rather than annually, the company insures you against defects in the title. It generally checks the county real estate records carefully to satisfy itself of the condition of the title before issuing the insurance.

If you're financing a house through a lending institution (see Section B, this chapter), it's likely that the lender (or "mortgagee," as it's often called) will require title insurance for itself. But this only insures the mortgage, not *your* interest in the property. You'd have to pay an additional premium if you want the title company to insure your rights in the property.

A great many real estate lawyers feel that if the lender is able to get title insurance for itself, then the buyer doesn't need it. Their reasoning is that the title insurance company has already thoroughly checked the records for the lender to make sure there aren't any defects. Since they're insuring the mortgage and issuing a policy to the mortgagee, the title must be O.K.; otherwise, they wouldn't issue the policy. So, according to this view, if the title has already been checked and found to be all right, why should you spend extra money on a separate title insurance policy?

While there's some logic to this argument, you can't completely rely on it. In the first place, title companies make mistakes. If the title is, in fact, defective, and you lose the property, you'll find that although the lender is protected, *you're* not. In the second place, title insurance covers you against types of flaws—such as forgeries—that aren't usually discovered even through careful checking of the land records. It also protects against unknown claims that don't appear from the records. For example, suppose Jones, who is selling to you, bought the property a few years ago from Smith, who is now dead. Smith, at the time, claimed he was unmarried, and signed the deed as a single man. You now innocently buy the property from Jones, relying on the *lender's* title insurance, and the fact that the title company has obviously looked into the title and certified that it was clear.

But now look what happens. Smith's widow appears, for the first time, to claim he was married to her all along, and especially at the time the original deed was signed. She claims that she's entitled to a widow's share (''dower'' rights) in the property. In many states, she'd be successful. You might be able to turn around and sue Jones, who sold you the property, but chances are he's not around anymore, or doesn't have a dime.

So the upshot of the story is that if you can afford title insurance, it's a good investment. The rates vary widely, but some typical charges are listed at the end of the chapter.

Be alert, though, to the fact that there are two principal types of title insurance policies issued. One insures against being dispossessed or losing title, but not necessarily against liens or defects. So even if the title turned out to be defective, you wouldn't necessarily be paid unless you actually lost the property. This isn't good enough, though. The particular flaw involved, and the potential future risk of loss, could block you from getting a purchaser.

The other type of policy insures you against unmarketability. Make sure this is the one you get. Many companies will give you the other policy unless you speak up. Ask for Form B, of the American Land Title Association Standard Owner's Policy. If they play dumb and claim they don't know what you're talking about, just tell them you want to be insured against unmarketability, and have them show you, in the policy, where it says that. A few companies may charge an extra premium for this, but most don't.

In many jurisdictions, abstracts are still used. These abstracts are summaries (sometimes photostats) of all the recorded instruments affecting a piece of property from a beginning date. While the abstract may be a complete résumé of what's *on* the record, it won't protect you from problems *outside* the record, such as the appearance of Smith's widow. In addition, abstracts are quite bulky, going back dozens of years in some cases; and you'll have difficulty in understanding what's in them, or interpreting them, without a lawyer's opinion. This can be expensive.

Sometimes, such as when you're buying an equity and making only a very small down payment, you won't be able to afford the cost of title insurance, or it may not be economically practical. In that case, you should usually demand at least an abstract, covering the period of time since the mortgage was placed on record. You'll need to assume that the title was good when the mortgage was made; the abstract will start from that point, and show you whether any second mortgages, tax liens, or judgments have been recorded since then. If so, these will need to be cleared up by the seller before you complete the sale.

A very small number of jurisdictions have experimented with a method of registering real estate titles. Called the Torrens System, for the man who introduced it in 1858 in Australia, it provides a system for the public recording office to register your deed and to check the title. Illinois, in 1897, was the first state to adopt the system, and although a few legislatures have tried it at one time or another, it's not widely used in this country.

In many states, the seller customarily pays for the title insurance, as part of the expenses of the sale. But there's no law that requires this, so you may have to pull up your belt and do some hard bargaining to get him to pay for it.

Ordinarily, a few days after the title insurance is ordered, you'll receive a title "binder," prepared by the insurance company. This is a preliminary commitment from the company, agreeing to insure the title, when the specified deed or document is placed on record.

Be careful about the binder, though. All too often it will contain exceptions or exclusions to your insurance, which means you're not covered for any of the items listed. If you've never seen a title binder before, it's easy to overlook the exceptions. Generally, there are some standard printed exceptions which appear in almost all binders. You'll find an exception for any claims by parties in possession of the property. In other words, the title company leaves it up to you to find out if anybody is living in the property, and what his interest is. To protect yourself, you should get an affidavit from the seller, at the same time he signs the deed, certifying that there are no other persons in possession. (See Form 6, at the end of this chapter, for a suggested affidavit.)

The company also excepts anything an accurate survey would show. This means that if the survey discloses, for example, that a neighbor has built on your side of the line, the title insurance usually won't protect you if there's a lawsuit over the boundary line. This is one of the reasons you should try to get a survey (see Section A).

Another exception in the title insurance is for any unfiled labor or material liens against the property. Most states allow workmen and suppliers, who have furnished materials or services for a house, to file a lien within a short period of time after they finish their work (usually 90 days). But since you may be buying the house within the 90 day period—and before the lien has run out—the title company isn't willing to gamble on this without some additional proof that there haven't been any repairs. This can be a dangerous gap in the insurance coverage, and could leave you vulnerable to unknown claims. About the only protection you have (other than the seller's solvency) is to require the seller to give you a sworn statement, at the closing, certifying that there have been no unpaid repairs, improvements, or work furnished to the property within the past 90 days. Some title insurance companies (but not all) will delete the "unfiled liens" exception if you furnish them this sworn statement. The suggested language for this statement is shown as part of Form 6. Even if the company won't take out the exception, the sworn statement is usually fairly good protection for you, since very few homeowners will knowingly give you a false affidavit. So always require such a statement, even when you're not getting title insurance.

There are also standard exceptions, in the binder, for current taxes (although *delinquent* taxes are usually shown); zoning restrictions (you'll need to check into these yourself, if you have any doubt, by talking to the appropriate governmental zoning department); and recorded restrictions (see discussion on restrictions, Section A).

While these exceptions are common to most binders, there can be others, which could substantially slice your coverage. Watch out for unpaid judgments (these are often listed inconspicuously), tax liens, and unpaid or unreleased mortgages. Always look on the back of the binder, since sometimes these exceptions are shown there.

F. What Type of Deed Should You Get?

Unless you're buying from an estate, or through some other unusual method, you should ordinarily receive a general warranty deed (see Section A). Such a deed may often have a lot of unnecessary legal lingo, but it needn't be complicated, as long as it contains certain representations, called warranties or covenants of title.

By this kind of deed, a seller warrants that he lawfully owns the property and has the right to deed it, that no one else has any claims or interests that would affect the title, that the buyer will have the "quiet enjoyment" of the property without interference, and the seller will defend the title.

Some states, by statute, authorize a "short form" warranty deed, giving the same full warranty protection, even though the covenants of title are not specifically set out in the deed. But unless you know that your state has such a statute, you should see to it that the deed contains the traditional covenants of title.

You can usually buy forms of deeds at a printing shop, and at some stationery stores. A form of warranty deed, that can be used in all states, is set out at the end of the chapter, as Form 7. You'll note, in the form, that the consideration is shown as "$10.00." The amount isn't particularly significant, as long as *some* figure is used, so it's been customary to use some small amount in deeds.

If your deed comes from an executor or administrator of an estate, you probably won't receive a warranty deed. Instead, you'll get an "administrator's deed," with a representation that the seller has complied with the requirements of the court. This isn't a warranty of title, and you should have some further safeguard, such as title insurance or an abstract of title (see Section E). Sometimes the administrator may not know what kind of deed is customary; if you're in a good bargaining position, try to demand, in the contract, that you be given a warranty deed.

If the seller proposes giving you a quit-claim deed, be careful.

This kind of deed warrants nothing (see Section A), and says, in effect, "I'm not claiming I own this property, or that I have any rights in it at all, but whatever I *do* have, is yours." Such an instrument is usually given when there is some doubt or dispute over a title (although it's sometimes used when one relative is conveying to another), and should not be accepted by you in the ordinary sale.

You may, on occasion, also run into a deed called a "special warranty deed." This isn't too much better than a quit-claim deed, and merely warrants that the seller hasn't done anything to adversely affect the title. But he's not really warranting that it's any good, or that the title is clear. As a general rule, don't accept a special warranty deed.

Regardless of the type of deed you get, it should accurately describe the property, by legal description. A deed that only lists the street address is risky at best, and may be considered void at worst, because of uncertainty.

Although there are a few cases when a deed doesn't need to be witnessed (for example, some conveyances by corporations), you should refuse to accept a deed that doesn't have two witnesses. In addition, to be able to record the deed, the seller must acknowledge his signature in front of a notary public or court official. In most states, the notary is required to imprint his seal of office on the deed. You should ask the notary to do this, since it's sometimes overlooked.

If the seller is a single person, always have his or her marital status recited in the deed, and in the acknowledgment by the notary, such as: "John Jones, unmarried," or "Mary Smith, a single person." If the seller is married, you'll usually need to have the spouse sign, except in a handful of states that don't require both signatures. However, both need to sign if the property is owned jointly. If you're in doubt, then have both of them sign. Beware of one of the spouses signing the other's name, by a power of attorney. Sometimes these are acceptable, but the power of attorney must meet certain tests, and be recorded. In the rare case where the seller wants to sign a spouse's signature under such a power of attorney, you better give your attorney a call.

G. Whose Name Should You Put on the Deed?

If you're married when you buy your house, you'll need to decide whether your wife's name should go on the deed. In the last thirty or forty years, with the increased independence of women, it's become quite common to take title in the names of husband and wife. In many places, this type of ownership creates a special relationship called an estate by the entireties (see Chapter 5, Section A). Although several states refuse to recognize all the legal consequences that flow from a true estate by the entireties, they do permit the chief characteristic of this type of joint ownership (and the probable reason for its popularity), namely, that when one of the parties dies, the survivor becomes the owner. This "right of survivorship" is automatic. You don't have to go through court, or file expensive administration or probate proceedings. About the only thing you might need is a death certificate to prove that the spouse has died; and sometimes an O.K. from the tax officer.

So then you should always put the deed in both names—husband and wife—right? Wrong. While this type of ownership has the advantage of being simple and avoiding probate, it can be tricky if you don't fully understand it.

Too many people use the device as an actual substitute for a will. But what happens if the husband and wife die in a common accident? The "right of survivorship" dies with them, and the house is then bogged down in court proceedings (see Chapter 5, Section A, for a more detailed discussion of this). There can also be serious tax consequences, particularly if your assets are large enough for estate taxation. While such considerations are dealt with more extensively in Chapter 5, you should be aware of them. If you're worth over $600,000, with life insurance, you should get some good tax advice before you blindly put a deed in both names.

Another potential trap with the joint husband-and-wife ownership is the problem of children by a previous marriage. Let's assume you have children, and your wife is dead or you're divorced. You remarry, plunk down a sizable sum for a new house, and put the deed in both names. Do your children share in the property if something happens to you? The answer is no; it all goes to the new wife under her "right of survivorship," and she can now even give it away if she wants to. This may be perfectly agreeable to you, but you should at least understand that this can happen under the joint ownership type of deed.

Let's consider, though, that you don't have children from a previous marriage, that you're not worried about estate taxes, and that you already have a will. Then joint husband and wife ownership is probably a good idea, and you'll come out ahead taking title in both names.

What about putting the names of minor children on the deeds? This brainstorm crops up from time to time, but can drench you in unbelievable legal difficulties, and should be done only in the most unusual situations.

To begin with, minors can't legally sign deeds or contracts, so if you later decide to sell the house, or borrow some money on it, you're boxed in. In a majority of states, even with your own child, you'd need to set up a formal guardianship in court, and you'll be stuck with expenses for filing fees, bond premiums, and even appraiser's charges.

So stay away from having a minor's name on a deed. Once it's done, you won't be able to have it undone (also see discussion in Chapter 5, Section C). If there are overriding reasons for transferring property to a minor, then at least consider setting up a trust, and giving the property to the trustee, for the benefit of the minor. Or you could try to transfer the title to a custodian, under a special law called the Uniform Gifts to Minors Act (see Chapter 5, Section G); but this law is generally restricted to personal property only (cash, securities, etc.).

Sometimes an older person (or anyone else, for that matter) may want to take ownership of property for his lifetime (a "life estate"), and have it go, when he dies, to a grown child or other relatives. This isn't as common as it once was, but is still possible. One advantage is the saving of probate and administration expenses. There's a risk here, too, though. If the "life owner" wants to sell or mortgage the property, he usually has to have the written permission or joinder of the "remainderman" (that is, the one who gets it when the life owner dies). The remainderman's wife will also have to sign, in a great number of states, and if the remainderman dies, his heirs will take over his interest. There can also be arguments about who pays for major repairs and other improvements to the property. If you still think you want only a life estate, just be positive you'll have no problems later on with the remainderman or his family.

Finally, you can buy a house with a relative, business associate, or friend. In such cases, title can be taken as "owners in common" (spoken of as "tenants" in common) or as joint owners with right of survivorship (joint "tenants"). Tenants in common each own a half-interest in the property, and each can sell his share or leave it to his heirs. In joint tenancy, on the other hand, the main characteristic is the right of survivorship, just as with husband and wife. When one of the joint tenants dies, his entire interest passes to the surviving owner, automatically. Some states don't permit this, but most of them do, if the intention is made clear in the deed.

Both types of ownership—tenancy in common and joint tenancy—have their places, but you should be aware of the differences before deciding how to take title.

The customary language for each of the types of ownership interests mentioned in this section is as follows:

1. Estate by the entireties: John Jones and Jane Jones, his wife, Grantors (or Parties of the First Part), to William Smith and Mary Smith, his wife, Grantees (or Parties of the Second Part). [NOTE: In a few states such as Kentucky and Mississippi, you would need to add, after the grantees' names: "as tenants by the entireties." In the other states recognizing this form of ownership, it's not necessary to use this language.]

2. Life estate: John Jones and Jane Jones, his wife, Grantors, to William Smith, Grantee, for life, remainder to Tom Brown and his heirs.

3. Tenants in common: John Jones and Jane Jones, his wife, Grantors, to William Smith and Tom Brown, Grantees, as tenants in common.

4. Joint tenants: John Jones and Jane Jones, his wife, Grantors, to William Smith and Tom Brown, Grantees, as joint tenants with right of survivorship, and not as tenants in common.

5. In trust: John Jones and Jane Jones, his wife, Grantors, to William Smith, as trustee for Tom Brown, Grantee.

H. Closing the Deal

You've carefully read the sales contract and made sure it protects you; you've been given a title insurance binder and a survey. Now comes the grand finale and culmination of your efforts: the "closing."

This is the completion of the sale, when you customarily pay the rest of the money, sign any mortgages and notes, and receive the deed. The closing, for a house, will usually take place anywhere from 10 to 40 days from the signing of the contract, in the average case.

If you're financing the purchase through a commercial lending institution, such as a bank or savings and loan association, you won't have to worry too much about the paper work. The lender's attorney or representative will already have prepared the note and mortgage, any affidavits or papers you're to sign, and a list of the expenses and costs (the "closing statement"). Many times, they'll also prepare the deed for the seller to sign. Even when they don't, they'll be as concerned as you are (probably even more so) to see that the deed is proper, since their mortgage is actually dependent on your getting good title. So if their lawyer says the deed is correct it probably is; but keep in mind that he's representing the lender, not *you*.

If you're dealing with a reputable lending institution, you won't have to study all the small print in the note and mortgage. They follow a standard format (see Section C), and they probably wouldn't change anything, anyway. But you'll need to check carefully to see that amount of the loan, the interest rate, and the repayment schedule are as agreed. Also look for the grace period and any prepayment penalty.

You should also be sure you understand the charges on the closing statement. Don't pay anything the seller is supposed to take care of. That may sound elementary, but in the rush of signing a batch of awesome-looking legal documents, it's often tempting to skim over the closing statement and assume it's right. Check all the expenses that are charged to you.

If you're not making a new loan, but are merely buying an equity and taking over an existing mortgage, then you'll have more of a burden to inspect the papers for the closing.

When the seller has a lawyer, he'll generally prepare the deed. Look it over to see that it's a general warranty deed (Section A), that the names are spelled right, that the property is what you agreed to buy (it's usually a good idea to match the legal description on the deed with the description in the title insurance binder), and that the deed is signed correctly. If a lawyer prepares the deed, it'll probably recite that it's subject to the mortgage, and that you, as the buyer, "assume" the mortgage and agree to pay it. In most states, this will make you just as liable for the payments as though you were the original signer of the loan. It'd be nicer if the deed just said it's *subject* to the mortgage, without any language about your *assuming* the mortgage (since you wouldn't then be personally liable if you defaulted on the payments). But the practice is widespread to require the buyer to assume the loan, and this shouldn't stop you from going ahead with the closing. Make sure, though, that if there's a "due-on-sale" clause (see Section D), the transfer has been approved by the mortgage company.

You should also receive the affidavit from the seller, certifying that there are no liens, or other parties in possession (Section E and Form 6).

In addition, the seller should furnish you with the termite clearance if this was agreed upon in the contract (see Section A). You should have previously received the evidence of title (either title insurance binder or abstract) and the survey, but if you haven't, then don't turn over the money until you do.

One very important item that you'll need at the equity closing, and sometimes overlooked, is an up-to-date status letter, or statement, from the lender or mortgage company. This letter should show the unpaid balance of the mortgage, whether it's current and in good standing, the amount of the payments, when the next installment is due, and whether the escrow account, if any (for taxes and insurance) has a deficit. If there's a shortage, the seller should pay it (see Section J).

Many lenders and mortgage companies, in the past few years, have been requiring the payment of a "transfer fee," ranging from $45 to as high as $500, before they'll change their records to show you as the new owner. If you don't pay the fee, they'll continue to carry the seller's names in their records. This may not sound like much of a problem to you—since you'll still be the legal owner—but you'll find it tough to get any information from them at any future time; so better see that the fee is paid.

Most of the lenders have their own "change of ownership notice," which they'll furnish to you, and which should be signed by you and the seller. You should return it to the lender, with the transfer fee, after the closing. This change of ownership notice is particularly significant since it serves as authority for the mortgage company to transfer the balance of the escrow account to your name.

If the mortgage company doesn't furnish you with any special forms to sign, or there isn't time to get it, then use the suggested form at the end the chapter (Form 8).

At the closing of an equity, you should also get the seller's copy of his fire insurance policy (unless you're getting your own insurance). If the policy is being transferred to you—which is the usual practice—then you should call or write the insurance agent and let him know. He'll issue an endorsement, without charge, showing you as the new owner.

Always get a copy of the mortgage that you're assuming. You really should have looked at it before you signed the sales contract, but if you didn't, then you should at least look at it by the time of the closing. If the seller doesn't have his copy, you can usually ask the mortgage company to furnish you a photostat. You can't be expected to understand all the small print, but you'll want to know whether there's a balloon payment (see Section D), and whether you have to be approved before the lender will allow you to assume the mortgage. Form 1, at the end of this chapter, contains a provision, making the purchase contingent on your being able to assume the mortgage.

The house you're buying may be entitled to some special property tax benefits, such as "homestead exemption" in some states. If so, don't overlook asking the seller for proof of such exemption. He should have a card or receipt from the local tax assessor.

The seller should give you a bill of sale for any personal property, furnishings, or equipment that go with the house. In place of this, it's probably acceptable to list these items in the deed, and this is the practice in some communities. A standard form of a bill of sale is shown in Form 9, at the conclusion of this chapter.

When the closing is completed, you should promptly take the deed to the appropriate local recording department or registrar of deeds (usually in the courthouse), and record the deed. If you're dealing with a commercial lender, their representative will usually record the deed, along with the mortgage, to be sure they're filed at the same time.

Also, don't forget to have the seller deliver all the keys to the house, and a list of the various people to call for utilities (water, electric, garbage, gas, etc.).

And finally, if you have a title insurance binder, you'll need to notify the company that the papers have been recorded, and request that the policy be issued. It's not unusual for them to take several weeks to send it to you. In some cities, it's not uncommon for the title insurance company to prepare all of the documents, including the deed, for an agreed fee.

A suggested "check-list," or summary of the things you should do at the closing, is shown at the end of this chapter, as Form 10.

I. Who Should Pay the Costs?

The question of who pays the costs can be a troublesome one. As strange as it may sound, some huge real estate deals have fallen through because the parties couldn't agree who should take care of a recording charge of a few dollars.

The contract, of course, should spell out whether you or the seller will pay the expenses, and which ones. In many communities, local custom determines the matter. Generally, though, the seller pays for documentary or revenue stamps on the deed; for evidence of title (either title insurance or abstract); and the cost of preparing the deed. Customarily, the buyer pays for recording the deed; transfer fee to the mortgage company; and the costs incurred in making a new loan. The expense of a survey is more often than not charged to the buyer, but the practice varies widely.

In areas where houses are plentiful, and there's a "buyer's market," the seller can often be persuaded to pay *all* the closing costs, even the expenses and costs incurred in your making a new mortgage. This was a common practice in Jacksonville, Florida for many years.

If you're making a new F.H.A. or V.A. mortgage, though, you'll probably have to pay so-called "pre-paid items." These are expenses covering a future period, but required to be paid at the closing, such as a year's fire insurance.

Sometimes the seller and buyer agree to split the closing costs. This is quite customary, in some locales, for the expense of drawing up the deed, and the transfer fee to the mortgage company. The dividing of the expenses probably works out well in practice, but if the biggest chunk of the cost is for items that would normally be the seller's expense (such as stamps and title insurance), don't be hustled into splitting everything, at least until you see who comes out ahead.

J. Things to Watch Out For

Many of the potential dangers in buying a house have been mentioned. There are some others, though.

When you buy an equity, be certain that the mortgage isn't delinquent. Don't accept the seller's word for it; insist on having a letter from the lender (see Section H). You'll also need to be on the lookout for an escrow shortage or deficit. This happens when the taxes or insurance premiums have been raised, and the escrow hasn't accumulated enough to cover the increase. If you're not careful, you may not even know about this until after you've completed the purchase, moved into the house, and found that the seller is already gone to parts unknown. How can you protect yourself? See that the letter from the mortgage company shows the escrow balance and whether there's a deficit. If the escrow is short, it should be the seller's responsibility to pay it.

Occasionally, the reverse situation happens; the escrow has built up too much, possibly because the taxes were overestimated. In that case, the seller may ask you for a refund (see Chapter 3, Section B).

Another hazard, seldom explained to a buyer, is your liability when you finance your home and make a new mortgage. You probably understand that if you don't make the payments, you'll lose the house. But in some situations, you can also be held accountable for a "deficiency," if the mortgage company sells the house for less than the mortgage balance.

As a practical matter, this probably isn't too much of a risk with many "conventional" mortgages, since it's likely that you've put in a substantial down payment (see Section B), and the house is probably worth at least the amount that's owing on it.

For many years, there wasn't too great a risk under the policy of the F.H.A., since that agency didn't pursue a deficiency after foreclosing. At the present time, though, the F.H.A. has indicated it will be changing its policy, and will seek a deficiency, if the circumstances warrant it.

The real danger in deficiencies is with V.A. mortgages. The Veterans Administration, for many years, has vigorously attempted to recover any loss if the foreclosed house sells for less than the mortgage balance. The V.A. makes its own appraisal, without giving you much of a chance to contest it, and then decides whether the mortgage balance is greater or less than their appraised value.

Since you've probably put only a very small down payment, if any, into the house, there's a good possibility you'll be hit with a deficiency.

To make matters worse, even if you sell the house to a buyer who takes over your V.A. mortgage, you might still be personally liable to the V.A. if your buyer defaults. About the only way to shield yourself is to try to get released by the Veterans Administration, and have the buyer substituted in your place. If the buyer's credit is good, you might be able to do it. But the V.A. is fussy about this, and your chances are less that 50-50 of getting released. There isn't too much you can do about it, although Congress at one time introduced some legislation to change the V.A.'s tough policy on deficiencies. The best you can do is try to get a financially responsible buyer, and hope he doesn't default. You should also ask the V.A. (or the mortgage company) to immediately notify you if the payments ever become delinquent. When that happens, if the house is worth salvaging, you might be able to get the buyer to deed the house back to you. If nothing works, and the V.A. demands a large amount of money from you to cover the deficiency, your best bet is to try to settle with them (see discussion in Chapter 3, Section B).

Another matter you should know about is the tax status of the house you buy. If you're in a state that allows a tax exemption to a homeowner, you should be positive that the seller has made the necessary application for the exemption, if he's eligible for it. Otherwise, your tax bill will be much higher than the year before. Have him produce the exemption receipt for you, or a letter from the local assessor.

Not all of these risks or suggestions will be applicable to your purchase. But if you're acquainted with the traps and pitfalls, and can recognize them, your chances of saving money and avoiding legal entanglements will increase considerably.

Form 1

CONTRACT OF SALE

[For Use in Buying Equity and Assuming Mortgage]

Date.............................

Seller ....
      (Names of Husband and Wife)

Buyer ....

Seller agrees to sell to Buyer, and Buyer agrees to buy, the following property in the County of ...., State of.............................:
Legal description:
(Shown on attached
sheet where de-
scription is too long)
Street Address of property:
Personal property included:

1. Purchase price is $............................., payable as follows:
   A. $............................. as a deposit, the receipt of which is acknowl-edged, to apply toward the purchase price.
   B. $............................. in cash, certified funds, or cashier's check, at closing.
   C. $............................. by the Buyer's assumption of the existing mortgage covering said property, held or serviced by ...., with monthly payments of .... Any variance in the amount of this mortgage, from the amount stated, shall be added to or deducted (whichever is applicable) from the cash payment (or the second mortgage, if any, at the Buyer's option). This contract is contingent on Buyer's being per-mitted to assume such mortgage.
   D. $............................. by the execution and delivery to Seller of Buyer's promissory note, dated the day of closing, with interest at ....% per year, payable $............................. per month, un-til the full amount of principal and interest has been paid; and Buyer shall execute and deliver a second mortgage, in the cus-tomary form used in the community, securing the note. Said note and mortgage shall contain provisions for acceleration of pay-ments, and payment of attorney's fees and court costs, in event of default for more than 10 days. The note shall allow Buyer the privilege of prepayment without penalty.

2. Seller shall, within 15 days of the date hereof, furnish to Buyer one of the following: (Check where applicable.)

__a. A title insurance binder from a reputable title insurance company, in the amount of the purchase price, insuring a marketable title, and insuring against defects and encumbrances, subject to exceptions for survey; current taxes; zoning; recorded covenants, easements and restrictions; rights of parties in possession; and unfiled labor and material liens. The title insurance shall be in the form of American Land Title Association Standard Owner's Policy Form B.

__b. A current abstract of title showing good and marketable title.

3. Seller shall, within 15 days of the date hereof, furnish to Buyer: (Check where applicable.)

__a. An up-to-date survey of the property, showing no encroachments.

__b. An up-to-date termite inspection report from a licensed local exterminator, showing all structures on the property to be free and clear of termite rot or other wood-boring pests. If such report shows such infestation, or damage from such infestation, Seller shall correct such damage and infestation, at his expense, within 30 days of notice thereof.

__c. An up-to-date inspection from a licensed local roofer, showing the roof and eaves to be in good repair and watertight.

__d. Other ....

(Insert any agreements regarding plumbing, electrical, heating, or other condition of property.)

4. __ (Check if applicable.) Seller warrants that the following shall all be in good working order at the time of closing and for 30 days thereafter:

__a. Appliances
__b. Heating
__c. Air conditioning
__d. Plumbing
__e. Wiring
__f. Other ....

5. If the title binder or abstract shall show any defects in title, or any matters rendering the title unmarketable, (and if the survey, if one is ordered, shows any encroachments), Seller shall use reasonable diligence to cure such defects or encroachments and to make the title good and marketable, and shall have 30 days to do so. If Seller is unable or unwilling to do so, this agreement shall be voidable, at Buyer's option, and in such event, Seller shall return the deposit forthwith to Buyer, and the rights of the parties shall terminate.

6. If the binder or abstract (and survey) show no defects or encroachments, other than those stated in this agreement (or, in the event Seller cures such defects or encroachments within the period specified in paragraph 5), then this transaction shall be closed within 10 days thereafter.

7. At closing, Buyer shall pay all sums due hereunder, and execute all required documents, and Seller shall execute and deliver to Buyer a general warranty deed conveying the property to Buyer free from all encumbrances and liens, except for existing mortgage, current taxes, and recorded restrictions, regulations, and easements common to the neighborhood; provided, the restrictions, regulations, and easements have not been violated or encroached by the existing improvements, and do not render the title unmarketable or subject to forfeiture.

8. If Buyer is unable or unwilling to complete the purchase for any reason not due to a default by Seller, the Buyer's rights in this agreement shall cease. In such event, Seller may keep the deposit as agreed liquidated damages, and Buyer shall return all documents to Seller.

9. Seller will pay for the following checked items:
    ___a. Revenue stamps on deed.
    ___b. Preparation of deed.
    ___c. Title insurance or abstract.
    ___d. Survey.
    ___e. Termite inspection and clearance.
    ___f. Roof inspection and repairs.
    ___g. Real estate commission.
    ___h. Mortgage company's transfer fee.
    ___i. Other ....

10. Buyer will pay for the following checked items:
    ___a. Recording deed.
    ___b. Stamps and expenses for second mortgage.
    ___c. Survey.
    ___d. Mortgage company's transfer fee.
    ___e. Other ....

11. The parties agree that the mortgage company's escrow fund, and the existing hazard insurance, shall be disposed of as follows: (Check where applicable.)
    ___a. Seller shall transfer all escrow funds and existing hazard insurance to Buyer, at closing, without additional payment.
    ___b. Buyer shall reimburse Seller for all escrow funds transferred to Buyer, and taxes and insurance shall be prorated as of closing. Such reimbursement shall be made at the following time:
        ___(1) At closing   ___(2) Other ....
    ___c. Buyer shall reimburse Seller for all surplus escrow funds not needed by the mortgage company for the actual payment of estimated taxes, insurance, or other "escrowed charges."

12. All taxes, insurance, rentals and other charges against the property shall be: (Check where applicable.)
    ___a. Prorated as of date of closing.
    ___b. Other ....
    ___c. If the actual tax bill, when issued, is higher or lower than the

amount used as the basis for proration, the parties shall make an appropriate adjustment between themselves.

13. Possession of the property will be delivered to Buyer as checked below:

__a. Date of closing.

__b. Other ....

__c. If Seller shall not deliver possession to Buyer at date of closing, Seller shall pay Buyer rent in the amount of $.............................. each ...., and shall maintain the house in good condition.

14. Seller shall deliver the property to Buyer in substantially the same condition as it is at the date of this agreement, and the risk of loss or damage to the premises by fire or other casualty, prior to the delivery of the deed, is assumed by Seller. If the premises are partially damaged and can be restored to their structural condition within 60 days after such damage, Seller shall so restore the premises, and the closing date shall be extended accordingly. If restoration cannot be completed within such period, or if the premises are substantially destroyed, this agreement shall terminate, at Buyer's option, and Seller shall return the deposit to Buyer; but if Buyer elects to purchase, he shall be entitled to the benefits of any hazard insurance on the property.

15. The terms "Buyer" and "Seller" shall include the plural, where applicable, and shall include the heirs, personal representative and assigns of the parties.

16. Other provisions: ....
....
....
....

....   SELLER:
.... (SEAL)
Witness as to Seller   .... (SEAL)
....
....   BUYER:
.... (SEAL)
Witnesses as to Buyer   .... (SEAL)

I hereby acknowledge receipt of $.............................., in escrow to be held by me pending the closing of the above transaction, and subject to the foregoing terms and conditions.

.... (SEAL)

CONTRACT OF SALE

[For Use with Refinancing]

Date.............................

Seller ....
(Names of Husband and Wife)

Buyer ....

Seller agrees to sell to Buyer, and Buyer agrees to buy, the following property in the County of ...., State of ....:

Legal Description:
(Shown on attached
sheet where de-
scription is too
long)

Street Address of property:

Personal property included:

1. Purchase price is $.............................., payable as follows:
   A. $.............................. as a deposit, the receipt of which is ac-
      knowledged, to apply toward the purchase price.
   B. $.............................. in cash, certified funds, or cashier's check,
      at closing.

2. This agreement is contingent upon Buyer qualifying for a mortgage loan (F.H.A., V.A., conventional) in the amount of $.............................., and if Buyer is not approved for such mortgage within 30 days after the date of this agreement, this agreement shall be void, and the deposit shall be returned to Buyer. Buyer agrees to use diligence in applying for such mortgage.

3. Seller shall, within 15 days after Buyer has been approved for the aforesaid mortgage, furnish to Buyer one of the following: (Check where applicable.)

—a. A title insurance binder from a reputable title insurance com-pany, in the amount of the purchase price, insuring a marketable title, and insuring against defects and encumbrances, subject to exceptions for survey; current taxes; zoning; recorded covenants, easements and restrictions; rights of parties in possession; and unfiled labor and ma-terial liens. The title insurance shall be in the form of American Land Title Association Standard Owner's Policy Form B.

__b. A current abstract of title, showing good and marketable title.

4. Seller shall, within 15 days after Buyer has been approved for the aforesaid mortgage, furnish to Buyer: (Check where applicable.)

__a. An up-to-date survey of the property, showing no encroachments.

__b. An up-to-date termite inspection report from a licensed local exterminator, showing all structures on the property to be free and clear of termite rot or other wood boring pests. If such report shows such infestation, or damage from such infestation, Seller shall correct such damage and infestation, at his expense, within 30 days of notice thereof.

__c. An up-to-date inspection from a licensed local roofer, showing the roof and eaves to be in good repair and water-tight.

__d. Other ....

(Insert any agreements regarding plumbing, electrical, heating, or other condition of property.)

5. __(Check if applicable.) Seller warrants that the following shall all be in good working order at the time of closing and for 30 days thereafter:

__a. Appliances
__b. Heating
__c. Air conditioning
__d. Plumbing
__e. Wiring
__f. Other ....

6. If the title binder, or abstract, shall show any defects in title, or any matters rendering the title unmarketable (and if the survey, if one is ordered, shows any encroachments), Seller shall use reasonable diligence to cure such defects or encroachments and to make the title good and marketable, and shall have 30 days to do so. If Seller is unable or unwilling to do so, this agreement shall be voidable, at Buyer's option, and in such event, Seller shall return the deposit forthwith to Buyer, and the rights of the parties shall terminate.

7. If the binder or abstract (and survey) show no defects or encroachments, other than those stated in this agreement (or, in the event Seller cures such defects or encroachments within the period specified in paragraph 6), then this transaction shall be closed within 10 days thereafter.

8. At closing, Buyer shall pay all sums due hereunder, and execute all required documents, and Seller shall execute and deliver to Buyer a general warranty deed conveying the property to Buyer free from all encumbrances and liens, except current taxes, and recorded restrictions, regulations, and easements common to the neighborhood; provided, the restrictions, regulations, and easements have not been violated or encroached by the existing improvements, and do not render the title unmarketable or subject to forfeiture.

9. If Buyer is approved for the mortgage, but is unable or unwilling to complete the purchase for any reason not due to a default by Seller, the Buyer's rights in this agreement shall cease. In such event, Seller may keep the deposit as agreed liquidated damages, and Buyer shall return all documents to Seller.

10. Seller will pay for the following checked items:
__a. Revenue stamps on deed.
__b. Preparation of deed.
__c. Title insurance or abstract.
__d. Survey.
__e. Termite inspection and clearance.
__f. Roof inspection and repairs.
__g. Real estate commission.
__h. Mortgage expenses and closing costs, except prepaid items, and except ....
__i. Other ....

11. Buyer will pay for the following checked items:
__a. Recording deed.
__b. Mortgage expenses and closing costs, except F.H.A. discount and except ....
__c. Survey.
__d. Prepaid items in connection with mortgage.
__e. Other ....

12. All taxes for the current year, rentals, insurance, and other charges against the property shall be: (Check where applicable.)
__a. Prorated as of date of closing.
__b. Other ....
__c. If the actual tax bill, when issued, is higher or lower than the amount used as the basis for proration, the parties shall make an appropriate adjustment between themselves.

13. Possession of the property will be delivered as checked below:
__a. Date of closing.
__b. Other ....
__c. If Seller shall not deliver possession to Buyer at date of closing, Seller shall pay Buyer rent in the amount of $............................... each ...., and shall maintain the house in good condition.

14. Seller shall deliver the property to Buyer in substantially the same condition as it is at the date of this agreement, and the risk of loss or damage to the premises by fire or other casualty, prior to the delivery of the deed, is assumed by Seller. If the premises are partially damaged and can be restored to their structural condition within 60 days after such damage, Seller shall so restore the premises, and the closing date shall be extended accordingly. If restoration cannot be completed within such period, or if the premises are substantially destroyed, this agreement shall terminate, at Buyer's option, and Seller shall return the de-

posit to Buyer; but if Buyer elects to purchase, he shall be entitled to the benefits of any hazard insurance on the property.

15. The terms "Buyer" and "Seller" shall include the plural, where applicable, and shall include the heirs, personal representative and assigns of the parties.

16. For F.H.A. and V.A. financing, it is expressly agreed that, notwithstanding any other provisions of this contract, the Buyer shall not be obligated to complete the purchase of the property described herein or to incur any penalty for forfeiture of earnest money deposits or otherwise unless the Seller has delivered to the Buyer a written statement issued by the Federal Housing Commissioner setting forth the appraised value of the property for mortgage insurance purposes not less than $..........................., which statement the Seller hereby agrees to deliver to the Buyer promptly after such appraised value statement is made available to the Seller. The Buyer shall, however, have the privilege and option of proceeding with the consummation of this contract without regard to the amount on the appraised valuation made by the Federal Housing Commissioner.

17. Other provisions: ....
....
....
....

....   SELLER:
.... (SEAL)
Witnesses as to Seller   .... (SEAL)

                                     BUYER:
.... (SEAL)
.... (SEAL)
Witnesses as to Buyer

I hereby acknowledge receipt of $..........................., in escrow, to be held by me pending the closing of the above transaction, and subject to the foregoing terms and conditions.
                                     .... (SEAL)

Form 3

CONTRACT OF SALE

[For Use When Seller Finances the Property and Takes Back a Mortgage Himself]

Date.............................

Seller ....
        (Names of Husband and Wife)

Buyer ....

Seller agrees to sell to Buyer, and Buyer agrees to buy, the following property in the County of ...., State of ....:

Legal description:
(Shown on attached
sheet where de-
scription is too
long)

Street Address of property:

Personal property included:

1. Purchase price is $..............................., payable as follows:
   A. $.............................. as a deposit, the receipt of which is acknowledged, to apply toward the purchase price.
   B. $.............................. in cash, certified funds, or cashier's check, at closing.
   C. $.............................. by the execution and delivery to Seller of Buyer's promissory note, dated the day of closing, with interest at .... % per year, payable at $.............................. per month, until the full amount of principal and interest has been paid; and Buyer shall execute and deliver a purchase money mortgage, in the customary form used in the community, securing the note. Said note and mortgage shall contain provisions for acceleration of payments, and payment of attorney's fees and court costs, in event of default for more than 10 days. The note shall allow Buyer the privilege of prepayment without penalty.

2. Seller shall, within 15 days of the date hereof, furnish to Buyer one of the following: (Check where applicable.)
   __a. A title insurance binder from a reputable title insurance com-

pany, in the amount of the purchase price, insuring a marketable title, and insuring against defects and encumbrances, subject to exceptions for survey; current taxes; zoning; recorded covenants, easements and restrictions; rights of parties in possession; and unfiled labor and material liens. The title insurance shall be in the form of American Land Title Association Standard Owner's Policy Form B.

__b. A current abstract of title, showing good and marketable title.

3. Seller shall, within 15 days of the date hereof, furnish to Buyer: (Check where applicable.)

__a. An up-to-date survey of the property, showing no encroachments.

__b. An up-to-date termite inspection report from a licensed local exterminator, showing all structures on the property to be free and clear of termite rot or other wood boring pests. If such report shows such infestation, or damage from such infestation, Seller shall correct such damage and infestation, at his expense, within 30 days of notice thereof.

__c. An up-to-date inspection from a licensed local roofer, showing the roof and eaves to be in good repair and watertight.

__d. Other ....
(Insert any agreements regarding plumbing, electrical, heating, or other condition of property.)

4.__(Check if applicable.) Seller warrants that the following shall all be in good working order at the time of closing and for 30 days thereafter:

__a. Appliances
__b. Heating
__c. Air conditioning
__d. Plumbing
__e. Wiring
__f. Other ....

5. If the title binder, or abstract, shall show any defects in title, or any matters rendering the title unmarketable (and if the survey, if one is ordered, shows any encroachments), Seller shall use reasonable diligence to cure such defects or encroachments and to make the title good and marketable, and shall have 30 days to do so. If Seller is unable or unwilling to do so, this agreement shall be voidable, at Buyer's option, and in such event, Seller shall return the deposit forthwith to Buyer, and the rights of the parties shall terminate.

6. If the binder or abstract (and survey) show no defects or encroachments, other than those stated in this agreement (or, in the event Seller cures such defects or encroachments within the period specified in paragraph 5), then this transaction shall be closed within 10 days thereafter.

7. At closing, Buyer shall pay all sums due hereunder, and execute all required documents, and Seller shall execute and deliver to Buyer

a general warranty deed conveying the property to Buyer free from all encumbrances and liens, except current taxes, and recorded restrictions, regulations, and easements common to the neighborhood; provided, the restrictions, regulations, and easements have not been violated or encroached by the existing improvements, and do not render the title unmarketable or subject to forfeiture.

8. If Buyer is unable or unwilling to complete the purchase for any reason not due to a default by Seller, the Buyer's rights in this agreement shall cease. In such event, Seller may keep the deposit as agreed liquidated damages, and Buyer shall return all documents to Seller.

9. Seller will pay for the following checked items:

__a. Revenue stamps on deed.
__b. Preparation of deed.
__c. Title insurance or abstract.
__d. Survey.
__e. Termite inspection and clearance.
__f. Roof inspection and repairs.
__g. Real estate commission.
__h. Stamps and expenses for mortgage and note.
__i. Recording mortgage.
__j. Other ....

10. Buyer will pay for the following checked items:

__a. Recording deed.
__b. Survey.
__c. Stamps and expenses for mortgage and note.
__d. Other ....

11. All taxes for the current year, rentals, insurance, and other charges against the property shall be: (Check where applicable.)

__a. Prorated as of date of closing.
__b. Other ....
__c. If the actual tax bill, when issued, is higher or lower than the amount used as the basis for proration, the parties shall make an appropriate adjustment between themselves.

12. Possession of the property will be delivered as checked below:

__a. Date of closing.
__b. Other ....
__c. If Seller shall not deliver possession to Buyer at date of closing, Seller shall pay Buyer rent in the amount of $............................... each ...., and shall maintain the house in good condition.

13. Seller shall deliver the property to Buyer in substantially the same condition as it is at the date of this agreement, and the risk of loss or damage to the premises by fire or other casualty, prior to the delivery of the deed, is assumed by Seller. If the premises are partially damaged and can be restored to their structural condition within 60 days after

such damage, Seller shall so restore the premises, and the closing date shall be extended accordingly. If restoration cannot be completed within such period, or if the premises are substantially destroyed, this agreement shall terminate, at Buyer's option, and Seller shall return the deposit to Buyer; but if Buyer elects to purchase, he shall be entitled to the benefits of any hazard insurance on the property.

14. The terms "Buyer" and "Seller" shall include the plural, where applicable, and shall include the heirs, personal representative and assigns of the parties.

15. Other provisions: ....
....
....
....

....   **SELLER:**

.... (SEAL)

Witnesses as to Seller   .... (SEAL)

....   **BUYER:**

.... (SEAL)

Witnesses as to Buyer   .... (SEAL)

I hereby acknowledge receipt of $.............................., in escrow, to be held by me pending the closing of the above transaction, and subject to the foregoing terms and conditions.

.... (SEAL)

Form 4 (Used with permission of the Jacksonville Board of Realtors, Inc. and not to be reproduced without their written consent.)

STANDARD AGREEMENT RECOMMENDED BY THE JACKSONVILLE BOARD OF REALTORS, INC.

DEPOSIT RECEIPT & PURCHASE AND SALE AGREEMENT

PARTIES: _____ (BUYER),

of _____ S.S.#/T.I.N.# _____,

and _____ (SELLER),

of _____ S.S.#/T.I.N.# _____,

which terms may be singular or plural and shall include the heirs, successors, personal representatives and assigns of SELLER and BUYER, hereby agree that SELLER will sell and BUYER will buy the following property, upon the following terms and conditions if completed or marked. In any conflict of terms or conditions, that which is added shall supersede that which is printed or marked.

The Property is in _____ County, Florida, and is legally described as follows (if lengthy, attach legal description.):

Address.

It is understood that the property will be conveyed by GENERAL WARRANTY DEED (unless otherwise required) subject to current taxes, existing zoning (unless specified otherwise in Paragraph 8), covenants, restrictions and easements of record

1. TOTAL PURCHASE PRICE to be paid by BUYER is payable as follows:

(A) Binder deposit, which will remain a binder until closing, unless sooner forfeited or returned, according to the provisions of this agreement .... $ _____

(B) Additional binder deposit due within _____ days after date of acceptance of this agreement $ _____

(C) Balance due at closing (not including BUYER'S closing costs, prepaid items or prorations) in U.S. cash or LOCALLY DRAWN certified or cashiers check approx _____ exactly _____ $ _____

(D) Proceeds of new note and mortgage to be executed by BUYER to any lender other than SELLER $ _____

(E) Purchase money mortgage and note to SELLER on terms set forth in paragraph 2C $ _____

(F) Other financing $ _____

(G) Existing mortgage balance encumbering the property to be assumed by BUYER (approximately) $ _____

Mortgage _____ Loan # _____ Int. Rate _____ P & I _____ approx _____ exactly _____ $ _____

(H) TOTAL PURCHASE PRICE $ _____

2. FINANCING

(A) ( ) APPLICATION: The application for the mortgage as described in paragraph 1D will be made with a lender selected by ( ) SELLER or ( ) BUYER. Unless such mortgage loan is approved without contingencies other than those elsewhere covered in this Agreement, SELLER or BUYER within _____ days of the date of acceptance of this Agreement, SELLER or BUYER shall have the right to terminate this Agreement, and BUYER will return to SELLER all the sale evidence and surveys received from SELLER and BUYER's copy of the Agreement. BUYER shall make application for financing within _____ days of the date of acceptance of this Agreement and timely furnish any and all credit, employment, financial and other information required by the Lender. In the event the original loan application is denied, BUYER, if requested by SELLER, will reapply within _____ days of such request at an alternate institutional Lender selected by SELLER.

1. ( ) FHA: It is expressly agreed that, notwithstanding any other provisions of the Agreement, the BUYER shall not be obligated to complete the purchase of the property described herein or to incur any penalty by forfeiture of earnest money deposit or otherwise unless the SELLER has delivered to the BUYER a written statement issued by the Federal Housing Commissioner setting forth the appraised value of the property (excluding closing cost) of not less than $ _____ which statement the SELLER hereby agrees to deliver to the BUYER promptly after such appraised value statement is made available to the SELLER. The BUYER shall, however, have the privilege and option of proceeding with the consummation of the Agreement without regard to the amount of the appraised valuation made by the Federal Housing Commissioner. **The appraised valuation is arrived at to determine the maximum mortgage the Department of Housing and Urban Development will insure. HUD does not warrant the value or the condition of the property. The purchaser should satisfy himself/herself that the price and condition of the property are acceptable.**

2. ( ) VA: It is expressly agreed that, notwithstanding any other provisions of this Agreement, the BUYER shall not incur any penalty by forfeiture of earnest money or otherwise be obligated to complete the purchase of the property described herein, if the Agreement purchase price or cost exceed the reasonable value of the property established by the Veterans Administration. The BUYER shall, however, have the privilege and option of proceeding with the consummation of the Agreement without regard to the amount of reasonable value established by the VA.

(B) ( ) MORTGAGE ASSUMPTION: BUYER understands that loan interest ( ) will ( ) will not escalate and is a ( ) variable ( ) fixed rate. If mortgagee approval of BUYER is required for loan assumption, BUYER shall, within _____ days, make required application and timely provide qualifying information as required by lender. BUYER'S obligation to close is contingent on lender's approval within _____ days.

(C) ( ) SELLER: The balance due to SELLER shall be evidenced by a negotiable promissory note of BUYER, secured by a valid purchase money mortgage on the property and delivered by BUYER to SELLER dated the date of closing, bearing interest at the rate of _____% per annum and payable $ _____ per _____. Privilege of Prepayment ( ) does apply ( ) does not apply. The mortgage will be ( ) due on sale ( ) not due on sale of the property. This contract is not assignable without the consent of SELLER. Within _____ days after the date of acceptance of this agreement, BUYER will furnish all credit, employment and financial information required by SELLER. SELLER shall within _____ days after receipt of the information, deliver a written decision to BUYER as to whether or not SELLER will make the mortgage loan.

3. BUYER WILL PAY:

(A) CLOSING COSTS: ( ) Recording fees ( ) Note Stamps ( ) Intangible Tax ( ) Credit report ( ) Mortgage transfer and assumption charges ( ) VA funding fee ( ) Mortgage origination fee ( ) Mortgage insurance premium ( ) Mortgage discount not to exceed

( ) _____ Attorney's Fee ( ) Wood-destroying organism report ( ) Photos ( ) Appraisal fee ( ) All other charges required by lender, unless prohibited by law or regulation, in which event they shall be paid by SELLER ( ) _____ . Title insurance policy

( ) _____

(B.) PREPAIDS: Prepaid hazard insurance, taxes, interest and mortgage insurance premiums, required by the lender, will be paid by BUYER.

4. SELLER WILL PAY.

(A.) CLOSING COSTS: ( ) Stamps on deed ( ) _____ Title insurance policy ( ) _____ Attorney's fee ( ) Real estate brokerage fee ( ) Mortgage discount not to exceed _____ ( ) Satisfaction of mortgage and recording fee ( ) Repairs or replacements required, in addition to those in paragraph 9, not to exceed $ _____ ( ) For VA sale only, wood-destroying organism report ( ) Charges required by Lender which BUYER is prohibited from paying by law or regulation. ( ) Survey ( )
( )

(B.) All mortgage payments and condominium and association fees will be current at SELLER's expense at the time of closing.

(C.) Seller shall deliver proof satisfactory that BUYER shall not be obligated to withhold any of the purchase price under the Foreign Investment and Real Property Tax Act OR shall provide funds at closing to enable BUYER to meet the tax obligation.

5. ( ) PRORATIONS: All taxes, rentals, condominium or association fees, prepaid hazard insurance premiums (if assumed), monthly mortgage insurance premiums and interest on assumed mortgages shall be pro-rated as of the date closing. If part of purchase price is to be evidenced by the assumption of a mortgage requiring deposit of funds in escrow for payment of taxes, insurance or other charges, BUYER agrees to reimburse SELLER for the escrowed funds assigned to BUYER at closing.

6. TITLE EVIDENCE: Within _____ days ( ) After date of acceptance ( ) After date of satisfaction of all conditions in paragraph 19, SELLER will deliver to BUYER or closing attorney:( ) Title insurance commitment for an owner's policy in the amount of the purchase price ( ) Title insurance commitment for mortgage policy in the amount of the new mortgage. Any expense of curing title including, but not limited to legal fees, discharge of liens and recording fees will be paid by SELLER.

7. SURVEY: Within _____ days ( ) after date of acceptance ( ) After date of satisfaction of all conditions in paragraph 19, SELLER will deliver to BUYER or closing ATTORNEY:( ) A new staked survey certified within 3 months of closing showing all improvements now existing thereon. ( ) A copy of a previously made survey of the property showing all improvements now existing thereon. ( ) No survey is required.

8. ( ) ZONING and RESTRICTIONS: Unless the property is zoned _____ and can be legally used for _____ or if there is notice of proposed zoning changes, deed or other restrictions that could prevent such use at the time of closing, BUYER shall have the right to terminate this Agreement. BUYER shall have 10 days from date of acceptance to verify the existing zoning and deliver written notice of objections to SELLER or be deemed to have waived objections under this paragraph.

9. ( ) WOOD-DESTROYING ORGANISM REPORT: "Wood-destroying organism" means arthropod or plant life which damages a structure. BUYER, at BUYER'S expense (unless VA), within time allowed to deliver evidence of title and examination thereof, may have the property inspected by a Florida Certified Pest Control Firm to determine whether there is any visible active wood destroying organism infestation or visible existing structural damage from wood destroying organisms in the improvements. If BUYER is informed of either or both of the foregoing, BUYER will have seven (7) days from receipt of written notice thereof or four (4) days after selection of a contractor, whichever occurs first, within which to have all such wood-destroying organism damages, whether visible or not, inspected and estimated by a licensed building or general contractor. SELLER shall pay costs of treatment and repair of all structural damage up to 1% of purchase price. Should such costs exceed that amount and SELLER declines to treat and repair, BUYER shall have the option of (a) cancelling the contract within five (5) days after receipt of contractor's repair estimate by giving written notice to SELLER, or (b) be deemed to have elected to proceed with the transaction, in which event BUYER shall receive a credit at closing of an amount equal to the total of the treatment and repair estimate not in excess of 1% of the purchase price, if approved by lender; if not, BUYER shall be deemed to agree to pay excess amount prior to closing.

10. (A) TITLE EXAMINATION AND TIME FOR CLOSING: If title evidence and survey, as specified above, show SELLER is vested with a marketable title, subject to the usual exceptions contained in title insurance commitment (such as exceptions for survey, current taxes, zoning ordinances, covenants, restrictions and easements of record), the transaction shall be closed and the deed and other closing papers delivered on or before ( )
( ) _____ days after date of acceptance ( ) _____ days after date of satisfaction of all conditions in paragraph 19, unless extended by other conditions of this contract.

(B) If title evidence and/or survey reveal any defects which render the title unmarketable, BUYER shall have 7 days from receipt of title commitment and survey to notify SELLER of such title defects and SELLER agrees to use reasonable diligence to cure such defects at his expense and shall have 90 days to do so, in which event this transaction shall be closed within ten days after delivery to BUYER of evidence that such defects have been cured. SELLER agrees to pay for and discharge all due or delinquent taxes, liens, and other encumbrances, unless otherwise agreed. If SELLER is unable to convey to BUYER a marketable title, BUYER shall have the right to terminate this agreement, at the same time returning to SELLER all title evidence and surveys received from SELLER and BUYER'S copy of the agreement; or BUYER shall have the right to accept such title as SELLER may be able to convey, and to close this transaction upon the terms stated herein, which election shall be exercised within 10 days from notice of SELLER'S inability to cure.

11. LOSS OR DAMAGE: If the improvements are damaged by fire or other casualty prior to closing, and cost of restoring same does not exceed 3% of the assessed valuation of the improvements so damaged, cost of restoration shall be an obligation of SELLER and closing shall proceed pursuant to the terms of this agreement with cost therefor escrowed at closing. In the event the cost of repair or restoration exceeds 3% of the assessed valuation of the improvements so damaged and SELLER declines to repair or restore, BUYER shall have the option of either taking the property as is, together with either the said 3% or any insurance proceeds payable by virtue of such loss or damage, or of cancelling this agreement.

12. SELLER agrees to deliver the property in its PRESENT AS IS CONDITION except as otherwise specified. SELLER does hereby certify and represent that he has legal authority and capacity to convey the property with all improvements. SELLER further certifies and represents that he knows of no latent defects to the property and knows of no facts materially affecting the value of the property except the following

_____ BUYER agrees that he has inspected the property and has not relied upon any representations made by any real estate agent in describing the property, and BUYER agrees to accept the property in its PRESENT AS IS CONDITION, except as herein otherwise specified.

13. ( ) OCCUPANCY: SELLER represents that there are no parties in occupancy other than SELLER. BUYER will be given occupancy at closing unless otherwise stated

       If occupancy is to be delivered prior to closing, BUYER assumes all risk of loss to persons and property from the date of occupancy, shall be responsible and liable for maintenance thereof from said date, and shall be deemed to have accepted the property, real and personal, in its existing condition as of time of taking occupancy unless otherwise agreed in writing.

( ) BUYER understands that property is available for rent or rented and the tenant may continue in possession following closing unless otherwise agreed in writing. All deposits will be transferred to BUYER at closing.

14. **PERSONAL PROPERTY:** Included in the purchase price are all fixed equipment including ceiling fans, drapery hardware, attached lighting fixtures, mailbox, fence, plants and shrubbery as now installed on the property, and these additional items: _____

Items specifically excluded from this agreement: _____

15. **DEFAULT AND ATTORNEY'S FEES:** If BUYER fails to perform this contract within the time specified (including payment of all deposits hereunder), the deposit(s) paid by BUYER shall be retained by or for the account of the SELLER as agreed upon liquidated damages, consideration for the execution of this contract, and in full settlement of any claim; (pursuant to provisions of the listing agreement on subject property) whereupon BUYER and SELLER shall be relieved of all obligations under this contract. If, for any reason other than the SELLER'S failure to make SELLER'S title marketable after diligent effort, SELLER fails, neglects, or refuses to perform this contract, the BUYER may seek specific performance or elect to receive the return of the BUYER'S deposit(s) without thereby waiving any action for damages resulting from SELLER'S breach. In connection with any litigation arising out of this Agreement, the prevailing party shall be entitled to recover all costs incurred, including a reasonable attorney's fee.

16. **PAYMENT OF EXPENSES:** If this transaction does not close through no fault of SELLER, all loan and sales processing and closing costs incurred, whether the same were to be paid by SELLER or BUYER, shall be the responsibility of BUYER, and the costs shall be deducted from the binder deposit. This shall include but not be limited to the transaction not closing because SELLER elects not to make the mortgage to BUYER as provided in Paragraph 2(C) of this Agreement, because BUYER does not obtain the required financing as provided in this Agreement, or because BUYER breaches this Agreement.

If this transaction does not close through no fault of BUYER, all loan and sales processing and closing costs incurred, whether the same were to be paid by SELLER or BUYER, shall be the responsibility of SELLER, and BUYER shall be entitled to the return of the binder deposit. This shall include but not be limited to the transaction not closing because SELLER is unable or unwilling to complete the transaction for a qualified BUYER, or because the property does not appraise for an amount sufficient to enable the lender to make the required loan, or because SELLER elects not to pay for the excess amount in Paragraph 9 or Paragraph 11, or repairs in Paragraph 4, or because zoning is not as required in Paragraph 8, or because SELLER cannot deliver a marketable title, or SELLER breaches this Agreement.

17. The offer of BUYER shall terminate if SELLER has not indicated his acceptance of the Agreement by signing and delivering same or telegraphing acceptance to BUYER or submitting agent before _____ :01 [ ] A.M. [ ] P.M., Date _____

18. **ADDITIONAL TERMS, CONDITIONS, OR ADDENDA** (Lettered A,B,C,D, etc.)

19. **TIMING:** The timing of paragraphs 6,7,9 and 10(A) will become operable after satisfaction of paragraph 2, if applicable, and these additional conditions lettered in paragraph 18 _____

20. There are no other agreements, promises or understandings between these parties except as specifically set forth herein. No alterations or changes shall be made to the Agreement except in writing and signed or initialled by the parties herein.

21. This legal and binding Agreement shall be construed under Florida Law, shall not be recorded and if not understood, parties should seek competent legal advice.

22. SELLER and BUYER give real estate agent authorization to advise surrounding neighbors who will be the new owner of the property.

23. TIME is of the essence in this Agreement.

24. SIGNED AND WITNESSED on the dates and in the year herein stated. SELLER's name, address, SS#/T.I.N.#, and phone number may be inserted in the first paragraph of this Agreement without constituting a counteroffer.

_____	_____
Date of Offer	BUYER
_____	_____
Date of Offer	BUYER
_____	_____
Date of Acceptance	SELLER
_____	_____
Date of Acceptance	SELLER

WITNESSES: (2 recommended but not required)

WITNESSES: (2 recommended but not required)

AGENT by the signature below acknowledges receipt of $ _____ ( ) cash ( ) check, as binder deposit, which is the amount mentioned in paragraph 1a of this Agreement. It will be held in escrow pending disbursement according to terms hereof, together with all additional binder deposits escrowed by terms of this Agreement.

Company _____ By _____ Title _____

SELLER agrees to pay listing agent a brokerage fee of $ _____ or _____ % of the total sales price(plus applicable sales tax.)Listing agent _____ agrees to pay _____ , cooperating agent $ _____ or _____ % of the sales price.

SELLER _____

This form is for the exclusive use of members of the Jacksonville Board of Realtors, Inc. unless its use is authorized in writing by the Board of Directors. Copyrighted by the Jacksonville Board of Realtors, Inc. Jacksonville, Florida. 1986 MLS Form I, Rev. #3 - 4/87

Form 5

TYPICAL TITLE INSURANCE RATES
[Subject to variation from state to state]

Amount of Insurance	Premium charged
$ 1,000	75–100
2,500	100–125
5,000	125–150
10,000	150–250
25,000	250–350
50,000	375–500
75,000	450–625
100,000	600–800

Form 6

SELLER'S AFFIDAVIT

STATE OF ....

COUNTY OF ....

Before me, the undersigned authority, personally appeared .... (and ....), who being duly sworn, say:

(He) (They) (is) (are) the owners(s) of the property located at ....; that (he) (they) (is) (are) in sole possession of such property; that there are no other persons in possession of such property, except: ....; that there are no unpaid material,
                    (put "None" if applicable)
work, labor, repairs, or improvements furnished to the property within the last past 90 days.

....
Signature
....
Signature

Sworn to and subscribed
before me this .... day
of ...., 19............

....
Notary Public, State and County
aforesaid. My commission expires: ....

Form 7

GENERAL WARRANTY DEED

THIS DEED made the .... day of .... 19............
by .... (and ...., his wife) hereinafter
called Grantor, to .... (and ...., his
wife), hereinafter called Grantee, whose mailing address is
....
(Wherever used herein the terms "Grantor" and "Grantee" include the
heirs, legal representatives, successors and assigns of the parties.)

WITNESSETH: That the Grantor, in consideration of $10.00 and other
valuable consideration, receipt of which is acknowledged, hereby grant,
bargain, sell, convey and confirm to the Grantee, all that certain land
in the County of .... State of ...., as
follows:

TOGETHER with all the tenements, hereditaments and appurtenances
thereto belonging or in anywise appertaining; to have and to hold the
same in fee simple forever. AND the Grantor hereby covenants with
the Grantee that the Grantor is lawfully seized of said land in fee simple;
that the Grantor has good right and lawful authority to sell and convey
said land; that the Grantor hereby fully warrants the title to said land
and will defend the same against the lawful claims of all persons whomsoever; and that said land is free of all encumbrances, except taxes for
the year ....

IN WITNESS WHEREOF, the Grantor has signed and sealed this deed
the date above stated.
Signed, sealed and delivered
in our presence:

                                          GRANTOR:

...., ... (SEAL)
.... (SEAL)

STATE OF ....
COUNTY OF ....

I hereby certify that on this .... day of .... 19............ before me, an officer duly authorized in the State and County aforesaid to take acknowledgements, personally appeared .... (and ...., his wife) to me known to be the person(s) described in and who executed the foregoing deed, and said person(s) acknowledged before me that (he) (they) executed the same.

....
Notary Public, State and County aforesaid. My commission expires:

....
(NOTARIAL SEAL)

Form 8

CHANGE OF OWNERSHIP NOTICE

Date.............................

To: ....
Name of Mortgage Company

....
Address

....
City and State

Re: Account #...............................

Property Address:

....

Gentlemen:

This is to notify you that the property described above has been sold by .... to ...., whose mailing address is ....

The sale was by deed dated ...., and recorded in the public records of .... County.

Recording reference .... (book and page no.)

It is agreed that any escrow funds shall be transferred to the buyers' account.

SELLERS:

....
Signature

....
Signature

BUYERS:

....
Signature

....
Signature

Form 9

BILL OF SALE

KNOW ALL MEN BY THESE PRESENTS: The undersigned, hereinafter called SELLER, in consideration of $10.00 and other valuable consideration, receipt of which is acknowledged, hereby grants, bargains, sells, transfers, and delivers to .... (and ...., his wife), hereinafter called BUYER (Wherever used herein the terms "Seller" and "Buyer" include the heirs, legal representatives, successors and assigns of the parties), the following goods and property:

TO HAVE and to hold unto the Buyer, forever. And the Seller hereby covenants with the Buyer that the Seller is the lawful owner of said goods and property; that they are free from all encumbrances; that Seller has good right to sell the same; and that Seller will warrant and defend the sale of the said goods and property to Buyer against the lawful claims and demands of all persons whomsoever.

IN WITNESS WHEREOF, the Seller has signed and sealed this instrument this .... day of .... 19.............

Signed, sealed and delivered
in our presence:

....

....

SELLER:

.... (SEAL)

.... (SEAL)

Form 10

CHECKLIST FOR HOUSE CLOSING

I. Papers to be delivered to you in advance of closing, so that you can have time to examine them:
    1. Title insurance binder or abstract.
      a. Look for any exceptions or liens.
      b. See that title binder insures "marketability" (use A. L. T. A. Standard Owner's Policy, Form B).
    2. Survey.
    3. Copy of existing mortgage and promissory note (if you're buying an equity).
      a. Check for "balloon" payments.
      b. Check for "due-on-sale" provision.
      c. Other requirements.
    4. Copy of any restrictions or easements.
    5. Any party wall agreements.

II. Things to do a day or two before closing:
    1. Make arrangements with utility companies to start service after closing.
    2. Arrange for necessary funds at closing.
    3. Make a final personal inspection of premises.
      a. Check physical condition, for any change.
      b. Make sure tenants, if any, are out.

III. Items to be delivered to you at closing:
    1. Any releases required by the title insurance binder.
    2. Seller's copy of his hazard insurance policy (or get new policy, where applicable).
    3. Copy of new note and mortgage (if new loan is being made).
      a. Check amount of loan, interest rate, repayment schedule.
      b. Check grace period and prepayment penalty.
    4. Last year's tax receipt, or proof of payment.
    5. Seller's copy of any service contracts (exterminating, garbage, etc.).
    6. Termite inspection report.
    7. Other reports on house condition (plumbing, wiring, roof, etc.) where applicable.
    8. Any applicable guarantees (roof, heating, appliances).
    9. Letter from mortgage company as to status of loan, and mortgage payment book used by seller.
   10. Change of ownership notice to mortgage company, signed by seller.
   11. Death certificate from seller, showing death of joint owner (where applicable; you'll also need proof of no estate taxes due, where this comes up).

12. Seller's affidavit of possession and no liens.
13. Closing statement: look over the charges.
14. Letter signed by the parties agreeing to adjustment of tax proration, when actual bill received (where applicable).
15. Current homestead exemption card or receipt.
16. Bill of sale for personal property.
17. Warranty deed with correct documentary stamps (or appropriate credit given to you for stamps).
    a. Check the description.
    b. Check names, signatures and marital status.
    c. Witnesses.
    d. Notary: seal, and date his commission expires.
18. Paid utility receipts (where applicable).
19. If possession will not be delivered at closing, get letter from seller, agreeing to keep house in good repair and to deliver possession by certain date.

IV. Things to do at closing:
    1. Have seller sign all papers.
    2. Buyer signs note, mortgage, and other papers.
    3. Deliver purchase price.
    4. Pay closing costs.
    5. Obtain keys.

V. After the closing:
    1. Record deed promptly.
    2. Notify title insurance company to issue policy.
    3. Send change of ownership notice to mortgage company, with transfer fee.
    4. Notify hazard insurance company to issue endorsement showing new owner.
    5. Notify utility companies.

CHAPTER 3

So You're Going To Sell Your House

BACK IN THE SEVENTEENTH CENTURY, SIR EDWARD COKE MADE his now-famous remark that a man's house is his castle. And down through the ages, it's been agreed that "there's no place like home." But even castles sometimes have to be sold. So suppose that one day you wake up and find that you need to part company with the old homestead.

How do you go about "putting it up for sale?" Where do you start?

Of course, it's easy enough to stick a For Sale sign on the front lawn. And maybe you're even well-prepared for a glib presentation extolling the physical virtues of your house. But you'll need to know more. You've got to have some idea what to tell a prospective buyer about financing, closing costs, taxes, recording, and a dozen other details.

Some owners decide they don't have the time, energy, inclination, or know-how to sell their house. So they turn it over to a real estate agent or broker. This is fine if you understand how such an agent works and what his charges are.

A. The Real Estate Agent

Usually the real estate agent will handle the advertising of your property, show the house to potential customers, prepare a sales contract, and in some cases, even draw up the deed. In return for his services in producing a buyer that's "ready, willing, and able"

78

to buy, you pay a commission, or fee, which is generally a percentage of the sales price.

Most agents have a written "listing" contract they ask you to sign, formally "listing" the house, or putting it in their hands, for sale. The agent will want you to do this before he gets started. These contracts are not uniform, and you shouldn't be bashful about studying it carefully.

You should first watch out for the amount of the commission. Don't let him use a phrase like "reasonable or customary charge used in the community." This tells you nothing, and you can end up litigating it in court. Make him tell you exactly what his charge will be. In the past, real estate agents commonly charged 5% of the total sales price. In recent years, the fee has climbed to 6% and sometimes 7%, especially when "multiple listings" are used (this means the broker refers the house to several other "cooperating" agents, who also try to sell the property, and split the commission with your broker).

Be careful about how the commission is figured. If you have a large mortgage on the property, and you're selling only your equity (that is, the value above the mortgage), you can get burned if you're not aware of how the brokerage is computed. Let's say your house is worth $70,000. It has a $60,000 mortgage on it, and an equity of only $10,000. If the agent's commission is 6%, it'll be figured on the whole $70,000, not on just the $10,000. So his commission would be $4,200 (6% of $70,000), and you'd only get $5,800. If you're willing to sell on that basis, well and good, but don't just plunge in without realizing how deep the water is, and how much you'll come out with.

Although the broker may tell you he's not allowed to "negotiate," or haggle over the amount of the commission, many of them will, especially when your equity is small. It's not unusual for him to cut the fee to as low as 3% to make the sale. Some will even take a "flat" fee of $750 or so if they can make a fast turnover. But you'll need to work this out before you sign up with him.

The listing agreement will specify how long it's effective. Some are for 90 days, but others are for as long as six months, and some don't even have a termination date. You're generally better off with a 90-day contract; if the house hasn't been sold in three months, you may want to turn it over to another broker. A few contracts require you to give written notice a certain number of days in ad-

vance, to discontinue the listing. Don't sign it unless you know
how you can cut it off.

Most agents will demand an "exclusive" listing. Under this type
of arrangement, they get their commission regardless of who sells
the house. This can be risky, especially when another broker tries
to claim that *he* found the buyer. You should try to give the agent
only an "open" listing, meaning the commission is open to whoever finds a buyer for you. If the agent objects to this (and many of
them will), then at least add a provision allowing you to sell it
yourself, without having to pay the commission. They won't give
in gracefully on this either, but try anyway.

When you're dealing with real estate salesmen, you'll need to
watch out for the so-called "oral" listing. In most states, even
without a written agreement, the courts can find an "implied"
contract, if the broker acts with your consent in getting a buyer.
Just a casual conversation with an agent could be enough to legally
bind you. If a broker introduces you to somebody, and you eventually sell to that person, the broker may be entitled to his commission if the court decides he's the "procuring cause." So when
you have a house for sale, be leery of overly-friendly brokers.

Also look out for the agent—whom you've never met before—
who knocks on your door and announces that he has a buyer who
"wants exactly the kind of house that you have." This can be tricky,
because he usually won't tell you the name or address of the buyer.
If you already have an exclusive listing with another broker, refer
all inquiries to the broker. If you have an "open listing," or none
at all, you're probably safe in telling the "door knocker" you'll
give him an open listing, with your right to cancel it at any time. If
he's sincere and really has a buyer, he shouldn't object. If he com-
plains that he has to have an exclusive agreement, then he's probably a phony, and you should close the door as fast as you can.

B. How Important Is the Contract?

As was explained in Chapter 2, the sales contract is the most
important part of your sale (Chapter 2, Section A). Why do you
need a contract at all? The primary answer is that without one, the
buyer isn't obligated to go through with the purchase, since a real
estate agreement has to be in writing (there are some isolated exceptions to this, but they're rare).

Even if you were sure of the buyer's integrity, and you knew he wouldn't back out, you still need a contract to provide for the various intricacies of closing costs, financing, possession, risk of damage, and so forth. Also, you'll find that most lending institutions, as well as the F.H.A. and V.A., require a signed copy of the contract before they'll approve any mortgage.

The F.H.A., in particular, has some specific requirements that you better know about before you agree to have the buyer finance the house through that agency.

For example, the F.H.A., even though it only *insures* the loan, rather than lends the money, has restrictions against your accepting a second mortgage, or deferred payments, from the buyer. It basically works like this: if the buyer applies for the maximum authorized F.H.A. loan, then he's not allowed to make a second mortgage for the down payment, although he can still borrow against other collateral (such as stocks, bonds, etc.). The restrictions are a little complicated, and the regulations have changed from time to time. So watch your step on this, and don't put anything in the contract that will violate this regulation. (See Chapter 2, Section B).

There's also an F.H.A. policy requiring you to get an appraisal of your house from one of its inspectors, before it will approve a loan. The cost runs around $200, which you pay to the mortgage company that will process the loan. The appraisal is good for only a limited length of time, generally nine months or less. The problem here, though, is that if the appraisal is for less than you expect, the buyer may have the right to back out of the deal and get his money back. The F.H.A. and V.A. require you to have a clause in the contract, relieving the buyer of his obligations, if the appraisal is less than a specified figure (see Form 2, Chapter 2).

Unfortunately, this rule indirectly serves to set your sale price. Technically, these government agencies claim they're not telling you what price to sell for; but in fact, it's a rare day when you can get more than the F.H.A. or V.A. appraisal. If the appraisal comes out way below what you hoped for, and you feel there may be a mistake, or that the inspector didn't consider all the factors, ask for a reevaluation. You may not get anywhere, but occasionally you can get the figure raised. It's especially helpful if you can show that some comparable houses were appraised higher.

You'll recall the discussion about an abstract and title insurance (Chapter 2, Section E). From your standpoint, as seller, it's usually cheaper to give an abstract, and have it brought up to date from the time you acquired the house. This isn't always true, though, and you should call a local title insurer and an abstract company (often the same company does both) to find out the charges. Better yet, see if the buyer will agree to pay the cost. Remember, there's no *law* that says you have to furnish title insurance or an abstract.

If you're selling an equity, and the buyer is taking over your mortgage, you should find out the status of your escrow account before you sign the contract. This is the account that the mortgage company holds, to use in paying taxes and insurance (see Chapter 2, Sections A and C). The escrow can catch you from both sides—whether there's a shortage or whether there's a surplus. If there's a shortage or deficit, the buyer will expect you to pay it. So you should know the exact balance in the account before you negotiate the deal, in case you want to raise the purchase price to make up for it. Have the mortgage company give you the information in writing, so that there can be no misunderstanding about it. On the other hand, the escrow frequently has a surplus. This happens when the mortgage company has overestimated the taxes or insurance during the year. In such a case, you should be entitled, as a minimum, to any moneys not needed to cover the estimated escrow items. The mortgage company usually won't give this back to you, since it's too much trouble for them to make refunds (they'll generally just continue to hold it until they eventually allow a credit on some future mortgage payment). But why should the buyer get the benefit of it? You should, therefore, add a provision to the sales contract, requiring the purchaser to reimburse you for any surplus in the escrow account.

A recommended clause (shown in Form 1, Chapter 2) is: "Buyer shall reimburse Seller for all surplus escrow funds not needed by the mortgage company for the actual payment of estimated taxes, insurance, or other 'escrowed charges.'"

Actually, the fairest way to handle the escrow—and the method used by many lawyers and realtors—is to require the buyer to reimburse the seller for *all* escrow money. This is really proper, since the escrow, in fact, *does* belong to the seller. The difficulty, though, is that in the typical equity sale, the buyer is purchasing the house on a "shoestring" and simply doesn't have enough money to pay you for the escrow. There are exceptions, of course, but if you insist on reimbursement, the whole sale may fall through. If you're only getting a couple hundred dollars for your equity, forget about getting reimbursed for the escrow. But if a larger amount is being paid to you, then you have a better chance to ask for the escrow.

As a matter of fact, probably a majority of equity sales are completed with no thought being given to reimbursing the seller for the escrow. The seller merely signs the "change of ownership notice" required by the mortgage company (Chapter 2, Section H), and the escrow account is automatically credited to the new buyer. But before you decide to agree to this, you should check on the exact amount of the escrow, and how much you'll be losing by agreeing to it.

When you sell a house with an existing mortgage on it, the ideal situation for you is to have the mortgage company release you completely from it. This involves having the new buyer substituted in your place (called a "novation"). You'll find, though, that a great many lenders won't agree to this, and it's not so easy to accomplish. Some savings and loan associations will release the seller and take the buyer in his place, but they'll charge a fee of around 1% of the mortgage. As a alternative, your sales contract should at least require the buyer to *assume* the mortgage (that is, be legally responsible for the payments), rather than merely taking the house "subject to the mortgage." You'd still be technically liable on the mortgage, since you haven't been released, but you'd have a claim against the buyer if the mortgage is foreclosed.

If your house happens to have a V.A. or F.H.A. loan, and you're selling your equity (rather than "refinancing"), you should make a special effort to get released from the loan. The V.A., for many years, has had a particularly harsh policy of pursuing everybody connected with the mortgage if there's a default. So even if the delinquency happens through no fault of yours, a few years after you sell, you may find yourself responsible for a deficiency (see Chapter 2, Section J). The V.A. and F.H.A. have the necessary application forms and financial data sheets for release and substitution of the buyer. It's generally wise to write in a provision in the sales contract, requiring the buyer to take all reasonably necessary steps to be substituted for your loan, and to allow you to be released. And don't forget the restrictions involving "due-on-sale" clauses (Chapter 2, Section D).

In preparing the sales contract, you might be confronted with a buyer who asks to have possession of the house before the closing date. Keep away from this, if possible. Some sellers have been good samaritans and allowed the buyer to move in a week or two before the final papers were signed, and before the final money was paid. Then something happens to prevent the closing—such as the lender's disapproval of the buyer's credit—and you can have a heckuva time getting him out of the house.

For other comments (and forms) on sales contracts, see Chapter 2.

C. How Much Deposit Should You Get?

Under the law of almost every state, any "consideration," or thing of value, no matter how small, is sufficient to make a contract legal. This is why many agreements and documents recite a consideration of only $10, or even $1.00 (see Chapter 2, Section F). So when you agree to sell your house, if you receive as little as a $10 deposit from the buyer, this is actually enough to make a binding agreement.

But should you be satisfied with that little? How much is "customary"?

You'll be taking a chance if you accept only a small deposit. In the first place, when a buyer has put up just $10 or $25, he isn't worried about forfeiting it if he finds a more suitable house between the signing of the contract and the closing. He may feel that he'd prefer losing twenty-five bucks, and getting the other house, rather than going ahead with his contract.

Can't you legally sue him for breaking the agreement? Or to force him to go through with it? In theory, yes, but in the average house sale, it just isn't practical. The suit would drag on for many months; it's expensive; the amount of damages is often unsatisfactory; and you may find the buyer is "judgment-proof" anyway. So in the overwhelming majority of such cases, you're better off to just keep the deposit and start over again. But if you get a large enough deposit to start with, there's less likelihood of your buyer backing out.

There's another reason to get more than $10 or $25. In the typical sale, you, as the seller, will have certain expenses in preparing for the closing. You might have to order title insurance or an abstract, possibly get a survey, pay for some termite exterminating, and the time and trouble of getting together various documents. So if the buyer backs out, you'll want to at least have enough money on hand to pay you for your out-of-pocket costs.

How much of a deposit should you get? In a number of sections, it's standard to ask for 5% to 10% of the purchase price. But don't be surprised if you can't get that much. Somewhere around $500 is probably a fair figure. If you're selling a fairly expensive house, though—say $75,000 or more—you should have a minimum of $1,000. On the other hand, if you're disposing of an equity and only getting $500 for the whole thing, it's not likely the buyer will be willing to put up the entire amount as a deposit. Around $100 is fair in that case.

If the buyer is giving a personal check for the deposit, you should always put it in the bank or cash it as soon as possible; never agree to just "hold it." Otherwise, the purchaser could stop payment if he changes his mind, and you'd have nothing (except an unsatisfactory possibility of suing him).

If you're getting a substantial deposit, the buyer may want the money held in trust by a disinterested third person (see Chapter 2, Section A). Try to discourage this, but if you can't, then find out if the third party will charge an escrow fee, before you agree. Sometimes the deposit is placed in an interest-bearing account.

When a real estate agent is handling the sale, he'll generally hold the deposit. He'll probably have a provision in the contract that if the buyer doesn't go through with the sale, the deposit will be divided equally between you and the agent. This is a common stipulation, but it's a little one-sided. See if the agent will agree to the following, instead: *"If the Buyer fails to complete the purchase, any expenses for closing costs or other items required to be paid by Seller shall be deducted from the deposit, and any balance shall be divided equally between the Seller and the agent."*

D. The Discount Trap

If you've been living in your house for several years, it's likely that your mortgage balance (if you're still paying on the loan) is low. Or to put it the other way, your equity is high. When that's the case, you'll often find that the typical buyer doesn't have enough money to buy out your interest. You'll either have to take back a second mortgage (see page 37 and Section F), or have the house refinanced. Of if you're able to finance it yourself, you might be willing to have the mortgage made to you and be paid monthly (see Section G).

In Chapter 2, the various types of available loans were discussed, with some advantages and disadvantages listed (page 33).

If you've decided to sell your house through a mortgage insured by the Federal Housing Administration, you should, of course, know that agency's requirements. Of those, one of the most puzzling for the unwary seller is the so-called "discount."

The discount is an amount of money charged by a mortgage lender when it makes the loan. In effect, you're paying the lender a premium or bonus for the privilege of borrowing the money. This sounds somewhat absurd, but the basic reason has to do with the availability of mortgage money, and the interest rates that a lender can charge for a loan.

The F.H.A. limits the interest rate that a mortgagee can charge, and the rate is usually lower than the customary interest charged by the lender for other types of loans. Result: he loses money by making the F.H.A. loan. Then why would a lender be willing to make such a loan at all? As a matter of fact, many don't; but since the F.H.A. stands behind the loan, and insures it, it's a fairly safe investment for a lender. Still, the lending institution feels it isn't getting a high enough return on its money. To make up for the lower interest rate, the lender charges the "discount," which is generally expressed as a percentage of the loan amount. The percentages are also spoken of as "points," with each point representing one percent. So if the loan, for example, is for $10,000, and the discount is 5%, for five "points," the lender would charge $500 (5% of the $10,000), even though the borrower has to pay back the full $10,000. Through this device, the actual interest "yield" is increased, and the rate is somewhat equalized with the higher charges made on non-F.H.A. loans.

So far, so good. But for a long period of time, the F.H.A.'s regulations required the *seller* to pay the discount, regardless of what the parties agreed on. That made no sense to most people, and fortunately that rule has been discarded. So the question of the discount, and who pays it, can now be negotiated between the parties, the same as the other closing costs.

If you're particularly anxious to sell the house, you may have to pay all or most of the discount yourself.

If that's the case, then another way around the discount is to raise the selling price so as to cover yourself. But the F.H.A. mortgage will still be based on the appraisal, rather than the selling price, and it's unlikely that you'll be able to get a buyer to go along with an inflated selling price. In many sales, then, you just have to absorb part of the discount. So be sure you at least have some idea how much the discount will be. It changes from day to day, and from place to place, and can vary by as much as seven or eight percent! When interest rates rose during the last few years, the discount could be as high as 10%, which obviously will take a whopping bite out of any expected profit on your sale.

Here again, it pays to shop around and call different lending institutions. Although many of them will have the same discount, this isn't always true. You can often find one with some surplus mortgage money, ready to give you a lower discount.

The discount, in fact, can be so costly to a seller that it can often make it completely impractical to sell through the F.H.A. at all. It sometimes pays to cut your price by a few hundred dollars, and see if the buyer can come up with enough cash to take over your existing mortgage, rather than refinance. Or you can consider the possibility of taking a second mortgage (see Section F).

If your equity is too large, though, and the only way you can sell is to have the house refinanced through F.H.A., find out in advance about the discount. Otherwise, it can hit your pocketbook pretty hard.

The closing costs on an F.H.A. loan can also be high. Get some estimate, from the mortgage company, about how much they'll be, especially if *you're* going to pay them. The costs can run well over $1,000 in many cases. Even if the buyer will pay them, you should have an idea of what they'll be, in case you're asked.

E. What Costs Should You Pay?

The best rule, of course, is pay as few costs as you have to. But there are certain expenses that are customarily your responsibility, and you should know which these are (see Chapter 2, page 50).

Usually the seller pays the revenue stamps on the deed. The amount differs from state to state, but is based on the selling price. Check with the local recording office to find out how much the stamps will be.

Several years ago, you had to put federal stamps, as well as state stamps, on the deed, but the federal charges are no longer required. Many states have now picked up these charges as a "surtax," or additional expense, so that you still have to pay the same amount in those states.

It's usually also your responsibility to give the buyer some evidence of clear title; so it's not out of line for you to pay for title insurance or an abstract. If you're not asked for it, though, don't volunteer it. Don't put it in the sales contract unless the buyer demands it. If he does insist on it, see if he'll agree to pay for it.

The question of who should be charged for a survey is not clear-cut. Try to get out of paying for it, if you can. But you should, beforehand, know how much it'll cost.

In areas where houses are scarce, you might be able to get by with a "net" deal; that is, a certain amount of money "net" to you, and the buyer pays all the expenses. Unfortunately, it works the other way too. The purchaser may say, "I have $10,000 to spend, which I'm willing to give to you, but you have to pay all the costs."

If you're not getting all cash, but are taking back a note and second mortgage (see Section F), the expense involved in this should be the buyer's. If he objects, explain to him that if he paid all cash, there wouldn't be any expense for this item, so since it's for *his* benefit, he should absorb the cost.

Taxes, insurance, and other charges attributable to the property are commonly prorated as of the closing date, but this isn't always true if there's an escrow (see page 30 and 36).

If a new mortgage is being made by the buyer, encourage him to take over your insurance policy, and have him pay you a prorated amount for the number of months left on the policy. Otherwise, he'd get his own insurance, and you'd cancel your policy. But your rebate, in that case, is based on a "short-rate" table used by the insurance company, and you won't get as much.

Expense for recording the various papers is usually the buyer's responsibility.

F. Should You Take a Second Mortgage?

With the high expenses involved in F.H.A. financing (such as discounts and closing costs), it's sometimes preferable not to have the house refinanced; but, instead, to sell your equity for as much cash as you can get, and then take back a second mortgage if necessary.

How does this work and what's involved?

Let's assume your house is worth $75,000, and your mortgage is down to $50,000. But you can't find a prospect with $25,000 cash. If you allow your buyer to finance through the F.H.A., you could be quickly losing as much as $3,500 to $4,000 on the discount (Section D), plus any closing costs you agree to pay.

Suppose, though, that the buyer has $15,000 he can give you as a down payment. You could allow him to pay you the other $10,000 over a period of time (several months, or a few years), in agreed-upon monthly installments. Since you'd need to have this agreement in writing, you'd have him (and his wife, if he's married) sign a promissory note for the $10,000, and a second mortgage (meaning that it's behind the original first mortgage), as security for the payments.

You'd need to decide, first, how much the buyer can pay each month. If he pays too little—$100 or $200 a month—it will take too long to pay off. Only in rare cases should you accept a second mortgage that will take more than five years to repay. Sometimes you can consider small payments, with a provision for the entire balance to come due, in a lump sum, in four or five years (a "balloon payment").

Many banks and insurance companies have "amortization" charts, showing how long it takes for a mortgage to be paid off at certain specified payments. Some samples are shown at the end of this chapter. If you can't get such a chart from your bank, you can write to City Computing Services, 25 S.E. 2nd Avenue, Miami, Florida, for a schedule. Their charge is nominal (about $4.00), and they list the payments and show the time it will take to pay off the loan, with a breakdown of how much goes to principal and how much to interest.

You'll also be entitled to interest on the mortgage, since you're indirectly making a loan to the buyer and financing his purchase. For many years, 10% was the going rate. But in recent times, higher charges of 12 to 14% have become common. WARNING: Most states limit the maximum allowable interest rate, and if you charge more in those places, you could be guilty of usury. Ask your bank, or a lawyer, what the permissible rate is, before you try 12 to 14%.

The note and mortgage would also permit you to make a "late" charge if the buyer doesn't pay on time, or within a certain number of days afterwards (15 days is a common grace period). In addition, you'll find it worthwhile to let a bank handle the collections for you. They'll send notices, mail out receipts, send the payments to you (or credit your account), keep a record of how much interest is being paid, and what the balance is at any given time. Most banks charge very little for this service: three or four dollars a month is typical. So it's a good investment, and saves you a lot of aggravation. In fact, it's not unusual to add a provision to the promissory note, requiring the buyer to pay the collection charge.

It's also routine to allow the note to be paid off in full at any time, without penalty. There are at least two exceptions to this rule, though. If you think you'll have a sizable tax gain from the sale, so that it'd be advantageous to defer any income, then you might prohibit any prepayment during the year of the sale. Also, if there's any chance that you'll want to sell the mortgage at some future time, you might want to provide a restriction against *partial* prepayments, and specify that any such payments will be applied to the *last* payments due under the note. This requires him to keep paying every month. Otherwise, the buyer could prepay six or seven months, and you might have difficulty selling the mortgage during that period.

It's also standard practice to provide that any partial payments must be made in multiples of the monthly installment. In other words, if the regular payment is $200 a month, then the buyer couldn't pay an extra $125; he'd have to pay another $200 or $400. Without this type of restriction, it can become difficult to compute the monthly interest, and can foul up an amortization table, if you're using one.

We've been talking about the details of a second mortgage. But a more important question is: how safe is a second mortgage, and should you really be involved in one at all? It's remarkable how many fallacies have grown up around such mortgages. Some people will tell you that you can't foreclose a second mortgage as long as the first mortgage is current (this isn't true); that if you do foreclose, you have to pay off the first mortgage in full (this generally isn't so, either; all you need to do, in the ordinary case, is keep the payments current on the first mortgage). You'll also hear that second mortgages aren't "worth the paper they're written on" (don't believe it; they can be good investments because of the high interest rate).

Of course, there are some disadvantages, too. If the first loan goes into default, you'll have to be ready to catch up the payments on it, or pay off the balance. If you don't, the first mortgage can be foreclosed, and your second note would be wiped out. So you do need to keep an eye on the first mortgage, and see that the payments are current. As some protection, it's customary to stipulate that any delinquency in the first mortgage will be considered a default in the second mortgage. That way, if you do have to make up a payment that's missed on the prior loan, you'll have the right to foreclose on your own second note.

Another disadvantage of a second mortgage is that your money is tied up, and not liquid. If you need to raise some cash in a hurry, it's not always easy to sell the loan, unless you're willing to do so at a big loss (often as high as 50%).

A third disadvantage is that if the mortgage isn't paid, you can't automatically take back the property in most states. You generally need to foreclose, which is a cumbersome and expensive legal proceeding in many parts of the country. Occasionally you can get the buyer to deed the property back to you, instead of your having to go to court; but you have to be certain there haven't been any other mortgages or liens against the property since the time you sold it. This involves having a title search of the property.

You'll find a suggested form of note and second mortgage at the end of the chapter (Forms 2 and 3). Remember to have the mortgage witnessed and notarized, and then file it with the local recording department. The charges vary, but should be paid by the buyer.

It's also important that you inform the holder of the first mortgage about your second lien, and ask that you be notified if there's ever a default. That way, you can protect yourself by making the payment, if necessary. Don't take a chance, though, on a telephone call; send the notice by mail. A form of notice is at the end of the chapter (Form 4).

If you're turning over any equipment or furnishings to the buyer, you should have your mortgage list the items, so that if you need to foreclose or take back the house, you can reclaim the personal property. In states where the Uniform Commercial Code is in effect, you should also file, with the appropriate recording office, a special "financing statement," listing the personal property.

It's also advisable for you to notify the insurance company agent that handles the hazard insurance on the house. Tell him you're holding a second mortgage, and request him to issue an endorsement to the policy, showing your interest. In case the house burned down, you'd be entitled to part of the proceeds (after the first mortgage).

When the mortgage is paid off, you'll need to deliver a release or "satisfaction" to the buyer, so that he can record it. Also, you should return the note and mortgage to him at that time. A form of satisfaction is reprinted as Form 5 at the end of this chapter.

A second mortgage can be a valuable tool in selling your property. Whether it's advisable in your specific case is a matter you'll need to determine from your own situation. But sometimes it works out very well, so don't sell it short. And as long as you understand what it is and how it works, you're less likely to get hurt by it.

G. How About Holding the First Mortgage?

Instead of being concerned with a second mortgage, you might be thinking about taking back a first mortgage. This might happen when your house is fully paid for. Maybe you're selling for $75,000, and the buyer needs to borrow $65,000. If you don't need the cash, you should seriously consider financing the sale yourself, and carrying the mortgage. As long as you treat it as a regular business transaction, with a reasonable rate of interest payable on the balance, it can be a good investment. You'll also be able to avoid the delays and uncertainty of having the purchaser apply to a commercial lender, and there'll be a large saving on finance charges and closing costs.

You must understand, though, that even a first mortgage has some drawbacks. Your funds are not liquid, for instance, and there are expenses in foreclosing or taking the property back. Also, if you're too friendly with the buyer, so that it might be embarrassing if he defaults, you better think twice.

But if these points don't worry you, and if you get a sizable down payment (at least 10%), and you feel the buyer is a reasonably good credit risk, you might do well carrying the mortgage. If you don't know anything about the buyer, though, try to get a credit report on him. Your bank can probably help you on this.

You can use the specimen form of note and mortgage illustrated as Forms 2 and 3, but delete the references to a second mortgage.

H. Things to Watch Out For

Finding a buyer for your house can be a long and drawn-out affair. But once you've caught him, don't feel you have to give in to everything he asks.

Be aware of the customary charges and procedures outlined in this chapter, and in Chapter 2. Don't let the real estate agent scare you or hustle you into accepting less than your house is worth; most of the agents are honest and reliable, but some are more interested in the commission than in helping you, and will play you off against the buyer.

If you're selling your equity, you don't need the consent of the mortgage company on old F.H.A. or V.A. loans, although you'll have to notify them and probably pay a transfer fee (page 48). But on the newer F.H.A. loans and on most conventional mortgages (and on some second mortgages), there are provisions entitling the lender to declare the whole balance due, unless the purchaser is approved. (See Chapter 2, Section D.) If you don't know whether your mortgage has such a clause, check with the lender.

In case the buyer is refinancing, so that you're paying off your present mortgage, get a letter from the mortgage company, giving you the exact payoff. You don't need their permission to pay it off, but you may end up with a penalty for prepayment (see page 37).

Also watch out for a weird requirement that the F.H.A. has, prohibiting you from leaving furniture or equipment in the house, for the buyer, unless you're paid for it. You might decide that to induce the purchaser to take your property, you'll throw in some of your furnishings without charge—maybe some drapes or a television set. What could be wrong with that? With some fancy mental gymnastics to justify its policy, the F.H.A. says it won't allow you to give these items away! The buyer has to pay for them! So if you list, in the sales contract, any movable personal property that you're including in the price, the F.H.A. may insist that you get paid for them separately. You might be able to get by this rule if you can certify that the items are so old that they have no value. Some sellers make a "gentleman's agreement" with the buyer to leave the goods in the house; but this is illegal and can get you in a pickle. In any event, you'd better look into the regulation, and have a representative of the F.H.A. explain it to you, before you agree to leave any equipment or furniture in the house.

Note, though, that some equipment may have originally come

with the house when it was built. It's likely that these items are actually included in the mortgage. Some examples are a water heater and a built-in oven. If you're selling your equity, you'll be required to leave these in the house if they're mentioned in the mortgage.

There are, of course, some tax consequences you should know about when you sell a house. If you make a profit, as defined by Internal Revenue regulations, you have to pay income tax on the gain. This doesn't apply, though, when you buy or construct a more expensive, or equally-priced, house within a certain period of time afterwards. There are also exemptions if you're over 55. The rules are somewhat detailed, so you should get qualified advice if you feel you're going to have a profit. If you sell your home and lose money, you can't deduct the loss from your tax (there are some exceptions if you've been renting the house or using it for business).

Internal Revenue also has special regulations that apply to "installment sales," when your profit is not received all at one time. In that situation, when you're paid over a period of time more than a year, there's a formula allowing the profit to be prorated, or divided, over a number of years, as you receive the installments. If you think this part of the law may apply to you, check with some competent tax people before you enter into the sales contract.

And, finally, whatever document or agreement you're asked to sign, read it carefully; don't sign anything with blanks in it; and make sure you understand what you sign.

Form I

SAMPLE LOAN AMORTIZATION

(Amounts Necessary to Pay Off a Loan in a Given Number of Years, with Equal Monthly Payments)

Interest at 10% Per Year

Amount of Loan	1 yr.	1½yrs.	2 yrs.	2½ yrs.	3 yrs.	5 yrs.
$ 500	43.96	30.03	23.08	18.91	16.14	10.63
1,000	87.92	60.06	46.15	37.82	32.27	21.25
2,000	175.84	120.12	92.29	75.63	64.54	42.50
3,000	263.75	180.18	138.44	113.44	96.81	63.75
5,000	439.58	300.29	230.73	189.06	161.34	106.24
10,000	879.16	600.58	461.45	378.12	322.68	212.48
15,000	1318.74	900.86	692.18	567.18	484.01	318.71
20,000	1758.32	1201.15	922.90	756.23	645.35	424.95
25,000	2197.90	1501.43	1153.63	945.29	806.68	531.18
30,000	2637.48	1801.72	1384.35	1134.35	968.02	637.42

Form 2

PROMISSORY NOTE
[For Use with Mortgage]

AMOUNT: $.............................   Date ....

FOR VALUE RECEIVED, the undersigned (jointly and severally, if more than one signer), promise(s) to pay to the order of .... (and ...., his wife), the principal sum of $.............................., with interest at ....% per year from date until maturity, said interest being payable (check applicable letter)

__a. Monthly

__b. Other ....

both principal and interest being payable in lawful money of the United States of America at .... or at such other place as the holder from time to time specifies by written notice to the maker, payments to be made as follows:

Not less than $.............................. per month (or not less than $.............................. per ....), on the .... day of each and every (month) (other period ....), commencing on the .... day of .... 19............, until the full amount of principal and interest has been paid, said payments to apply first to interest accruing from pay period to pay period, and balance to principal.

Maker(s) shall pay collection charges if this note is turned over to a bank or collecting agency. If any payment is not made within 15 days after the due date, Maker(s) shall pay a late charge of 5% of the payment.

If default is made in the payment of any of said sums, within 15 days after the due date, then, at the option of the holder hereof, all sums then remaining unpaid, with accrued interest, shall immediately become due, without notice, time being of the essence, and the principal shall bear interest at the maximum legal rate from such time until paid.

Each maker and endorser waives presentment, protest, notice of protest and notice of dishonor, and agrees to pay all costs, including a reasonable attorney's fee, whether suit be brought or not, in the event of default in this note or the security thereof.

Maker(s) may, without penalty, prepay all of this note at any time, or may make partial prepayments in multiples of the regular payment, such prepayments to be applied to the last payments due under the note.

                        .... (SEAL)

                        .... (SEAL)

Form 3

MORTGAGE

THIS MORTGAGE made the .... day of ....
19............ by .... (and ...., his wife)
hereinafter called Mortgagor, to .... (and
.............................., his wife), hereinafter called Mortgagee (Wherever
used herein the terms "Mortgagor" and "Mortgagee" include the heirs,
legal representatives, successors and assigns of the parties)

WITNESSETH: That the Mortgagor, in consideration of $10.00 and other
valuable consideration, receipt of which is acknowledged, hereby grant,
bargain, sell, convey and confirm to the Mortgagee, all that certain land
in the County of .... State of ...., as
follows:

TOGETHER: with all the tenements, hereditaments and appurtenances
thereto belonging or in anywise appertaining; to have and to hold the
same in fee simple.
(This is a second mortgage, and any default in the terms of payment of
the first mortgage shall constitute a default hereunder)*

And the Mortgagor hereby convenants with the Mortgagee that the
Mortgagor is lawfully seized of said land in fee simple; that the Mortgagor has good right and lawful authority to sell and convey said land;
that the Mortgagor hereby fully warrants the title to said land and will
defend the same against the lawful claims of all persons whomsoever;
and that said land is free of all encumbrances (except the first mortgage)*

PROVIDED, ALWAYS, that if the Mortgagor shall pay to the Mortgagee
the certain promissory note, of which the following is a copy, to wit:
(copy of note attached)
and if the Mortgagor shall promptly and fully perform and comply with
each covenant and condition of the promissory note and of this mortgage, then this mortgage and estate hereby created shall cease and
be void.
The terms "Mortgagor" and "Mortgagee" shall include the plural,
where applicable.

The Mortgagor covenants and agrees:

1. To pay all sums required under the note and this mortgage promptly
when they become due.

*Use this clause only in connection with a second mortgage; delete this clause
if you're using a first mortgage.

2. To pay all taxes, assessments, levies, liabilities, obligations, and encumbrances of every kind now or hereafter imposed on the mortgaged property, when due and payable, and before they become delinquent; and in the event that any are not so paid or discharged, the Mortgagee may pay the same without waiving or affecting any option or right under this mortgage; and the full amount of each such payment shall be immediately due and payable, with interest as set out in the note.

3. To place and continuously keep on the buildings now or hereafter situated on said land hazard insurance in the usual standard policy form, in a sum not less than the amount of the first mortgage, if any, and the second mortgage, in such company as may be approved by the Mortgagee; and all such insurance policies shall contain the usual standard mortgagee clause making the loss thereunder payable to said Mortgagee as its interest may appear; and each policy, or a copy, shall be promptly delivered to and held by the Mortgagee; and not less than 10 days in advance of the expiration of each policy, to deliver to Mortgagee a renewal thereof, together with a receipt for the premium; and in the event any money becomes payable under such policy, the Mortgagee shall have the option to receive and apply the same on the note or to permit the Mortgagor to receive and use it; and in the event Mortgagor shall fail to keep the premises insured or fail to comply with this paragraph, Mortgagee may place insurance on the premises without waiving or affecting any right under this mortgage, and the full amount of any such payment shall be immediately due and payable, with interest as set out in the note.

4. To permit, commit or suffer no waste, impairment or deterioration of the mortgaged property or any part thereof.

5. To pay all costs and expenses, including reasonable attorney's fees and cost of title search, incurred at any time by Mortgagee in the event of failure of the Mortgagor to fully perform each covenant and condition of the note and this mortgage; and such costs and expenses shall be immediately due and payable, and shall be secured by the lien of this mortgage.

6. That (a) in the event of any breach of this mortgage or default continuing for 15 days after written notice from the Mortgagee, or (b) if any of the sums of money referred to herein or in the note not be paid within 15 days after due, without demand or notice, then the aggregate sum mentioned in the note then remaining unpaid, with accrued interest, and all moneys secured by this mortgage, shall become immediately due and payable, at the option of the Mortgagee, without further notice or demand.

7. If, during any suit to foreclose this mortgage, or to enforce payment of any sums hereunder or under the note, the Mortgagee shall apply for the appointment of a Receiver, such court shall forthwith appoint

such Receiver of the mortgaged property and the rent, income, profits and revenues, and such Receiver shall have all the powers entrusted by a Court to a Receiver; and such appointment shall be made as an admitted equity and a matter of absolute right to the Mortgagee, without reference to the adequacy of the value of the property or the solvency of the Mortgagor; and such rents, income, profits and revenues shall be applied according to the lien of the mortgage and the practice of the Court.

8. To duly, promptly and fully perform each agreement, condition and covenant in the promissory note and this mortgage.

If the mortgaged property, or any part thereof, is taken by eminent domain or condemnation, the Mortgagee shall have the right to receive any moneys paid by the condemning authority for the property or part taken, up to the principal balance and accrued interest owing to Mortgagee, plus attorney's fees if any are paid by the condemning authority.

IN WITNESS WHEREOF, the Mortgagor has signed and sealed this mortgage the date above stated.

Signed, sealed and delivered
in our presence:

....   MORTGAGOR:

.... (SEAL)

STATE OF .... (SEAL)

COUNTY OF ....

I hereby certify that on this .... day of ....
19............ before me, an officer duly authorized in the State and County aforesaid to take acknowledgments, personally appeared
.... (and ...., his wife) to me known to be the person(s) described in and who executed the foregoing mortgage, and said person(s) acknowledged before me that (he) (they) executed the same.

....
Notary Public, State and County aforesaid. My commission expires:

....
(NOTARIAL SEAL)

Form 4

NOTICE TO HOLDER OF FIRST MORTGAGE

Address:
Date:

XYZ Mortgage Company
100 Main Street
New York, N. Y.
Gentlemen:

Re: Your mortgage on
123 Oak Street; Name of Payer

I am presently holding a second mortgage on the above property,
made by _____(and _____, his wife), who also
(has) (have) a mortgage with your company.

Please notify me if any payment is not made on time, or if there is
any default in the mortgage.

Thank you.

Sincerely yours,

Form 5

SATISFACTION OF MORTGAGE

KNOW ALL MEN BY THESE PRESENTS: The undersigned, being the
owner(s) and holder(s) of a certain mortgage executed by
.... (and ...., his wife) to
.... (and ...., his wife), dated the
.... day of .... 19__, recorded in Book ....,
page ...., of the public records of .... County, State
of ...., securing a certain note, and being a lien on the
property described in such mortgage, hereby acknowledge full payment and satisfaction of said note and mortgage, and surrender the
same as cancelled, and hereby direct that the mortgage be cancelled
of record.
IN WITNESS WHEREOF, the undersigned (has) (have) set (his) (their)
hand and seal this .... day of .... 19............

Signed, sealed and delivered
in our presence:

....
....   Mortgagee
STATE OF ....
COUNTY OF ....   Mortgagee

I hereby certify that on this .... day of ....
19............ before me, an officer duly authorized in the State and County
aforesaid to take acknowledgments, personally appeared
.... (and ...., his wife) to me known to
be the person(s) described in and who executed the foregoing instru-
ment, and said person(s) acknowledged before me that (he) (they) executed the same.

....
Notary Public, State and County
aforesaid. My commission expires:

....
(NOTARIAL SEAL)

CHAPTER 4

So You Think You Want A Divorce

A CYNIC WAS ONCE ASKED TO NAME THE GREATEST CAUSE OF DI-
vorce. Without hesitation, he responded, "Marriage." The philos-
opher Voltaire, in the same vein, said, "Divorce is probably as old
as marriage, or perhaps marriage is a few weeks older."

The dissolution of a marriage, though, isn't funny. It can be a
tragic, painful experience. All too often there are long, drawn-out
court battles, with sordid accusations and bitter custody fights.
Many studies and efforts have been made to improve divorce laws
and to rehabilitate broken marriages. But despite these enlightened
attempts, the divorce rate continues to climb.

Whether you're still single; or have been through a divorce one
or more times; or are still happily married, having steered your
matrimonial ship through calm and sometimes stormy seas, you
need to know a little about our divorce laws and the rights of husband and wife.

A. What Are the Legal Grounds?

It's probably safe to say that in most marital breakups, both parties are at least partly to blame. Yet, in the past, very few courts
would grant a divorce when both spouses were at fault, or when
neither was at fault. Our statutes were based on the somewhat naive
and archaic notion that one party must be guilty of wrongdoing,
and the other, innocent. Sometimes, of course, this is exactly the
situation. But more often, both sides have contributed to the

problem: the husband drinks too much, so the wife nags him. Or the wife is indifferent to her husband's caresses, so he seeks entertainment elsewhere. Or the wife flirts at parties, so the husband sulks and curses her. Sometimes the difficulties are less dramatic, and a small disagreement can be blown out of proportion.

The roots of a marital problem, of course, can run deep, and can spread slowly until love and respect wither. Until recently, though, there had to be "grounds" for dissolving a marriage. But the national trend is now toward "no-fault" divorce, upon a showing of "irreconcilable differences" or an "irretrievable breakdown" of the marriage, without the traditional requirement of "fault" or misconduct. And an even newer move is to "administrative divorces," without a court hearing, when there are limited assets and no children. In fact, many states now use the term "dissolution of marriage," instead of "divorce."

But there are still states that require legal grounds. In those places, merely showing that you don't get along, or that "we don't love one another," is generally not enough.

The recognized grounds vary considerably from state to state. For a complete list, by state, see the chart at the end of this chapter.

A majority of the states still list adultery as a ground. As you might expect, this can be difficult to prove. But it's generally not required that you have any pictures, or even "eye witnesses." In many jurisdictions, you only need to show that the guilty spouse had the "opportunity" and the "desire" to commit adultery. It's usually enough to prove that he (or she) spent the night in a motel room with a person of the opposite sex. This is "circumstantial" evidence; but in most places, if the circumstances would lead the "guarded discretion" of reasonable men to conclude that there's guilt, that's sufficient.

The defendant may have an explanation. He or she may have only been playing gin rummy all night in the motel room (that excuse has been used more than once), but such defenses have not met with any spectacular degree of success.

Adultery is no longer used as a ground for divorce as often as in the past. This is partly due to the liberalization of divorce laws, and the addition of new grounds in a number of states (in New York, for example, for many years, adultery had been the only way to get a divorce; now this has been changed by legislation). For other reasons—because of property settlements, custody of children, embarrassment, and difficulty of proof—adultery is now used only in a very small number of divorces.

Desertion, or abandonment, is a basis for divorce in more than half the states. Merely living apart from each other, though, doesn't meet the test. To prove desertion, you have to show an intentional or deliberate absence or abandonment by one of the parties, usually against the will of the other.

The length of time needed to establish desertion isn't the same in all states. The shortest period of time is six months, but in other places it's as high as three years. The most common requirement is one year.

The desertion has to be continuous for the required statutory period. In other words, if the husband and wife reconcile and live together for even a day, this will cut off the desertion, and you'd have to start counting all over again if the spouse leaves.

When one of the parties separates involuntarily from the other, or through no fault of his own, there's no desertion. This comes up in cases where the husband leaves because of military orders, or is transferred by his employer to another city.

Sometimes the wife will refuse to follow her husband even though his job requires him to move. Basically, the man has the right to decide the family residence, even against the wife's will. This sounds a little old-fashioned, but the law still recognizes the husband as the head of the household. And the wife has the duty of living with him, if reasonably possible. In one court case, the parties had been living in England. The husband returned to the United States, but the wife refused to go and wouldn't leave the home. The husband claimed desertion, and was granted a divorce.

In some circumstances, the man's choice might be unreasonable. With the present world situation, if a husband wanted to move to Soviet Russia, it's unlikely he could successfully prove desertion against an unwilling wife.

What happens when one party is *forced*, by the other, to leave the home, or is locked out? The courts in many states recognize a doctrine known as "constructive desertion," allowing a divorce to the one who's forced out (provided that the required statutory period passes). It's often hard to decide when one spouse is forced out. If he or she is driven out by actual physical compulsion or genuine fear, this is all that's needed. But if the husband, for example, raises his voice a time or two, so that the wife packs her bags, she ordinarily wouldn't be legally justified in leaving. No two cases are exactly alike, though, and a slight change of facts can bring about a different result.

Many courts require a husband to make a reasonable attempt at a reconciliation after the parties have separated, even though he may have been the one abandoned. It's not always clear, though, what is a "reasonable" attempt. The offer must at least be in good faith with no unduly restrictive conditions.

Suppose the husband and wife mutually agree to go their separate ways and live apart. Can one of them sue for desertion after the required statutory waiting period? Legally, no. But this probably happens in many cases, with no objection raised by the spouse being sued.

A more liberal approach to the desertion problem, in force in about one-third of the states, is the recognition of mere separation or absence, as a ground for divorce, without intent or wilfulness. The required minimum length of time for such separations differs from state to state. It's one year in some, to as high as five years in Rhode Island, under some conditions. Many states don't permit it at all.

Probably the single most commonly used ground for divorce in the United States has been "cruelty." Approximately 60% of the states permit some form of this charge, and it runs the gamut from physical abuse and "personal indignities," to the milder "mental cruelty" allowed in several places.

What constitutes "cruelty"? No all-inclusive definition has been given, and thousands of cases are passed on each year by judges trying to decide the question.

Conduct that's cruel to one person of a sensitive nature won't necessarily be cruel to another. The key, apparently, is what effect the actions have on the particular person involved. Clearly, behavior that brings about serious injury to a spouse would be sufficient. This would include beatings, severe slapping, and other similar actions. Slight acts of violence, though, especially committed very infrequently, would not meet the test in most places. But actual physical violence or injury doesn't have to be present in the majority of states.

The prevailing view is that if the conduct impairs or endangers the health of the affected spouse, it's grounds for divorce. This includes the so-called mental cruelty that has become increasingly popular.

Some courts have said that cruelty is any "unjustifiable" course of conduct which "utterly destroys" the legitimate ends of marriage. But this definition doesn't tell you what behavior meets the test. There are other broad definitions by the courts. It's often said, for instance, that cruelty is any action that makes living together unsafe or intolerable. Yet mere inconvenience or unhappiness doesn't authorize a divorce.

Under most of the statutes, threats of physical violence, causing a reasonable fear, will constitute cruelty. The threats have to be of serious mistreatment, though. It probably wouldn't be enough to prove a threat of an ordinary spanking.

Certain acts, when standing by themselves, might be insufficient as cruelty. But with other behavior, or when committed over a long period of time, they'll satisfy the average court. Consider a case of a wife who nags her husband and constantly criticizes him in front of his friends. Is that cruelty? Maybe, when combined with other elements—such as frequently raising her voice and cursing him.

In particular cases, some of the following actions, often in combination, have been used to prove cruelty:

1. False accusations of unfaithfulness or other immoral conduct.
2. Habitual fault-finding and nagging, without cause.
3. Cursing and use of obscene language.
4. Statements of love for another person.
5. Repeated refusal of affection or love.
6. Remaining away from the home for long periods of time without explanation.
7. Continuous coldness and indifference to the wants or needs of the spouse.
8. Persistent offensive habits (such as constant gambling, refusal to bathe or keep clean, or continuous neglect of normal household duties).

Usually, to establish cruelty, you need to prove a "course of conduct," or repetition of the behavior, rather than one isolated episode. This is particularly true in the mental cruelty complaints. If the isolated episode happens to be serious enough, or especially flagrant, then it might be sufficient. In one case, a divorce was granted for a single false accusation of adultery, made in front of mutual friends.

What about refusal to engage in sexual intercourse? If the refusal is unjustified, and continues for a long period of time, it can be the basis for a divorce in a number of jurisdictions. But again, the specific facts of a given case can alter the outcome.

From time to time, cruelty is claimed because of "perverted" or "abnormal" sex practices of the other spouse. If these make the marriage revolting to the innocent party, the court might grant the divorce. In a few cases, sodomy by the husband was considered cruelty. In another case, active homosexuality was the basis for a divorce.

A number of states still recognize impotency as a ground to dissolve a marriage. This has been variously defined as inability to consummate the marriage, or incapacity for sexual intercourse. Every now and then the courts have struggled with some delicate distinctions as a result of this definition, and the reported cases are not always illuminating. For instance, how about imperfect or unnatural sex relations? The answer is not clear-cut, but usually this constitutes impotency, according to the courts. There are cases holding that if sexual union can't be natural and complete, because of some defect or malformation, then impotency has been proved.

The reasons for the incapacity apparently don't bother the courts too much. In one reported Alabama case, the proportions of the husband's sexual organ were "abnormally excessive." In a Massachusetts decision, the court found impotency because of the wife's extreme pain during the sex act, making coitus practically impossible.

In one famous case, there had been no consummation of the marriage for a number of years, and the husband and wife had never had intercourse. The wife sued for divorce, accusing the husband of being impotent. He denied the charge, claiming that he hadn't wanted to "hurt" her or cause her pain or discomfort. The court, in a restrained understatement, found this conduct most gallant and solicitous in a suitor, but not believable in a husband. The divorce was granted.

Is impotency the same thing as sterility, or inability to beget children? No, say the courts. If you're able to have normal relations, but can't have children, that's not impotency.

There's not too much dispute, either, over when the impotency must exist. If it's not present at the time of the marriage, then it's not a ground for divorce. To put it another way, if the problem comes up later, it's usually not a basis for an impotency complaint.

And in most states where the matter has been litigated, the impotency has to be incurable. So if the condition can be removed or corrected by medical treatment or surgery (provided there's no great danger), the court will deny the divorce. If the incapable spouse doesn't consent to the cure, though, then the refusal would be sufficient ground.

An interesting quirk is that several cases have said that the impotent party can't terminate the marriage for his own incapacity; only the other spouse can use this as a complaint.

In several states, nonsupport is a ground for divorce. Some statutes call it "neglect of duty" or "refusal to provide." Traditionally, the wife has to show that the husband has the ability to support her, but that he's failed to do so intentionally. If the man isn't able to provide support because of misfortune or sickness, the divorce will be denied.

A spouse's insanity for a prescribed period of time is cause for divorce in about half of American states. But the statutes are strict about what insanity is, and many of them require confinement in a mental institution for several years.

In most jurisdictions, habitual drunkenness, alcoholism, or "intemperance" is a ground for divorce. The court requires more than an occasional drink, though; usually the complaining party must show excessive drinking, for a substantial length of time. The cases, in fact, refer to a "fixed habit," or an "irresistible temptation." One court pointed out dramatically that the drinking must be to the point where "the will is dethroned by frequent indulgence and failure to control one's appetite for strong liquor." It's probably not necessary to go that far in the average case.

Some of the states require the habit to have continued for a minimum period, such as a year or two. But this isn't a standard requirement.

With the increasing use of drugs and narcotics, a few states have broadened their definition of "intemperance," or added a separate category to include habitual drug usage as a ground for divorce.

Sometimes the wife or husband wants to avoid the embarrassment and scandal of a public charge of "excessive drunkenness." It's not uncommon for such misconduct to be listed with other improper behavior as a basis for a cruelty charge.

Suppose the husband or wife is convicted of a serious crime and imprisoned for a number of years. Grounds for divorce? Yes, in most states, but not all. Several recognize varying degrees of crimes as a sufficient basis. In a few states, the sentence has to be life imprisonment; in others, as little as two years.

Not every crime, though, will qualify. Some statutes refer to "infamous crimes," a somewhat nebulous term at best, while others refer to offenses involving "moral turpitude." And different courts sometimes come to opposite conclusions over the same crime. In one state, assault to commit rape was found to be an infamous crime, while in another, it was not.

In fact, about the only uniformity in divorce law is the lack of uniformity. Each state sets its own public policy as to which marital offenses will justify the dissolution of a marriage.

Here's a list of some other grounds found with less frequency, but in use in some of the states:

1. Bigamy (even though this allows you to get an annulment—a decree which says, in effect, there never was a legal marriage—a few jurisdictions also list it as a basis for divorce).

2. Fraud or force (also used as a ground for annulment).

3. Marriage to a close relative.

4. Pregnancy at the time of the marriage (required to be from someone other than the husband, and undisclosed at the time of the marriage).

5. Violent and ungovernable temper (this overlaps with cruelty in many cases).

6. Incompatibility (probably the *actual* ground in most divorces, but recognized in very few states).

So despite the tremendous increase in divorces, some states still require that one of the marital partners be innocent, with "clean hands," and that the other be "guilty" of some recognized misconduct. Recently, though, there has been a strong nationwide movement to discard the ancient concept of "blame," and to sanction "no-fault" divorces if the court finds the marriage is really "irretrievably broken" or that the differences are "irreconcilable." (See divorce chart following the chapter.)

B. Suppose the Spouse Won't "Sign"; Then What?

Movies and television have popularized the idea that if the spouse won't "sign," the other can't get a divorce. Or it's sometimes put the other way: if one *does* "sign," the other automatically gets the divorce.

Both notions are wrong.

The "signing" that's supposed to take place refers to the spouse's agreement that the husband or wife can have a divorce. One party technically signs a waiver, a stipulation, or other document signifying he or she is not contesting the proceedings.

But what if the spouse doesn't sign? Is that the end of it, forever? "My wife won't give me a divorce," the husband moans to the "other woman" in the soap operas. What he really means is that in such circumstances, a divorce might be harder to get. But not impossible. Because now he really has to *prove* the grounds, and whatever charges he makes will probably be vigorously denied and contested. But in a state with "no-fault" divorce, it won't make too much difference either way.

To illustrate, suppose the husband and wife just don't hit it off. No major flaws; but he likes sports and cards; she likes to read. He enjoys parties; she prefers knitting. Finally, he decides he has to break away. The answer? Divorce.

But she won't agree. Can he get it in those circumstances? In the "no-fault" states, generally yes. But where fault is still required, he'd have to sue on one of the prescribed legal grounds in his state. His best bet would probably be cruelty (see Section A). He'd claim that she criticizes his cardplaying, nags at him when he loses, won't go out with him, fusses if he comes home late, and generally makes his life miserable. But what happens? In court, she'd no doubt deny all this, and have friends testify what a good and devoted wife she is. Unless he has a batch of corroborating witnesses (see Section C), it's likely he'll lose. Meanwhile, he's spent a large wad of money on fees and costs.

So, in this type of "weak grounds" situation, there's some merit to the concept that you won't get the divorce unless she agrees. But even in this very kind of case, many divorces are actually granted in some parts of the country, over strenuous objection by the wife. The judges in such cases often reason that it's unlikely the parties will get back together; that they'll be better off unmarried. Obviously, not all judges agree with this philosophy. But the point is that even if a wife (or a husband, for that matter) won't "sign," you're not out of the ball game. You still have a chance, and shouldn't always give up, if you genuinely feel the marriage is hopeless and really can't be saved.

Of course, your chances improve substantially if you have some strong ground, such as drunkenness, physical violence, or adultery. You might still have difficulty *proving* the charges, since the bulk of marital misbehavior takes place behind closed doors, and very few people like to get involved as witnesses in a domestic squabble. But if you can present some outside evidence to back up your charges, the odds shift to your side. Even though the spouse won't "sign," you have a good shot at a divorce.

Now take the case of the "agreeable" spouse. She wants out as much as you do, and is ready to sign the papers. She's so eager, she'd probably sign a long-term agreement to rent a room from the Boston Strangler if you put it in front of her. So it's automatic, right? Probably yes, in the "no-fault" states. But elsewhere, you still have to allege some ground for the divorce. This isn't always as simple as it sounds. As mentioned previously, in New York, for many years, adultery was the only recognized ground. Also, in a state where cruelty isn't a legal basis, you might have a tough job. And even where cruelty is a recognized ground, some statutes require more than just "mental suffering." Still worse, in a number of states, you have to have some corroborating witnesses confirming your testimony go to court with you, even if the divorce is not contested (see pages 110–112). And in every state, there are certain minimum residence requirements before you can qualify to even file the suit (see chart at the end of this chapter).

So in very few places does the divorce go through just by "signing." And in any event, there's still a court hearing, as a general rule.

Certainly it's a lot easier when there's no fight; there's not as much strain, it's less expensive, and the chances are that you'll be able to get it, once the spouse agrees to it. But don't expect to be completely home-free without any hurdles at all.

C. Witnesses

The old ecclesiastical courts of England wouldn't grant a divorce unless the complaining party (the plaintiff) had some confirmation or corroboration of his charges. This doctrine, with some alterations, has been adopted in a great many areas. Even in uncontested divorces, some states require some corroboration. The theory is to prevent collusion, and to make sure there is, in fact, a legitimate cause for dissolving the marriage. Sadly, instead of making more divorces "honest," the rule has had the opposite effect. It's a common sight in divorce courts to find the plaintiff dragging in a friend or neighbor to "stretch" the truth, and in some cases to actually commit perjury, so that an uncontested divorce can be obtained. A philosophical defense of the corroboration rule is best left to other forums; but until changed or modified, the principle remains imbedded in most divorce statutes and laws.

How much corroboration do you need? And what part of the evidence has to be backed up by witnesses? Basically, the corrobative testimony has to support the essential elements of the case, but not every detail. For example, if you're the plaintiff, you need to substantiate your residence in the state. You'd ordinarily have a friend, business associate or relative testify that you've lived in the state continuously for the required minimum period, and that it's your "home" (this is often somewhat of a sham in states that have very short residency requirements, with the plaintiff planning to leave as soon as the divorce hearing is over).

In a cruelty case, the witnesses would testify, typically, that they were present on a number of occasions when the offending spouse committed some dastardly act of misconduct, and that they saw or heard the defendant do one or more of the following:

1. Holler at you (this is good);
2. Curse you (the more profanity, the better);
3. Threaten you (better still, especially if a weapon was used);
4. Strike you (best);
5. All of the above (divorce granted).

For a desertion case, the witness' testimony might go something like this:

1. The husband left the house more than (a year ago) (two years ago) (longer);
2. When he left, he said he was going for good;
3. He hasn't been back;
4. She never gave him any cause to leave.

Adultery can get a little stickier. Sometimes hired investigators are used. Once in a while, the "third party" or "correspondent" testifies, although the courts receive such testimony with caution.

Very often, circumstantial evidence is relied on. Testimony that the husband spent the night in a hotel room with a woman will generally prove the point.

In fact, circumstantial evidence is commonly relied on in divorces to establish grounds for the breakup, since eyewitness corroboration is generally difficult and not required. In a cruelty case, for example, a neighbor is often called as a witness to establish that she (or he) saw bruises or marks on the plaintiff, even though the witness didn't see the injury actually take place.

Certain grounds are obviously awkward, if not impossible, to corroborate. As a hypothetical case, try proving a charge of impotency with corroboration. In this type of case, the courts have had some predictable difficulty. Sometimes they've considered admissions by a spouse, or a refusal to submit to a medical examination.

The requirement, in some localities, for more than one corroborating witness, has caused problems. The practice in Duval County (Jacksonville), Florida, for a long period of time, was to have two witnesses, especially to prove the plaintiff's residency. This has been changed, and only one witness is now required. Apparently, most jurisdictions don't specify the *quantity* of corroborating witnesses, but are more concerned with the *quality* of the evidence.

Now and then, an unhappy spouse is confronted with the embarrassing prospect of being unable to find even one corroborating witness. He may have lurid tales of his wife's misconduct—ranging from temper tantrums, to infidelity—but alas, there's nobody who saw it! In states with a strong policy of corroboration, he'll have serious difficulty. This is true even when the spouse will "sign" for the divorce (see Section B). To get around this enigma, some determined plaintiffs have taken up residency in the "easy-divorce" states (notably Nevada and Idaho), or have tried a Mexican divorce. Others have stayed where they are, but have persuaded friends to "exaggerate" a little in court, enabling the judge to grant the divorce.

So, unfortunately, the corroboration requirement, which started out as a noble device to keep divorces aboveboard, has now gone full circle the other way, and has probably been responsible for more fabricated testimony in American courtrooms than any other cause. Until the divorce laws are changed, the practice will no doubt continue.

D. Defenses

The most common defense to a divorce action is a simple denial. "I didn't do it, Judge," has probably knocked out more divorces than all else combined. But there are other defenses, some of them technical; some bizarre.

To start with, the complaining party must meet strict residency requirements in each state (see the chart at the end of this chapter). These rules can be complicated, and many a plaintiff has slipped up at this stage of the game.

"Residence," as used in most divorce statutes, means physical presence within the state, and the intention of staying there indefinitely. This sounds clear enough, but it isn't. What happens when a plaintiff leaves the state for a short time during the residency period? This is permissible, if there's no intention to move away; so a traveling salesman, a railroad conductor, or an airline pilot are all protected. But suppose you're in the armed forces, and your military orders send you to another country or state for several months. Do you lose your residency or domicile? The general rule in most states is that you don't, but in a few jurisdictions, the answer would be different, since some states require actual "physical" presence for a divorce.

The standard way to maintain residency intact when you're away on military orders, or other temporary job assignments, is to keep up a house or apartment in the state, continue your voting registration there, bank accounts, church membership, and other affiliations to show your intention.

What if you're a "career" serviceman, or have been away from your home state for several years? It's possible for you to establish a new legal residence in the state where you're stationed. You'd need to be there for the required statutory time, and you'd have to intend to make it your home. Several states have special laws for servicemen, creating a presumption that they're legal residents of the state where they're stationed.

If you're in a "transient" type of business, where you spend six months in one place (like a waiter in Florida during the tourist season), and then several months somewhere else, you'll have some difficulty with the residence requirement. Your domicile, for divorce purposes, will usually depend on where you've established "the chief seat" of your household affairs or home interests.

Another defense to a divorce action is forgiveness, or "condonation," as it's called by lawyers. The innocent spouse "condones" or excuses the misconduct of the other, usually on the implied condition that the offensive behavior won't be repeated.

It works this way: let's say the husband has committed adultery. The wife is willing to give him another chance. If she resumes cohabitation (living together as husband and wife), knowing he's been unfaithful, then she's condoned the offense. If she changes her mind a few days later, it's too late; the husband could then successfully defend a divorce on the ground of condonation. But if he "strays" again, or commits other acts of marital misbehavior, this can "revive" the original offense as a basis for divorce.

Condonation applies to other misconduct, as well. If a husband beats up his wife, but she goes back to him, she condones the offense. Or if he drinks excessively, but she keeps living with him, she condones his drinking. Remember, though, that the forgiveness is conditional, and if the spouse starts the misconduct again, it wipes out the condonation.

Each state, as well as the church, has a strong public policy that seeks to preserve marriages. For this reason, our laws traditionally disallowed a divorce by "consent" of the parties (see Section A). If the evidence before the court indicated that the parties had aided or assisted each other, in some improper way, to obtain a divorce, the judge could throw out the case. This unlawful assistance, or aid between the spouses, is known as "collusion." This is an agreement, between husband and wife, to illegally promote or bring about a divorce.

It's rare, of course, for one of the partners to raise this defense, since he'd be admitting that he's a party to it. Collusion is usually brought up by the judge, if he feels the testimony shows it.

Note, though, that merely agreeing to a divorce is not collusion. Neither is failing to object to a divorce. Collusion involves an actual meeting of the minds of the parties, basically to perpetrate some fraud on the court. A typical situation would be the husband's agreement that the wife will give false evidence against him, or that certain testimony will be suppressed.

Fifty years ago, a judge would have probably called it collusion if he thought the parties had "agreed" to the divorce. But now, the vast majority of divorces are really "agreed upon" beforehand, in the sense that property settlements and custody matters are carefully worked out in advance, and it's clearly understood that the divorce won't be contested. Although this is fairly close to being collusion, in the classical sense, don't worry about it. Almost everywhere, judges now accept the idea that if a ground for divorce can be proved, it's not collusion for the parties to have an uncontested court hearing, agree on alimony, support, and the other marital matters.

Very similar to collusion is a companion doctrine known as "connivance." This refers to the unlawful consent or approval by one spouse for the other to commit an act constituting grounds for divorce. The standard connivance is for one of the parties to consent to adultery by the other. This sounds fairly ridiculous, at first blush, but it was quite common in places like New York, where adultery was once the only ground for divorce. Connivance isn't restricted to infidelity, though. In one Florida case, a husband kept his wife supplied with whiskey and continuously encouraged her to drink. When he brought suit for habitual drunkenness ("intemperance"), the court denied him relief, because of connivance.

Probably the strangest divorce defense of all is "recrimination," which means countercharge. Roughly speaking, if the complaining spouse was *also* guilty of a ground of divorce, neither party would be granted a decree. The theory was that the plaintiff had to have "clean hands," and be innocent of wrongdoing, to be entitled to a divorce. If he wasn't, then the court would leave him where he was before he brought the suit: still in a state of marital bliss.

The rule operated this way: if the man proved the woman committed adultery, but she proved that he did the same thing, neither one was granted a divorce.

The doctrine has been criticized by many courts, but it still survives. Critics argue that if both sides have committed serious acts of misconduct, it's unlikely the marriage can be saved, and a divorce should be granted. Some writers have claimed that the rule encourages collusive divorces and perjury, increases adultery, and is completely illogical.

Several courts and legislatures, in recent years, have tried to back away from the harshness and folly of recrimination. They've decided that it's not an absolute bar, and that the judge still has discretion to grant the divorce. In a number of states, a rule called the "doctrine of comparative rectitude" is in force. This permits a divorce to the party who is "less at fault."

There are some other defenses also available on occasion, such as:

1. Provocation (the plaintiff's misconduct provoked the defendant).

2. Unreasonable delay in bringing suit (waiting too long, so that the key witnesses die or move away; or the misconduct happened so long ago as to be too remote).

3. No valid marriage to begin with (this can happen when a prior divorce isn't final, or where there's no marriage ceremony or "common law" marriage).

4. Knowledge, before marriage, of the other spouse's misconduct (such as the husband's awareness that the wife was pregnant when they married).

E. How Much Does It Cost?

There are no standard fees or charges that will apply to every divorce case in every city. The attorney's fees can vary enormously, depending on the time spent, the value of the property involved, the difficulty of the case, how much of a contest there is, and other circumstances (see Chapter 11).

The fees are also based, to some extent, on the particular locality. The charges in urban areas are uniformly higher than in small communities.

Several sections of the country, for a time, used suggested minimum fee schedules, but even these varied. The attorney's charge for an uncontested divorce, without any unusual problems or complicated property settlements, probably runs from a low of $150 to a high of $750. More typically, the cost usually is in the range of $300 to $500.

But if there are time-consuming agreements to prepare (even though there is no dispute between the parties), or deeds and other documents to draw up, the fee can run higher.

In a contested divorce, it's hard to predict what fee you'll have to pay. Some lawyers charge for the time spent, the rate starting at about $75 an hour (occasionally lower), and up to $175 an hour. In large metropolitan law offices, fees of up to $250 per hour are not uncommon. The cost of a contested divorce can start at $350, and go as high as several hundred thousand dollars, in the more spectacular cases that make front-page headlines.

A run-of-the-mill divorce contest (if there is such a thing), with the parties in a middle income bracket, arguing over child support, alimony, and grounds for divorce, can be quite expensive. It's not easy to give an average fee in such a case, but it could easily go above a thousand dollars. About all you can do to protect yourself is to get an understanding from your lawyer, in advance, about how he'll charge, and his estimate of the expense. Don't demand a "top" figure, though. This can backfire against you. The average lawyer, if he's pinned down to quoting a maximum fee ahead of time, will tend to make it higher, maybe subconsciously, to cover himself. But later you may end up being billed that amount, since the quoted "top figure" sticks in his mind. Or if he gives you a figure that turns out to be too low for the number of hours he's spending, he may have to cut the time he's devoting to your case since he'll be losing money. So just try to get his best estimate of what it'll cost you, and what his hourly rate is, and don't insist on a definite maximum fee.

If you're the husband, there's a good possibility you'll also have to pay your wife's legal bill, or a portion of it. See if you can get an estimate of that, too. More than one unhappy male has agreed to a settlement after he found out how much a contested divorce would cost. (For a more detailed discussion on paying your wife's attorney fee, see Section J.)

There are also court costs in every divorce case. These differ in each locale, too, but in an uncontested case will roughly range from $75 to $150. In a contested divorce, with hundreds of pages of testimony, and possible depositions (see Chapter 8), the court costs can be astronomical, and you'll need to ask how high they can go.

In many areas, it's traditional for attorneys to be paid in advance for a divorce, especially an uncontested one. This is so they won't have to hound you for the fee when the case is over. Don't be offended if you're asked to pay before any papers are even filed. In some places, the lawyer may agree to a "retainer" or deposit, in advance, usually between 25% to 50% of the total fee, with some understanding about payment of the balance.

Occasionally, a question comes up about "contingent fees" in divorce actions; that is, fees based entirely on the outcome. This is not as common in marital cases as the general public believes. In fact, in many states, if the fee agreement is directly and expressly contingent on the amount of alimony or property settlement, the agreement is considered unenforceable and against "public policy."

On the other hand, the amount of money or property involved

usually does have at least some bearing on the fee. The more money at issue, the greater the lawyer's responsibility (see page 324).

So even though it's almost impossible to tell, in every case, exactly what you'll have to spend, make sure you talk it over at the beginning.

F. How Long Does It Take?

An uncontested divorce, in theory, should move along smoothly and be over in a matter of days. In some states, it does, and is. In Florida, for example, the divorce—from start to finish—can be signed, sealed, and delivered in 30 days or less. But in other states, because of court congestion, waiting periods, and various delays, it can take as long as eight months, even when nobody's fighting it.

A few of the states also have "interlocutory decrees," which are temporary court orders, finding that grounds for divorce exist, but leaving the marriage intact until a certain number of months pass. Primarily, this is to allow a "cooling-off" period and to stop hasty divorces. The typical "waiting period" is 60 days, but it's as high as six months in some states, such as in Wisconsin. In most places, though, there's no interlocutory decree, and the parties are free to remarry immediately. But don't jump into matrimony again unless you know, for certain, whether your divorce is final. A chart, listing the various waiting periods, can be found at the end of this chapter.

G. Who Gets Custody of Junior?

Child custody cases are among the bitterest of all court battles. The usual rule is that the welfare and best interests of the child are the prime concerns of the court. So fundamental is this policy, that even when the husband and wife agree on who should have custody, the court isn't necessarily bound by it. But in the ordinary case, such an agreement will be recognized, unless there are overriding considerations to the contrary.

The ancient principle was that a father had a superior right to the custody of his children. This has given way, though, to the more modern maxim, that each parent has an equal right to custody. In practice, though, the mother usually gets the care and control of young children, if she's a fit parent. But, again, not every case is the same, and the rule doesn't always hold up. If the welfare of the child demands it, a judge will grant custody to the father. Lately, a number of courts have been ordering "shared parental responsibility," or "joint custody," so that the parents share major decisions about the upbringing of the child. Also, it's not out of the ordinary for the custody to be awarded to a third party, such as a grandparent or aunt, when neither of the natural parents can properly care for the offspring.

If the parties have agreed on who will have custody (even when the court approves), this isn't final for all time. If the circumstances change, the judge can alter the custody award. It usually requires some substantial change, and the court won't allow the same evidence to be rehashed before him.

Suppose the child, himself, prefers to stay with one of the parents. This doesn't carry much weight if the child is young (under 10), but if he's sufficiently mature, the court will consider his desires. The preference of the minor, though, is only one factor the judge will weigh, and it's not controlling.

When custody is awarded to one of the parents, the other has the right of "reasonable visitation." There can be some juicy brawls over what's "reasonable." Twice a week? Every Sunday? If the parties can't agree between themselves, the judge will set the ground rules. Most courts are reluctant to spell out the visitation rights in great detail, preferring to leave such matters to the parents. But when necessary, the judges will do it. It's not unusual for the decree to set forth specific hours of visitation; which holidays will be reserved for the father; a schedule for summer vacation; and other similar items. In recent years, some states have also been granting visitation rights to grandparents.

Some courts have granted "divided" custody: the child stays with the mother for six months, and with the father for a like period. This is usually impractical and can be harmful to the child. Most judges will avoid this "solution," and you shouldn't agree to it, except as a last resort, in the most exceptional circumstances. When the parties can't agree on custody, it's not uncommon for a court to require mediation by a trained counselor, in a more informal atmosphere than a courtroom.

Can the mother—or other custodian—move out of the state with the child? Normally, yes, unless there's some special restriction in the court's order. If the decree is silent, as is true in most cases, the mother usually has the right to move, although she's generally supposed to let the other parent know.

What if the mother moves for the sole reason of depriving the father of visitation rights? If that's really happening, it might be possible to get an injunction, preventing the move. But it's extremely tough to prove, and the effort is usually unsuccessful.

If you're the father of young children, and you're ready for a divorce, you may feel you're going to fight for custody of the kids. It happens, of course, that a father can win a custody contest. But the odds are heavily against it, and you'll have to prove that the mother is unfit. This can be a nasty and cut-throat business. Even if she's committed some marital misconduct, this doesn't necessarily disqualify her from caring for junior. A bad wife isn't always a bad mother. How about adultery by her? While this is a matter that the judge will consider, even that factor, alone, won't invariably knock out the mother's custody, if she properly looks after the child. Her adultery would probably win for you, though, if you could show she did it in front of the children; or she locked them out while "performing"; or if the act was so open and flagrant that it's commonly known in the community.

If the mother is a heavy drinker or a drug addict, the husband will have the upper hand in a custody fight. Probably his best chance, though, is to show that the mother has actually neglected the child a number of times (such as leaving it alone for long periods; not properly feeding or bathing the child, etc.).

What happens if the mother works, and has to leave the children in a nursery or with a third person? The courts seem to still lean to the mother, if she's not unfit in other ways. She'll get custody as long as her employment is reasonably necessary (that is, she's not doing it just to get away from the kids), and provided the child is well cared for while she's away.

H. Who Gets the House?

When the husband and wife agree in advance on child custody, support, alimony and on who gets the property, there's not much of a problem, and the court will usually go along. But let's assume they don't agree on anything. This brings on a batch of legal wrangling, including the age-old hassle over who gets the house.

If the home was purchased in both names, the husband and wife each own a half interest in it, in theory, at least. But the court can give the house to the wife under at least three different principles:

1. As "lump-sum" alimony. Instead of monthly or weekly support payments to a divorced wife, the judge can award a lump-sum allowance, either in the form of cash or property, including the husband's interest or title to the house.

2. As a "special equity." When the wife can show she's put her own money into the house, or contributed some unusual or special services, above ordinary household duties—such as doing all the major repairs or upkeep—she might be able to establish a special claim to the house, and be given the husband's interest.

3. For the care and maintenance of the wife and minor children, the court can award the wife the exclusive use and possession of the home and furniture, without actually giving her the ownership. When the judge makes such an order, he can specify that the wife can remain in the house for some designated period, say until she remarries or the youngest child becomes an adult. The husband still retains his interest in the property, and if the house is sold, he'd get a share of the proceeds. The judge also has the power to bar the man from selling his "part" of the house as long as the wife and children, if any, live there.

Often, the court will find some way to award the home to the spouse who gets custody of the children. Since that's customarily the wife, she ordinarily gets the house, under one of the theories set out above.

Even when the title to the house is entirely in the husband's name, the court can still transfer the property to the woman, under the same reasoning. A newer trend is to award the house to the wife as an "equitable distribution" of the couple's assets.

Happily, more often than not, the husband will agree that the wife can have the use of the house; or when the equity isn't large, he frequently will deed his interest in the property to her. This probably happens in the majority of cases, since it's too expensive to fight it out in court, or the husband realizes the wife needs the house to rear the children.

In some states, particularly when children aren't involved, the judge can award the use of the house to the "innocent party." There are also procedures permitting the property to be "partitioned," or divided. When this happens, the house is put up for sale, and the proceeds split between the husband and wife.

I. Legal Separations: Should You Get One?

A "legal separation" is somewhat of a misnomer. Any separation is technically "legal," since there's no law that can *force* a husband and wife to live together. Most people, though, speak of a legal separation when they mean one that's been approved by the court, with no divorce being entered; or a separation based on a written agreement signed by both parties.

In some states, a court-approved separation is called "separate maintenance." A few jurisdictions refer to it as a divorce from "bed and board," or a "limited divorce." In each of these situations, the parties are still legally married, but are bound by certain obligations and duties.

The legal separation can actually come about in at least three different ways. The first, and most informal, happens when one of the partners moves out, and the couple lives apart. There's no divorce, and not necessarily any agreement; in fact, it's an even bet that they're not even talking to one another. Sometimes the husband may pay some support money; sometimes not. The separation might last a day, or for years.

The second type of legal separation may start the same way as the first, but this time the parties agree on support money, custody of the kids, use of the house, and other related matters. There's still no divorce or other court proceeding, but they'll either have an oral understanding between themselves, or they'll enter into a formal agreement, often in a lawyer's office. A suggested form for use in such a situation is shown at the end of this chapter.

The third, and most expensive, separation procedure is the one filed in court—either the separate maintenance action or limited divorce. The parties will often agree on the terms, and the court's decree is merely a formality, adopting the provisions of the agreement. More frequently, the judge sets the terms, fixing the amount of support and the other obligations.

Why would anyone want a legal separation in the first place, and what's its purpose? Mainly, it's a procedure to make the husband support the wife and family. But from a practical standpoint, it's used for other reasons.

A wife might try it as a "cooling-off" technique, if she's not sure she really wants to break up the marriage for keeps. Or she might use it to shock the husband into a reconciliation.

In a few cases, it's resorted to when the parties, because of religion, are unwilling or unable to get a divorce.

In point of fact, some wives use a legal separation to further their own interests, either financially or emotionally; for instance, as a weapon to force the husband into a better divorce settlement. He's apt to give in when he sees that he has to keep supporting her, yet he's still legally married.

Some wives will choose a legal separation for "spite"; they won't live with the husband, but they won't give him the supposed satisfaction of a divorce.

A few think that by staying married, they'll be able to inherit from the husband and collect his insurance (to some extent, this is true; see Chapter 5, page 145).

The relative ease, though, of getting a "no-fault" divorce (page 103) has decreased the use of legal separations.

From the husband's side of the fence, a legal separation is not particularly desirable, in the ordinary case, except as a possible cooling-off arrangement, or if his religion prevents a divorce.

The separation agreement, itself, usually provides that the parties will live apart and will not bother or interfere with each other. Matters of child custody, as well as disposition of the property, are also set out. The husband is required to support the wife, and usually in a fixed amount per week or month. Sometimes the woman will agree to a lump-sum payment instead of regular periodic amounts. But if you're the husband, you're making a mistake if you consent to a lump-sum, unless a divorce goes along with it. If she spends the money, or loses it in a poor investment, she can generally come back against you for additional moneys, since you might still have a duty to support her as long as you're married. Also, the lump-sum payment is not deductible from your income tax.

You should know something about the other tax consequences of a separation agreement. If the husband files a separate tax return, he can deduct the payments to the wife for her support—and by the same token the amounts are taxable to her, provided that certain specific requirements are met. These are somewhat complex, and have changed from time to time, so you should consult your tax advisor.

You can't deduct voluntary payments, meaning amounts not required under a court order or within a written separation agreement. Also, amounts paid as child support—rather than for the wife's support—are not deductible. So it's important to expressly point out which sums are for the wife and which for the child. Actually, from the husband's standpoint, if none of the payment is broken down to show which part is for the child, the entire amount is probably deductible. But the wife would be taxed on all of it. So it's best to sit down and carefully decide how much should be alimony and how much is child support.

The legal separation isn't necessarily binding and final for the rest of your life. The parties are still free to reconcile, or to modify the terms, or to eventually seek a divorce. But the consequences can be far-reaching, and it pays to consider them carefully before deciding whether a legal separation is "right" for you.

J. Alimony and Support

Alimony has been defined, by a wit, as the high cost of leaving. Historically, it was based on a man's obligation to support his wife, and could be granted as part of a divorce or separation. But not every wife receives alimony. And nowadays, in most places the judge can award alimony to *either* spouse. The dominant rule in the United States is that such an award rests in the discretion of the court. Basically, alimony depends on the spouse's needs and conduct, and the other spouse's ability to pay. (Texas bars long-term alimony unless both parties agree.) In recent years, many courts have granted "rehabilitative alimony," for only a short period of time (six months to a few years), to give the spouse time to find work or to complete his or her education. This is especially true if the marriage is not a long one.

If the woman is self-supporting, or is wealthy, alimony is usually denied. But if she's not able to support herself, the judge will customarily consider her expenses and bills, in the light of the husband's income and net worth.

It's also proper for the court to give weight to the husband's future earning capacity and prospects. So if the man is making $350 a week now, but he's scheduled for a raise to $500 in a few weeks, the judge will no doubt base the award on the future potential, rather than the present figure.

What's the alimony situation when the wife is the guilty party in the divorce, or is the one that's committed the misconduct? Does she get alimony? The old rule was that she didn't. But this has been softened in most states, and not every type of misbehavior will disqualify her. The serious offenses, such as adultery, might still bar her. The wife's desertion is, more often than not, ground for denying alimony, but even for that, there are several cases that have granted an award..

One key reason that a husband would, in the past, contest a divorce, and counterclaim against a wife, was to defeat her alimony efforts. If he could beat the wife's accusations, and at the same time prove she's committed adultery or some kind of serious cruelty, he'd have a good chance of walking home scot-free, without paying alimony. Under "no-fault" divorce, though, this practice is no longer as common.

It's not easy to predict what part of the husband's income will be granted to a wife as alimony. It depends on how much he makes, what assets he has, the social status of the parties, and the standard of living they've been accustomed to. The amount of child support also has a bearing. As a rule of thumb, the range of total payments (alimony and child support) falls somewhere between 15% and 50% of the man's pay. More commonly, the average would probably be from 20% to 40%, although there necessarily is a wide variation, based on the individual case.

In certain circumstances, a court will award lump-sum alimony (see Section H), sometimes called an "allowance in gross." Some judges prefer this, since it closes out the case, and the parties go their separate ways. But usually the lump-sum award isn't granted unless there are special reasons not to give periodic payments. Some of the factors considered are: the age of the couple, their life expectancy, the total assets of the husband, whether the wife has contributed money or property to the marriage, and whether there are children.

If you're the husband, should you agree to a lump-sum award? Note that this is different from such a payment in a legal separation (see page 124), and the considerations are not the same. In a divorce, a lump-sum is more common. Whether to agree or not depends on a number of factors, not the least of which is the tax aspect; such payments, though, must meet IRS requirements, so you'll need to check the rules carefully. But in a given case, particularly if there are no children, it may be cheaper for the husband to agree to the lump-sum. By paying it, he'll generally be free of harassing payments and petitions for increases, and he can make a fresh start. But no two cases are identical, and it's not possible to say, in all situations, which set-up would be best.

Another factor that can influence the parties is the circumstance under which alimony stops. The guiding rule (with exceptions in a few states) is that alimony ceases on the death of either spouse, or upon the remarriage of the wife. This principle can seriously affect your strategy. If you're a young woman, and expect to remarry in the future, you'll probably be better off with a lump-sum, since if you accept monthly payments, you'll lose them when you find a new mate. Another time for a wife to consider a lump-sum is when her husband is old or seriously ill. There's a way, though, for the wife to continue getting alimony even after the husband dies. If, as part of a divorce settlement, she can get him to agree that his estate will be responsible for paying alimony *even after his death*, then she'll keep getting it (provided, of course, he leaves some assets). How does she do it? Simple. Merely by insisting on it. If the husband is the one that wants the divorce, or is agreeable to the wife's suit, he'll very likely go along with most of her demands. So if you're the wife, and you're wondering what would be a reasonable alimony agreement, add one more demand: that the payments will continue after his death. Another good strategy is to have the husband carry life insurance for the wife, to replace the lost alimony if he dies.

As part of his duty to support his wife, a husband very often gets nicked with paying his wife's attorney. It's not true in all cases, but he'll usually have to come across if he's financially able to, and the woman can't afford it. The man may feel this is adding the proverbial insult to injury, but he might as well include this expense with the other costs he'll have.

An award of alimony can be modified by a court, after divorce, even if the parties have agreed on the amount. But it takes a strong showing to alter the figure—either to raise it or to lower it—and the courts require a "substantial change in circumstances." It can work this way: you're the husband and you agreed on $100 weekly alimony at the time of the divorce four years ago, when you were making $500 a week. Now you've been seriously ill and you can't work full time. Your income is down to $150 per week, with no immediate prospects of an increase. If you apply to the court, it's reasonably certain that the payments will be reduced.

The change in circumstances, though, has to be one not contemplated or expected by the parties. For instance, if the man earns $300 a week, but he'll get a $100 raise in a month, and a $5,000 bonus at the end of the year, what effect will this have? If the wife knows all this when she signs the agreement, it won't do her much good. After the divorce is over, if she comes back to the judge, hollering "changed circumstances," she'll lose, because the raise and bonus were "in the contemplation of the parties."

It can work the opposite way, too. Take this case: a working wife, making $200 a week, agrees to accept $75 weekly alimony. A year later, she's hospitalized, unable to work, and has no savings. She'll have a fairly good chance of increasing the alimony because of the changed circumstances.

In almost all states now, property obtained during the marriage ("marital property") is equitably divided by the court, and it usually doesn't matter whose name the property is in. Certain items are often excluded—but not always—such as gifts and inheritances received by one spouse. The "marital property" can even include pension and retirement benefits.

Closely related to alimony is child support. The law of every state requires a divorced husband to support his children. The factors considered are pretty much the same as those in an alimony case: the needs of the children, and the ability of the father to pay. Even if the mother has substantial earning capacity, the father isn't relieved of his obligation.

If the husband and wife agree on the amount of support for the children, the judge will usually ratify it. But he doesn't have to. If he feels the wife isn't getting a fair deal, he can discard the agreement and award what he thinks is reasonable.

How much is "fair"? The amounts fluctuate, depending on the section of the country, the income and living standards of the couple. The usual scale, in the average case, is from 20% to 40% of the husband's income, for child support and alimony, combined.

Some courts traditionally set a fixed dollar amount for child support (unless there's a substantial change in circumstances later). Others, though, will require the father to also pay expenses such as unusual medical bills or education.

It's becoming fairly commonplace for the parties to agree that the husband will not only pay support of a set amount, but will carry hospitalization insurance on the children, or pay their medical bills.

In a great many cases, a husband will tell the wife he'll pay "X" number of dollars for alimony and child support together. If the figure sounds fair, she'll probably agree, without any breakdown of how much is actually for the children, and what part goes to her as alimony. Does it make any difference? To Uncle Sam, it does.

Here's the rule: if it's *alimony*, it's deductible by the man, on his federal tax return; and it's taxable to the wife. But if it's *child support*, he can't deduct it, and she doesn't pay taxes on it; instead, he may be able to claim the children as dependents, but his ability to do this is now severely limited, unless the wife agrees in writing. The regulations for claiming the tots as dependents are loaded with traps, and the husband can quickly lose the deduction unless there's an agreement on a special tax form. Without such an agreement (or a court order, in some cases), the *custodian* of the child generally claims the exemption.

You need to go a step further to get the whole story on alimony–child support payments. If you call the payment "alimony," the wife loses it if she remarries; but if you say it's child support, she keeps getting it until the children become of age. So how do you decide whether you should call it "alimony" or "child support"? You actually have to do a little fancy figuring to make the right choice.

From the husband's side of the table, if he's paying a sizable amount per year, he's probably better off calling most of it alimony, so that he can deduct it (this is especially true if the wife is young, and likely to remarry, since he can stop paying if she ties the knot again). But remember, the wife has to pay taxes on alimony. So she'll usually prefer treating it all as child support (which isn't taxable to her). Again—there are exceptions. Example: 44-year-old wife, two children, ages 17 and 14. If she agrees to consider all the payments as child support, she'll lose everything in about four years, when the youngest child is grown. If she calls it alimony, it continues until she remarries—which might never happen.

Now consider a 24-year-old divorcee; two children, ages 3 and 1. She'll be smarter calling almost all of it child support. Caution: the wife should leave her foot in the door at least an inch, and never waive all alimony entirely. She should insist on at least "token" alimony of even as low as a dollar. Why? That way, if there's a change in circumstances later, she can petition the court for an increase. But if she closes herself out completely and waives her right to any alimony, she loses her standing, in many states, to ever come back and ask for any, in the future.

Suppose you're the wife. You've carefully balanced all the financial choices, and made your decision between alimony and child support. Everything's fine. Except for one minor problem. Your ex-husband doesn't pay. He just stops completely. What can you do? You can sue him for it, but this is often long and cumbersome. In most states, the wife can file a motion or petition to hold the husband in contempt of court for nonpayment, and the judge can sentence him to jail. This doesn't guarantee that you'll get your money, but the average deadbeat husband can usually find some way to scrape together the back payments when he finds himself behind bars.

If he's left the state, you'll have a much rockier road. The state you're in won't have much ammunition for you, since he's now beyond its jurisdiction. You can either hire a lawyer in the city where he's moved; or contact the local state attorney in your own county to help you. He can file a special proceeding under the "uniform nonsupport statute," which has been passed in every state, to force payment from a husband that's skipped.

K. A Few Final Comments

If you've come this far, you'll know something about the myriad rules and complexities of divorce. Above all else, remember that the laws in each state are vastly different, with a batch of exceptions and peculiarities. As one writer once put it, "It's so complicated, you're better off staying married." In any case, don't rely on what the cousin of your brother-in-law's uncle, on his father's side, told you. Chances are he doesn't know the law.

Form 1

STATUTORY GROUNDS FOR DIVORCE (1987)

	Adultry	Bigamy	Cruelty	Crime against nature	Desertion or abandonment	Drunkenness or drug addiction	Felony or imprisonment	Fraud or force	Incapacity or impotency	Insanity	Incompatibility	Irreconcilable differences	Irretrievable breakdown	Nonage	Nonsupport or neglect	Physical violence	Pregnancy at time of marriage	Separation	Separation under court decree	Violent temper	Other
Ala.	X			X	X	X	X			X	X		X		X	X	X		X		
Alaska	X		X		X	X	X			X	X	X	X								
Ariz.													X								
Ark.	X	X	X		X	X	X			X	X					X		X			*
Cal.										X		X									*
Colo.													X								
Conn.	X		X	X	X	X	X			X			X					X			
Del.	X	X	X		X	X	X			X	X							X			a
D.C.																		X	X		a
Fla.										X			X								
Ga.	X		X	X	X	X	X		X	X	X		X				X				b
Hawaii													X					X	X		
Idaho	X		X		X	X			X		X		X			X		X			
Ill.	X	X	X		X	X	X				X		X								c
Ind.							X		X	X			X								
Iowa													X								
Kans.											X	X				X					
Ky.													X								
La.	X						X											X	X		
Maine	X		X	X	X				X				X		X						
Md.	X		X	X	X		X		X									X			d
Mass.	X		X	X	X	X	X						X		X						
Mich.													X								
Minn.													X								
Miss.	X	X	X		X	X	X		X	X			X				X				b
Mo.													X								
Mont.													X								
Nebr.													X								
Nev.											X	X						X			
N.H.	X		X		X	X	X			X			X		X						e
N.J.	X		X		X	X	X				X								X		f
N.M.	X		X	X								X									

Statutory Grounds for Divorce (1987), *continued*

	Adultry	Bigamy	Cruelty	Crime against nature	Desertion or abandonment	Drunkenness or drug addiction	Felony or imprisonment	Fraud or force	Incapacity or impotency	Insanity	Incompatibility	Irreconcilable differences	Irretrievable breakdown	Nonage	Nonsupport or neglect	Physical violence	Pregnancy at time of marriage	Separation	Separation under court decree	Violent temper	Other
N.Y.	X		X	X	X													X	X		
N.C.										X								X			
N.D.	X		X	X	X					X		X			X						
Ohio	X	X	X		X	X	X	X							X			X			g
Okla.	X		X		X	X	X	X	X	X	X				X		X				g
Ore.													X								
Pa.	X	X	X		X				X	X			X								
R.I.	X	X	X	X	X	X				X					X			X			d
S.C.	X	X	X	X														X			
S.D.	X	X	X		X	X				X		X			X						
Tenn.	X	X	X	X	X	X				X		X			X			X	X	X	h
Texas	X	X	X						X			X						X			
Utah	X	X	X		X	X			X	X		X			X			X		X	
Vt.	X				X					X					X			X			i
Va.		X	X	X		X												X	X		
Wash.												X	X					X			
W.Va.	X		X		X	X	X			X		X			X	X		X			
Wisc.													X								
Wyo.										X	X										

Other grounds, where specified by letter, symbol or *

    *—allows dissolution by agreement, if certain requirements are met

    a—homosexuality or V.D.

    b—marriage to a relative

    c—attempt on life; communicating V.D.

    d—cruelty of minor child

    e—religious belief opposing cohabitation

    f—deviant sex conduct

    g—obtaining divorce in another state; also, Ohio allows dissolution by agreement, if certain requirements are met

    h—attempted murder of spouse

    i—intolerable severity

Form 2

CHART SHOWING MINIMUM RESIDENCE REQUIREMENTS; AND NECESSARY WAITING PERIODS BEFORE REMARRIAGE

	Residence	*Required waiting period after divorce*
Alabama	6 mos. (some exceptions)	60 days (some exceptions)
Alaska	none	none
Arizona	90 days	none
Arkansas	60 days	none
California	6 mos.	none
Colorado	90 days	none
Connecticut	1 year (some exceptions)	none
Delaware	6 mos.	none
D. C.	6 mos.	none
Florida	6 mos.	none
Georgia	6 mos.	none (some exceptions)
Hawaii	6 mos.	none (some exceptions)
Idaho	6 weeks	none
Illinois	90 days	none
Indiana	6 mos. (some exceptions)	none (some exceptions)
Iowa	1 year (some exceptions)	none
Kansas	60 days	none
Kentucky	6 mos.	none
Louisiana	no special requirements	none
Maine	6 mos. (some exceptions)	none
Maryland	no special requirements (some exceptions)	none
Massachusetts	varies	90 days (some exceptions)
Michigan	6 mos. (some exceptions)	none
Minnesota	6 mos.	none
Mississippi	6 mos.	none (some exceptions)
Missouri	90 days	none

	Residence	Required waiting period after divorce
Montana	90 days	none
Nebraska	1 year (some exceptions)	none
Nevada	6 weeks (some exceptions)	none
N. H.	varies	none
N. J.	1 year (some exceptions)	none
N. M.	6 mos.	none
New York	1 year (some exceptions)	none
N. C.	6 mos.	none
N. D.	6 mos.	as permitted by Court
Ohio	6 mos.	none
Oklahoma	6 mos.	6 mos.
Oregon	6 mos. (some exceptions)	30 days
Pa.	6 mos.	none
R. I.	1 year	none
S. C.	1 year (some exceptions)	none
S. D.	no specific time	none
Tenn.	no specific time	none
Tex.	6 mos.	30 days (some exceptions)
Utah	3 mos.	during appeal
Vermont	6 mos. (some exceptions)	none
Virginia	6 mos.	varies
Washington	no specific time	none
W. Va.	1 year (some exceptions)	none
Wisconsin	6 mos.	6 mos.
Wyoming	60 days (some exceptions)	none

Form 3

FORM OF SEPARATION AGREEMENT

[Check applicable lines where more than one choice is listed]

THIS AGREEMENT made the .... day of ....
19............ by ...., Husband, and
............................., Wife.

WITNESSETH: Because of differences and disputes between the parties, and their desire to settle their mutual rights and duties, Husband and Wife agree as follows:

1. Husband and Wife shall live apart, at such place as each may select, and neither shall molest, interfere with, nor harass the other.

2. Husband shall pay to the Wife, for her support, the sum of $.............................
   __a. Each week
   __b. Each month
   __c. Twice a month
   __d. Every other week
   __e. Other ....

beginning on the .... day of .... 19............ Such payments shall
   __a. Terminate at Husband's death
   __b. Continue after his death

In any event, such payments shall end when the Wife remarries or dies, except the Husband shall remain liable for arrearages.

3. __a. The Wife
   __b. The Husband
   __c. Other ....

shall have custody of the minor child(ren) of the parties, subject to the other spouse's right to:
   __a. Visit said child(ren) and to be visited by said child(ren) at reasonable times and places.
   __b. Visit said child(ren) and be visited by said child(ren) during the following times (list specific dates, holidays, vacations and other special hours).

....
....

4. Each party shall promptly notify the other of any serious illness or accident suffered by the child(ren).

5. Husband shall pay to the wife, for the support of each child, the sum of $............................., or a total of $............................. for the support of the children
   __a. Each week

___b. Each month
___c. Twice a month
___d. Every other week
___e. Other ....

beginning on the .... day of .... 19............, until

___a. Each child, respectively, reaches 21 years of age, marries, or be-
comes self-supporting, whichever occurs first.
___b. The youngest child reaches 21 years of age, marries, or be-
comes self-supporting, whichever occurs first.
___c. Other ....

6. In addition, Husband shall
___a. Carry and maintain hospitalization and medical insurance on
............(1)Wife; ....(2) The child(ren).
___b. Pay for all reasonable and necessary medical, dental and drug
expenses of said child(ren).

7. From the child support payments, the Wife shall pay all sums
needed for the education and maintenance of the child(ren) except
....

8. The property owned by the parties shall be disposed or used as
follows:
___a. The home located at: ....
....
___b. Furniture and furnishings: ....
___c. Joint checking or savings accounts: ....
___d. Automobile(s): ....
___e. Other: ....

9. Husband shall pay the following debts, indemnify and hold the
Wife harmless from any claims thereon:
....

10. Wife shall pay the following debts, and indemnify and hold the
Husband harmless from any claims thereon:
....

11. Except as set forth in this agreement, each party releases the
other from all other claims and demands to the date hereof, and
relinquishes all rights in the other's property or estate
___a. Including dower and inheritance rights
___b. Except ....

12. The parties agree to
___a. File separate tax returns
___b. File joint tax returns, if either requests it. Any tax refunds, in
such event, shall be paid as follows:
___(1) Equally to the parties
___(2) Other ....

__c. If a joint return is filed, and any taxes or deficiencies are due or are incurred, they shall be paid as follows:

.... and (Husband) (Wife) shall indemnify the other from any claim or deficiencies.

13. Husband shall carry and maintain the following life insurance policies: .... and shall name as beneficiaries thereunder the following:
__a. The Wife
__b. The child(ren) of the parties

14. Each party has made a full disclosure to the other of his current finances and assets, and each enters into this agreement in reliance thereon.

15. Nothing in this agreement shall be interpreted so as to prevent the other from filing for divorce. If a divorce is filed, then the parties agree that this agreement:
__a. May be offered in evidence, and the terms incorporated in any judgment or decree rendered.
__b. Shall not be binding on the parties.
__c. Other ....

16. Other provisions: ....
....
....
....
....   HUSBAND:
....
Witness as to Husband   .... (SEAL)
....   WIFE:
....
Witness as to Wife   .... (SEAL)

CHAPTER 5

So You're Wondering About A Will

IF YOU'RE TYPICAL OF MILLIONS OF AMERICANS, YOU'VE THOUGHT up some pretty good excuses for not having a will.

You may have felt that you don't have enough property to worry about; or that everything will go to your wife anyway, since "it's all in both names." You may even figure you don't give a hoot what happens after you're gone. Or if you're superstitious, you might even believe that once you make a will, that means you're ready for the undertaker to come and carry you off. And most likely of all, you probably have said you'll make a will "later," when you have the time.

What's the real story about a will? How important is it, and what happens if you don't have one?

A. Do You Need One At All?

When a person dies without a will ("intestate," the law calls it), his property passes to certain specified relatives, as set out in the statutes of each state. Sometimes, for example, if a man dies intestate, leaving a wife and children, the wife and children share equally, with the woman getting a child's share (or, if she prefers, she can claim a "dower" interest of about one-third of the estate). If you're lucky, it may work out that you would have decided to leave your property the same way, even if you had a will. But suppose you wanted your wife to have it all? Or you'd rather that one child receive more than the other?

138

This is where the will comes in. It allows you to leave your property the way you want to, and to the people you select (although there are some restrictions to this; see Section J).

What about having everything in "both names"—husband and wife? As pointed out in Chapter 2 (page 44), this type of joint ownership creates a special legal relationship, in most states, spoken of as an estate by the entireties, or a "tenancy" by the entireties (although the word "tenancy" is a little deceiving; you're an owner, not a tenant in the usual sense of the word). If one of the spouses dies, under this kind of ownership, the survivor gets the property automatically. Does this do away with the need for a will? In most cases, no. For at least two important reasons:

1. If something happened to you and your wife at the same time, such as in a common accident, the joint ownership wouldn't do you much good. The property would now go to the relatives mentioned in the intestate statutes, and you'd have no say-so about it.

2. You might overlook or neglect putting some assets in both names. This can happen when you buy a new car, and unconsciously take the title just in your name. Or you inherit or are given some property, so that it's now owned by you alone. If this occurs, these assets would again be governed by the inheritance laws, rather than by what *you* want, if you leave no will.

There are other important reasons for having a will. One is to save money. If you die intestate (no will), and the property goes to certain relatives that the law designates, that part may be O. K. with you; they may even be the ones you would have picked. But when there's no will, it's up to the probate court to appoint an administrator (the person that takes care of your estate), and it may or may not be the one you would have chosen. The administrator might have to pay for a bond, to protect the heirs and creditors. If he has to sell any property to pay bills or expenses, he needs a court order, and usually an appraisal. If there are minor children, a guardian may have to be appointed (see Section C). All of this is expensive and takes time. But with a will, you can slice through a good portion of these costs and procedures.

Another important saving can be on taxes. With a properly executed will and estate plan, it's possible to legally cut estate and inheritance taxes by thousands of dollars, even in a middle-sized estate, and still carry out your intentions.

So although you might not have much property, and even if you think everything is in "both names," you should still have a will.

You'll need to realize, at the outset, though, that certain assets will not be directly affected or controlled by the will. Life insurance proceeds, for instance, usually pass "outside the will." Your policy is a contract with the insurance company, and they've agreed to pay to a designated beneficiary. Even if you said in your will, "I hereby change my mind about my insurance, and I want the proceeds to go to my old Aunt Gussie," they wouldn't. The company will still give the money to the person named in the policy. So if you think you should change the beneficiary, the will isn't the place to do it; notify the insurance agent. It *is* possible, though, to have your insurance payable direct to your "estate," if you wanted it that way, or to your "personal representative," which is the same thing as the administrator or executor. If you did that, then the provisions of your will would take over. This is sometimes done for special reasons, such as to provide the personal representative with enough cash to pay bills and taxes (otherwise, he might have to sell some property at a loss). Occasionally, the insurance is made payable to your estate when you'd like the proceeds to go to minor children. You can set up a trust for them in your will, naming a trustee, and giving him certain instructions (see Section C). But having the insurance paid to the estate can be dangerous and expensive, too. By going through the personal representative, there can be additional court costs and fees. The eventual distribution to the heirs might be delayed. And in some states, the money is subject to the claims of creditors and to local taxes. So even in situations where you'd like the money to go to your minor children, in trust, as mentioned above, you may be better off setting up a separate "insurance trust," rather than having the proceeds payable to your estate or personal representative. Don't let an insurance agent fast-talk you into having the money payable to your estate, unless you thoroughly understand the consequences.

Another type of property that passes "outside the will" is jointly-owned property, with right of survivorship. To illustrate: if you've set up a savings account this way (such as in your name and your brother's), then when you die, the money would go directly to him, and your will would have nothing to do with it. In some situations, this can be a convenient and inexpensive way of transferring property without a will. But there are booby traps here, too: you don't have complete control of the property this way; there can be some gift tax consequences (as well as possible estate taxes); and this type of ownership seems to be a fertile field for litigation, the contention being made that such an account was for convenience only, rather than actual joint ownership.

B. Should Everything Be in Both Names?

It's becoming increasingly common for husband and wife to acquire property in both their names, with the right of survivorship. If you don't have a large estate (not over $500,000), you shouldn't have any real problems with this method, and it can work out quite well in the average situation, although you should still have a will (see Section A). But as your assets approach $600,000, then you need to know that there can be serious tax consequences. These days, it's not so unusual, with life insurance, to have an estate higher than that figure. In adding up the value of your property, you have to include the face amount of such insurance on your life (there's an exception if you've made an outright gift of the policy, or have no rights of ownership in it). In general, you also have to add in the *full* value of all jointly-owned assets, not just *one-half* of them (unless your survivor's funds were used, or the property was acquired by gift or inheritance). There's also an exception if the survivor "materially participates" in a jointly-owned business or farm.

Let's assume that with insurance, your estate is $800,000. If it all goes to your wife, there won't be any federal estate tax under present law. But when she dies later, leaving an $800,000 estate to the children, the tax bite could be in the neighborhood of several thousand dollars. Are there any ways to save the tax? There are, although the expense and other disadvantages sometimes make it impractical. One way is for the wife to make gifts to the children while she's alive. But this takes it out of her control, and is often unappealing. Another way is for the husband, while he's still living, to convert the joint ownership either to his name alone (and then he wills it, partly outright and partly in trust, to the wife), or put it in a special kind of ownership known as "tenancy in common" (see page 46). Another method recommended by some writers is a revocable trust (see Section D). But none of these alternatives are really too attractive in many situations.

If your estate passes $600,000, though, you begin to feel the federal estate tax impact. And at this point, you won't want to indiscriminately take title to everything in both names. Watch what can happen: say your estate is now $800,000, after expenses and debts, and all your property is owned jointly with your wife. At your death, there are still no taxes. Okay so far. (Your estate is allowed to deduct an unlimited amount, as long as it's left to your spouse outright, or if the spouse has general control over it.) In other words, you could leave your wife the whole $800,000 without paying estate tax. But now assume that your wife passes away ten years later and still has $700,000. The tax could then become quite substantial. This is because an *unmarried* person doesn't have the benefit of the "marital deduction" permitted for married people. (If she dies *within* ten years of your death, the Treasury Department allows some credits against the estate tax, but only if *your* estate had to pay any taxes.) Is there a realistic way to avoid this tax, when the property eventually goes to your children or other heirs, with your wife still getting the benefits of all your property?

There is. Here's how it's done: only a portion of your assets—depending on the size of your estate—is left to your wife, enough to take maximum advantage of the so-called "unified credit," which presently works out to $600,000. But what you're aiming for is to avoid having the other portion of your estate taxed when your wife dies, so that it passes to your children free of taxes. The only way to accomplish this is to keep it from being legally considered your wife's property. Yet at the same time, you want her to have some control over it. How do you go about it?

The answer is through the so-called testamentary trust. This "other portion" is left to the wife, but in trust. By this device, it will no longer be taxable to her when she dies. Yet she can be lawfully given the following control or powers: 1. She can receive all the income from the trust, for her life. 2. She can have the right to withdraw $5,000 per year, or 5% of the trust, whichever is more. 3. She can take out additional amounts to meet unusual medical expenses or to maintain her customary standard of living. 4. If an independent trustee is used (one who has no interest in it), he can distribute even additional sums to her, in his discretion, for any reason whatsoever. 5. She can be given certain powers to approve or veto investments by the trustee. 6. She can choose which of the family will get the balance of the trust at her death (called a "power of appointment").

You can see, then, that the wife can keep reasonably good dominion over the trust, and accept substantial benefits, yet it won't be considered part of her estate. So through this method, your heirs can save thousands in taxes.

But remember, there's no way to get this sizable tax saving if your property is all "jointly-owned," with right of survivorship. Why not? Because under the right of survivorship set-up, it all goes outright to the wife. You'd be unable to establish the trust machinery, and the government would clip the estate for the second tax when your wife died.

Setting up a trust to save taxes gets pretty tricky, and since the IRS rules change fairly rapidly, you really need expert help before you tackle this.

So the moral is: if you're worth less than $500,000, and you're sure you'd like it all to go to your wife, you can generally take title in both names. But as your net worth increases, and finally approaches or passes $600,000, tax planning becomes a major element, and you need to think carefully before you blindly take joint title to everything.

C. What About Minor Children?

If you've never made a will, you probably have a hazy notion that you'd like everything to go to "the wife and kids." If the children are grown, you can do this, without too many complications (although even here there are reasons not to do it; see page 145). But if it's done while the children are minors, you're opening a Pandora's box of legal problems.

As a general rule, the law says that children aren't capable of owning property in their own names. So if you were to leave assets, outright, to a child, the court would have to appoint a guardian. It's fairly certain, of course, that your wife, as the mother, would be the guardian. But in most states, the guardian—*even for her own children*—has to put up a bond, file inventories, prepare yearly accountings, and go through an incredible assortment of legal mumbo-jumbo, red tape, and expense (except in rare cases). And if your wife died or became incapacitated while the children were still underage, a successor guardian would have to be appointed by the court. There would be more costs, and the guardian might even be someone not sympathetic to your children's needs.

Occasionally, situations arise when you do want to leave property to a minor, such as: when you're divorced or widowed; when you'd like to benefit a grandchild; or when your wife is independently wealthy. In fact, even when you *do* plan to leave everything to your wife, you should consider the possibility of a common accident, in which case your assets would go to the children.

How, then, can you get around the formal guardianship proceedings? The solution is by using a trust in your will. Don't let the idea scare you off. The trust can be fairly simple. It would provide, basically, for the appointment of a trustee—a person or bank that manages the property; it would authorize the trustee to use the funds for the welfare and care of the minor; it would set out the powers and authority of the trustee (he's usually given broad discretion); and it would specify at what age and under what conditions the money should be paid to the child. A form of will, with this kind of trust, is shown at the end of this chapter as Form 1. NOTE: Such a will is intended for use only when the estate is not large enough to be subject to federal taxes.

A trust of this kind will not only save money at the outset (for bond premiums and court costs), but the trustee can be given authorization to deal with the trust property—invest, mortgage, or even sell it—without a court order that a guardian would normally need.

By setting up a trust for your children, in the will, you can also give the trustee discretion to distribute or pay benefits according to a child's needs, rather than by any rigid and fixed formula that divides everything into equal shares (as a guardianship requires). This provides much more flexibility, and permits the trustee to use the assets as you, yourself, would have done, based on the welfare and special requirements of the children.

Through a trust, you can also provide for holding back payment to a child even past age 21. You can, if you want to, specify that the trust be continued until the *youngest* child reaches 21 or, if you prefer, until the children reach some later age. It's not uncommon to provide for only part of the principal to be paid at 21; then another part at 25; and a final share at, say, age 35. There are several variations of this.

Another advantage of a trust for children is that you can usually name an out-of-state relative as the trustee, if you feel he'd be best. But if a guardianship were used, instead, you might very likely find that the guardian had to be a resident of your state.

You can visualize, then, that it can be a mistake to leave property outright to minor children. Even if your estate is small, your will should have a trust provision for any minor beneficiaries.

At the beginning of this section, reference was made to leaving property to grown children, on occasion. Even in those situations, a trust can be useful, on the chance of a common disaster, or if the child dies before you. In that case, if you have grandchildren, or expect to have them, the trust will come into play until the grandchildren reach maturity. And again there'll be a substantial saving in guardianship expense and entanglements.

Be careful about leaving most of your property to your grown children, if your wife survives you. If you don't have a large estate, it's usually better to leave most, or all, of your assets directly to your wife, and then to the children if she dies. Why? Because your widow has probably been dependent on you for support, and will have financial difficulty when you're gone. If you give a large portion of your estate to the adult children, your wife may end up having to ask them for assistance, which can be embarrassing to her, at best.

There are, naturally, times when it's desirable to provide for grown children. If you've been divorced or widowed, so that your present wife isn't the mother of the children, you may feel you'd like to leave them something. Or if your wife has ample financial resources of her own. Or if you have a large estate, with enough to go around for everybody.

You should be aware, too, of the rule that you can't cut off a wife completely. She's entitled to a ''widow's interest'' (usually called dower), which customarily is a third of a man's property (it can be more). So even if you wanted to leave *everything* to your children, and nothing to your spouse, you normally can't do it. (There's one time when you can: if, before marriage, your wife signs away her rights in an ''antenuptial agreement.'' This is sometimes done prior to a second marriage, where one or both of the parties have children by a prior marriage. It requires a complete and open disclosure, to the other, of what you have.)

Can you go the other route, though, and disinherit your children? If you're sure that's what you want, there's nothing to stop you from doing it (except in Louisiana; and even there, you can do it if you have good cause). You can also make an unequal distribution; more to one child, less to another. In most jurisdictions, if you don't want to leave a child anything, you might have to say, though, in your will, that you're making no provision for him, or that you're leaving your property to your wife "to the exclusion of your children." If you don't say this, the law might presume that you forgot the child, and he may still be able to claim a share of your estate. That's why there's a popular idea that you have to leave a child at least a dollar, to show that you didn't overlook him. But that's not necessary. You don't even have to leave him a penny, as long as there's some reference in the will to the child. In fact, you're really better off not using the old-fashioned "dollar" bequest. There can be unnecessary and absurd complications if the child has died, leaving descendants (technically, they could each demand a share of the dollar, causing delay in closing the estate). It's customary to use language something like this: *"I intentionally make no provision for my children, whether living now, or born after the execution of this will."*

Since many states give certain rights to children born after a will is signed, it's important to refer to such "after-born" children, to avoid any problems.

Don't make the mistake of using any disparaging language. Clauses such as "I leave nothing to my son John, because he has not been respectful," are an invitation to challenge.

D. Should You Really Avoid Probate?

A number of years ago, a best seller explained how to bypass the expenses and delays of the administration of your estate in court (a procedure known as "probate"). The author's suggestion for avoiding probate was to establish revocable trusts while you're living—so-called inter vivos trusts.

A trust, as we've seen before, is a device by which you transfer certain assets to a trustee, who holds the title and manages the property under your instructions (see Section C). "Revocable" means you can revoke it, or terminate it, at any time. The book even proposes that you can act as your own trustee, so that your control of the property won't be affected. The trust would provide that, upon your death, the assets would pass to your named beneficiaries, without having to go through the probate process. In effect, says the author, you have your cake and can eat it too.

The book's description of the revocable inter vivos trust, on the surface, sounds logical and persuasive. But is it as good as it sounds? First, let's look at the advantages.

If the trust cǎn really enable you to avoid probate, your beneficiaries will save court costs and cut the delay in receiving the property. Publicity will be kept to a minimum (if this is important to you), since there's no "public record" required, as there is in probate.

There are some other claimed benefits: you might be able to set up the trust in another state whose laws are more favorable (a will, on the other hand, is governed by the statutes of your residence). Also, since there's more privacy in the trust, it's argued that there's less likelihood of an attack in court.

All of the supposed advantages make the revocable trust sound like the miracle drug of the century. But before you gulp it down, you better find out whether there are any harmful "side effects." As a matter of fact, there are.

In the first place, the courts in some states, when the issue was raised, ruled that if you attempt to set up a trust, and yet keep complete and unlimited control of the property, then you haven't created a trust at all. Even though you've labeled it as a trust, those courts treat it as a will, and you're tossed right back into probate.

To get around this "complete control" obstacle (and, coincidentally, to make some money), many banks and trust companies have been drumming up business for their version of a revocable trust. Under their plan, you name the bank or other institution as the trustee and turn over your assets to them to manage for you. The bank makes the investments, but you have the right to change the trust or to cancel it at any time. The income will be paid to you—or to anyone you choose—and when you die, the assets are distributed to whomever you've designated, without going through the probate process. Sounds simple enough. Any disadvantages? Yes, if your primary goal is to avoid the expense of probate. The bank, obviously, must make a charge for its services as trustee. The fee—which is usually an annual charge, based on a percentage of the trust—is generally not exorbitant; but if you pay it for five or six years, it very likely will be about equal to the cost of probate. Of course, if you like the idea of the bank managing your property and securities, and saving you the chore of investing, well and good. But don't expect the service to be free.

It's also not true that an inter vivos trust is immune to litigation. A court has the power to set aside such a trust on the same grounds that a will could be challenged—undue influence, mental incompetence, fraud, and duress. Many of such trusts have been successfully attacked.

Does the revocable trust allow your heirs to avoid the delays of probate? Not entirely. The bank trustee will be reluctant to distribute the property immediately after your death, until they're sure there are no unpaid bills or debts. In all states, there's a statutory period allowed to creditors to file claims against the estate. This varies, but it could be six or eight months. If the bank distributed all of the trust assets before the claims period expired, they'd be on the hook—and could be sued—if a creditor filed a claim. So even if you avoid probate, there can still be delays in getting the assets into the hands of the eventual heirs.

In fact, this very delay can sometimes be an advantage in an estate that's subject to federal tax. An executor has an option of using varying periods to value the assets. With stocks and other properties that fluctuate in value, a delay in distribution can actually produce a tax saving.

You should also realize that if there are to be any savings at all, with a revocable trust, they won't be on taxes. Since you have the right to cancel the trust at any time, the law says that the assets are still legally yours, for tax purposes. When you die, they'll be considered part of your estate—and subject to taxes (unless you're under the statutory minimum).

Incidentally, another type of trust—an irrevocable one—is sometimes used in estate planning. If you set this up properly, it's probable you'll save taxes, but the assets can no longer be called back by you, and you can't ordinarily terminate the trust in your lifetime. So you shouldn't consider this type of irrevocable arrangement, unless you're certain you won't want or need the property back.

The revocable trust has some other flaws. It's not practical to include all of your property in such a trust (for example: if you turned over your car title to a trustee, you'd probably have to deliver the car along with it). So you'd still need a will to cover the "loose ends."

Actually, the probate procedure in many states isn't half as evil as the villain it's been pictured. There are, quite naturally, expenses and some abuses in certain areas. But by its requirement of public disclosure, it protects heirs and creditors. They're given a chance to examine the will and to decide whether there's any legal ground for declaring it void (such as forgery, fraud, duress). There are also safeguards on the hasty sale or disposal of assets (usually the heirs are notified). While a trustee is not subject to court supervision in many states, an executor is responsible to the court. The probate process isn't completely heartless, either, contrary to some of the representations made. There are statutes in many states permitting a partial payment or allowance to the widow and children during the probate period, to prevent financial hardship.

In most jurisdictions, the court appoints as the executor the person named in your will, or a near relative (some states still have a "public administrator," a system which is generally criticized, but reforms are gradually coming). When you've named your wife or a close relative, it's likely he or she will serve without pay, so that the administration costs are cut considerably. The executor will no doubt have to pay some legal expense (see Section E). But many states have a statutory scale of fees, and they're usually not as high as you've been led to believe.

If you recognize the limitations of a revocable trust, it can be a valuable tool in planning your estate. But to adopt it solely for the sake of avoiding probate can be risky and foolhardy. Find out, first, what a bank will charge you to act as trustee. Then get an estimate of what the probate costs will be (a lawyer can tell you; in fact, the bank can give you a pretty close computation, too). Then decide whether you're willing to pay the bank's annual trust charges, for what could be many years, to save on probate costs.

E. How Much Does a Lawyer Charge?

As with most legal matters, an attorney's fee for preparing a will usually is based on how much time he spends; and that depends on how complicated your ideas are. If you make a "simple will" (see Section G)—all to the wife, and if she doesn't survive, then to the children—the average cost runs between $75 and $250, probably below $150 in most places. In some of the bigger northern cities, it might be a little higher, but not always. If you add some unsophisticated trust provisions to protect your children (see Section C), the expense increases, usually another $100 to $250 more.

When your estate gets large enough to be vulnerable to federal taxes (it can be affected by your marital situation, as said before), then you'll have to figure on higher legal fees. It's fairly likely a trust would need to be set up to save a second set of taxes when your spouse dies (see Section B). This is ordinarily more complex and time-consuming than the trust for children. Depending on the lawyer's hourly charge, and the size of your estate, the fee can run from $350 to $1,000. In situations where the value of your property justifies it, a lawyer may have to devise an elaborate estate plan, to minimize the tax impact, and his fee could jump much higher than $1,000. It's always best to get an estimate in advance. But it's not practical to "shop" around, calling several lawyers. Most of them won't quote a fee over the phone, since they don't know how much time will be involved; or they'll often realize you're comparing prices, and will ask you to make an appointment.

While you're figuring the expense of having a will prepared, you should add the cost of drawing up a will for your mate. Even if there's no property in his or her own name, it's a good idea for your spouse to have a will. When you pass away, your spouse will be inheriting or acquiring your property. But if he or she outlives you by only a few months (or less), and doesn't have a will, the death will be "intestate" (Section A), and the costs, expenses and involvements of probate will mushroom. In case you have children, guardianship expenses would also be incurred. If you have no kids, your property would probably pass to your *spouse's* relatives, rather than yours, since all your property would then be legally your spouse's.

So don't skimp on having wills for both of you. When it's prepared at the same time as yours, you usually get a break on the fees. If a simple will would cost $150, then the cost of the second will would probably be around another $50 or so.

But don't sign a "joint" will with your spouse (that's when you both sign the same document). Many states don't allow them, and they cause all kinds of problems even where they're legal.

F. What Other Costs Are There?

The actual expense of probate varies from state to state, and is based mainly on the size of the estate that's administered. Remember, though, that not all of your assets go through probate; as we've seen, insurance and jointly-owned property customarily pass outside the court (see Section A). The amount spent on court costs isn't too high, in the ordinary administration of an estate. They'll range from about $50 to $200, unless appraisers need to be appointed. Not all jurisdictions require them. Their fees usually start at around $150, but can be much more if there are large assets—either in quality or quantity—to appraise.

The executor, or personal representative, is also entitled to a fee, paid from the assets of the estate. Unless you'll have intricate investment problems, it's usually advisable to choose, as executor, the chief beneficiary under the will. If you're leaving everything to your spouse, that person should be the personal representative, in most cases. That way, additional fees can be avoided. The executor will need to rely on a lawyer, anyway, and there's usually no sense in having two fees—one for the executor and one for the lawyer. Generally, the attorney's charge is roughly comparable to the executor's fee, although sometimes more.

Obviously, if the wife is disabled, or incapacitated, then you'll need to appoint someone else. Even in that situation, rather than appointing a brother or uncle (unless you feel that he'll waive his fee), you might consider appointing your attorney as executor. If the estate is not large, he'll generally agree to charge only one fee for both jobs.

If you do appoint a third party as executor—such as a relative or a bank—you ought to have some idea of the fees they'll receive. The charge is traditionally set by the court, although it's not unusual to get a written fee commitment from the executor (especially a bank) when you prepare the will. On an estate of under $100,000, with no unorthodox problems, you can expect that the fee would go from a low of $1,000 to a high of about $3,500, depending on the state, the exact nature of the assets, and the amount of work to be done. The average for such an estate would probably be between $1,500 and $2,500.

Over $100,000, the fee would increase roughly two to three percent per thousand. Each jurisdiction is different, though, and you shouldn't be shy about asking your bank or attorney what the charges will be.

G. Is a Simple Will O.K. for You?

You've added up your property, and you have less than $500,000, counting insurance and jointly-owned assets. Is a "simple will" O.K. for you? The answer is a qualified yes, but you have to be sure you know what a "simple will" means in your particular case.

Basically, such a will leaves everything to the spouse. It then usually itemizes who gets the property if he or she doesn't outlive you. Some lawyers, incidentally, suggest adding a requirement that your mate must survive you for a specified period—either 30 days or 60 days—before he or she can inherit. That way, only *your* estate would have to be probated if you both died in the same accident (unless your spouse had separate property that had to be administered). Watch out for this danger, though: if you require your spouse to survive you by more than six months, you can lose important tax benefits. Make sure the "survival" period, if you use one, is under six months.

You would also customarily direct that if your spouse didn't survive you for the specified period, your property would go to your lineal descendants. If they're minors, you should consider having an uncomplicated trust provision (Section C) to avoid guardianship expenses. This possibly takes your will out of the pure simple will category, but it's better to do it, and it's worth the few extra bucks.

It's also sound planning to go a step further, and list who's to get the property if you leave no descendants (this could happen if you and your spouse and children were all killed in a common accident). If such a tragedy occurred, you might not care too much about what disposition should be made of your property, but why let your state law of inheritance choose for you, especially if it's contrary to what you'd prefer?

In a number of households, the husband and wife decide that if they and their children all die together, their property should be split into two parts, rather than all going to the husband's relatives. One share would pass to the husband's side of the family (his parents, or brothers and sisters, etc.), and the other share to the wife's relatives. This is usually the fairest solution when the marriage has lasted several years, with the husband and wife mutually contributing to their possessions. But you'll need to discuss your situation with your wife to decide if that solution would be practical in your own case.

The simple will should also name an executor. As we've noted earlier, this is the person or institution who sees that the will is filed, debts and taxes are paid, and the property is distributed to the appropriate heirs. Unless there's a special reason to the contrary, you should have your spouse as the executor (see Section F). Aside from saving on expenses, you'd name the spouse because he or she is the one that will ordinarily gain the most from the will, so is naturally most interested in seeing that there's no delay, and that everything is handled properly. If the executor doesn't know what to do, she'll be relying on an attorney, anyway.

Not all writers agree that the wife or chief beneficiary should be appointed as executor. Some feel that an institution should be picked. In fact, many banks and trust companies advertise widely in an effort to be named as executor. In all fairness to this position, it should be pointed out that there are a number of advantages in having such an executor, particularly when the estate is large, with extensive investment decisions and inventory problems to tackle. But if you have a small estate, you're better off not choosing the bank.

You should also provide for at least one successor executor (and generally a second successor) in case of death or disability of your first choice. Ordinarily, a trusted relative is named, but be careful, because some states require the executor to be a resident. If you do pick a relative, make sure he's at least financially responsible, so that he won't be tempted to "borrow" any of the assets. If he's always short of money, he'll be a dangerous choice. It's helpful if he has some business experience, but this isn't even essential in the ordinary estate. If you have the slightest qualms about the stability of the relative you're considering, then reject him. If he's the only possible one available, then you might consider having him serve under bond (you do this by simply not making any mention of the bond in the will; unless the bond is waived by you, the law will require him to get one).

In some cases, it's also not a bad idea to pick your lawyer as a successor executor (see Section F). As a final alternative, even in a modest estate, you can name a local bank or trust company, in case none of the other designated executors survive or are able to serve.

In the absence of any clause to the contrary, your executor will usually have to post a bond with the court, guaranteeing that he or she will faithfully perform the required duties and won't run off with any money. This is an expense that's paid out of the assets of the estate. But if you have confidence in the person you pick (and you shouldn't choose him if you have any doubt), it's not unusual to waive the bond requirement. This is especially true if the executor is the chief beneficiary under the will. You'll also find that in most places a bank or trust company isn't required to put up a bond.

An executor has certain rights and powers set by statute. But unless your will gives him broad discretion and authority to act, he won't be able to accomplish very much without a court order. In most states, if the executor feels that a piece of property or some shares of stock should be sold—maybe they're declining rapidly in value—he couldn't do it without the judge's approval. This is an expense, and time-consuming, at best. So ordinarily, you should see to it that the will gives the personal representative the power and authorization to sell, invest, and manage your property, without court order. In some situations, he might still need the judge's permission, but not nearly as often.

If you have minor children, your will should name a guardian to take care of them and to have their custody. The guardian would be your wife, if she survives, but in case she doesn't, you'll need to pick a successor. Your choice isn't 100% binding on the court; certain people are disqualified: convicts, insane persons, sometimes nonresidents unless they're blood relatives. But the judge will usually go along with your choice. So give some serious thought to who would be best qualified to look after the children. And it's not necessary that the trustee or guardian of their money be the same as the guardian of their ''persons.'' If Aunt Gussie would be the logical one to raise the kids, but you don't feel she could properly manage the cash, you might consider someone else, or a bank, as the guardian of the property. But keep in mind that Aunt Gussie would have to work closely with the property guardian in deciding how much support will be needed. So don't pick somebody whose personality will clash with Aunt Gussie's.

As mentioned previously, it's preferable to have a *trustee* for the children's assets, rather than a *property guardian* (see Section C). Actually, it seems silly that the *label* you give the person (''trustee'' instead of ''property guardian'') can make such a difference. But it does.

Even with a trust, though, your will should still name a property guardian, in case the children acquire some money or assets from another or unexpected source. The trustee, if you've named one, would be the logical choice as the property guardian.

We've been assuming that you're married and have children. Suppose, though, you're single. Does any of this apply to you, and how complicated a will do you need? The simple will can probably be used, with some modifications. Chances are you won't be too concerned with trust provisions and guardians, but even if you're unmarried, you might like some of your property to go to nephews or nieces, who may be minors. If you're making just a small bequest (say under $500), you might feel it's not practical to start up with trusts. You might prefer to leave it to the parent of the minor (or some other relative) with the instruction that it be used for the child, in the discretion of the relative, but without legally requiring the relative to account to the court. This type of language is probably not binding on the relative, but will normally accomplish your purpose. If you felt you had to be guaranteed it would be used for the child, then you'd either leave it in trust, without making it too complicated, or a better alternative might be to leave it to a named adult, as custodian for the child under a special law known as "the Uniform Gifts to Minors Act" (it's also called "the Uniform Transfers to Minors Act" in several states). The money or property would lawfully belong to the minor, but would be held by a custodian (which can be a member of the child's family or an institution) until the child becomes of age. In many states, the age is 18; in others, it's 21. Most jurisdictions only allow cash and securities to be included, but some states (such as Florida) now permit real estate, as well.

If you're married, but have no children, you won't need an intricate will, provided your estate is under $500,000. Over that amount, and up to between $550,000 and $600,000, you might still want it all to go to your spouse, outright (see Section B), under present law. You'll have no federal estate taxes, but your heirs may have to pay a bundle when your wife dies, if she doesn't remarry or give away a hunk of the estate. You'll need to decide whether you want to set up a trust with part of the property, so that it's not taxed at her death (see Section B), or whether you'd just as soon leave it all to her, direct. Unless it's important to you that your relatives share in a part of your estate after you're gone, you're probably better off letting it go to your wife. There could be other reasons, though, for establishing a trust for your wife: for instance, you may feel she wouldn't know how to invest any hefty amount of dough, and that you'd feel more comfortable having a bank handle it for her.

H. Signing Your Will

The signing of your will is a special kind of ceremony, and if you don't follow the rules of your state, right down to the dotting of the "i" and the crossing of the "t," all of your carefully worded directions may go down the drain.

You'll need to have witnesses. While almost all states require only two, you should have an extra one along, since a few jurisdictions require three. It's not necessary, though, that the will be notarized, but it's advisable to have it done, if you can.

What kind of witnesses should you have? Don't just call somebody in off the street, unless you have no alternative. At some later time, the witness may have to testify about your signature and competency, so you should try to have witnesses who know you, and who will be available, if needed. But avoid using one of your heirs or a beneficiary under the will as a witness. Such a person is either not legally qualified, or could end up losing his bequest. Whenever you can, get people who are younger than you are, or at least ones who aren't elderly.

In most states, all of the witnesses have to be present at the same time when you sign, and they're required to sign in the presence of each other. Even if your state doesn't require this, it's best to follow the practice.

Stay away from signing a copy of the will; just execute the original. If you sign more than once, all of the copies might need to be filed for probate. In case one is misplaced or can't be produced, there may be a presumption that you intended to revoke the will. You might want to argue with the logic of this rule, but it's not worth trying to be a pioneer and making new law.

If your will is more than one page, you should sign each of the pages. This will make it difficult for anyone to substitute a page, and will deflate any argument that somebody fraudulently *did* slip in a phoney page.

Keep the original signed will in a safe place. A safety deposit box is often used, but you should be sure that your spouse, or some other trusted person, has the right to open the box if something happens to you. Otherwise, a court order may be needed to open it. If you've chosen a bank as trustee or executor, they'll usually keep the will for you, without charge. Your lawyer will probably also take care of it for you, if you ask.

It's advisable to keep a photocopy of the will at home, or some convenient place. That way, if you need to check it over, you won't have to go to your safety deposit box, or bother anybody else. Incidentally, you should make it a habit to look over your will once a year. The odds are it won't need changing, but it's a good idea to read it over again, to be sure.

You may have wondered whether you should specifically itemize all of your property in the will—bank accounts, stocks, car, and so forth. This is done on rare occasions, but it's unwise. Anytime you changed or added to your holdings, you'd have to revise or amend the will. So it just isn't practical to do it. The best way to handle this is to make a separate memorandum (it can be handwritten or typed), listing such information as: where you bank and have savings accounts; companies you have insurance with, and policy numbers; stocks and bonds, and the name of your broker; real estate; pension and profit-sharing benefits; and other assets that your heirs should know about. This inventory isn't a part of your will, but can be kept with it (usually paper-clipped to it), so that your property can be easily located. If you don't do this, your executor can easily miss some of your assets, or have to be an expert sleuth to track them down.

I. What If You Change Your Mind?

The law demands certain rigid formalities for a will to be effective. There have to be witnesses (page 156), although some states allow, as an exception, an entirely handwritten will. In addition to the witness requirement, you have to be of "sound mind"; the will must be written or typed (a few courts allow an "oral will" if a person is on his deathbed). But although these rules all emphasize the solemnity and gravity of a will, there's an equally important principle you need to know: a will doesn't have any legal effect until you die.

This means that you have the right to change your mind as often as you like. You can make a new will every month if it suits you. But watch out for this pitfall: after the will is signed, and witnessed, don't write in some extra language later, or cross something out. This could void the entire will.

If you'd like to make a minor change or addition, you can do it by a "codicil," which is an amendment to a will. It has to be signed with the same formalities as the will. (See Form 4.) If you need to make several changes, it's best to draw up a new will. The most recent will that you make automatically revokes the earlier one, if you specifically say so in the will. Once you sign the new one, you should destroy the old will, particularly if you've made any substantial changes. If you leave both of them around, it's possible that only the first one will be found, or that a disinherited (and dishonest) heir may destroy the later one, and produce the first one.

If you haven't made any major changes, it might be all right to keep the old one, but you should mark across it, ''Revoked by will of (such and such a date).'' Occasionally such an earlier will can be of some help in court in case of a contest over your intention.

J. Can You Leave Your Property Any Way You Want To?

It's been said, generally, that you can leave your property any way you want to. But that's not entirely true.

As we've seen earlier (Section C), you ordinarily can't completely disinherit a wife—although, interestingly enough, in some jurisdictions, a woman can cut off a husband entirely.

And in several places, there are restrictions on your being able to dispose of your ''homestead,'' other than to your wife and family.

Can you give your property away to charity? Yes—except for the wife's claim. But there are some conditions attached. A number of states invalidate such gifts if made shortly before death, when you have a wife or children. This apparently is based on the law's fear that a person who's dying may want to ''buy'' his way into heaven, at the expense of his family. But if the bequest isn't made ''in contemplation of death'' (say, for example, a year before), it's generally legal. In several states, you can't give more than a limited percentage of your property to charity, such as a third or a half.

This type of will, with bequests to charity, is often a fruitful source of legal attack by disgruntled heirs. But merely disinheriting a relative isn't enough to knock out a will; the heirs have to show some disqualification—mental incapacity, undue influence, fraud, duress.

Sometimes the gifts are so ''unnatural'' that a question is raised whether the will, by itself, is some evidence of mental weakness. Just because a will may be foolish or unjust isn't grounds for setting it aside. But its unnaturalness is a factor that the court can consider in determining soundness of mind. In one case, an elderly man cut off his children without a nickel and left all his money for the breeding of cats. The will was thrown out. In another case, a father left nothing for his son except a transcript of the boy's divorce, with an insinuation that the son had lied. The will was upheld.

Every now and then you'll have an asset that you can lawfully leave to your family, but you either won't want to, or they won't know what to do with it. To illustrate, let's say you own a thriving business, in partnership with two other men. Your wife, though, doesn't have the ability or interest to help run it if something happened to you. If you leave your share to her, there would be problems for everybody concerned. The solution is a "buy-and-sell" agreement, made while you're living, between you and your partners, committing each of you to buy out the share of any partner who dies (see more detailed discussion in Chapter 6, page 194). A good way to handle this is for the partners to buy life insurance on each other's lives. If you were to die, the insurance proceeds would go to your wife, or family, as payment for your share of the business.

There are a few other types of assets that you might own, and yet not have enough control over to be able to leave to somebody in your will. We've already talked about joint ownership with right of survivorship (Section A); if you happen to be such a co-owner, your share or "half" can't be willed away. If anything happens to you, it goes to the survivor.

A life estate in property (see page 45) is another possession that you can't regulate in your will. Your rights in the life estate last as long as you live, but no longer. When you go, the life estate goes; and it then passes to the "remainderman," or person who survives you. If you'd like to leave it to someone in your will, forget it. You can't do it.

Knowing what you're *not* able to do with your property should give you a little better idea of what you *are* able to do. If you've learned enough to spot some of the trouble areas, you're two jumps ahead of the crowd. But tax laws are complicated and strict, and so are the rules governing wills and estates. You might need to use the services of some experts in this field—primarily an attorney, accountant, insurance agent, and banker. All of them can give you help in staying out of court and away from lawsuits. And if their services—and what you've read here—can help you do that, then that's the best way, in the long run, to avoid lawyers.

Form 1

LAST WILL AND TESTAMENT

[For Married Man with Minor Children; No Estate Tax Problems]

I, ..., a resident of the City of ....,
County of ...., State of ...., do make,
publish, and declare this to be my Last Will and Testament, and hereby
revoke all former wills and codicils made by me.

ARTICLE I

I direct that all my legal and enforceable debts, including funeral
expenses (and including the cost of a suitable monument at my grave),
expenses of last illness, and the expense of the administration of my
estate, be paid by my (Executor) (Executrix) hereinafter named, or (his)
(her) successor, as soon after my decease as may be practical.

ARTICLE II

I give and bequeath the following: (for use when applicable)
1. To ...., that certain property described as: ....
2. To ...., that certain property described as: ....

ARTICLE III

All the rest, residue, and remainder of my property, real, personal,
and mixed, at whatever time acquired by me, and wheresoever situated
(hereinafter called my residuary estate), including all property over
which I have testamentary power of disposition or appointment, I give,
devise and bequeath to my wife, ..., to the exclusion
of any child or children now or hereafter born or adopted, provided that
my wife shall survive me for 60 days. The proceeds of any insurance
on my life, payable to my estate or to my executors and administrators,
shall be considered a part of my residuary estate, and are hereby specifically bequeathed as a part of said residuary estate.

ARTICLE IV

In the event my wife shall predecease me, or not survive me for 60
days, then I hereby give, devise and bequeath my residuary estate to
my Trustee, hereinafter named, in trust for the use and benefit of my
children, whether now or hereafter born or adopted, upon the following
terms and conditions:

1. I authorize my Trustee to sell at public or private sale, for cash or
credit, with or without security, invest, reinvest, mortgage, lease, pledge
and dispose of all property, at such times and upon such terms and
conditions as my Trustee may determine, all without court order.

2. I waive compliance with any law requiring qualification, administration, or accounting by my Trustee to any Court.

3. I authorize and direct the Trustee to pay over or apply the net

income of the trust for the maintenance, education, and support of any or all my children at such times and in such proportions as the Trustee shall determine, in the discretion of the Trustee, keeping in mind the interest and welfare of my children. If the income shall be insufficient to provide any of my children with adequate maintenance, education, and support, the Trustee shall have the discretion to invade the principal of the trust for this purpose, and such invasion shall be according to the needs of my children, rather than according to any pro rata scheme of distribution.

4. I direct that the trust shall be administered and treated as one trust for all purposes until my youngest child shall reach the age of: (use applicable letter)

__a. 21 years.

__b. 25 years.

__c. Other ....

At that time, the Trustee shall divide the trust into as many equal shares or parts as there are children of mine surviving at that time, or lawful descendants of a deceased child per stirpes; and the Trustee shall, at that time, pay over to each child his equal share of the then remaining residuary estate, and his interest under the trust shall cease.

5. If any child dies before becoming entitled to his full share of the principal of the trust, the interest of such child in the trust shall cease, and his share shall be transferred to my child or children surviving at that time; provided, however, the share of said decreased child shall be paid to his lawful descendants, if any, that survive him, per stirpes. If all my children shall die before becoming entitled to their respective shares and shall leave no lawful descendants, then the trust shall terminate, and the principal and income shall descend as set forth in Article VI of this will.

6. The trustee shall have discretion, during the term of the trust, to pay, transfer, or assign the income or corpus of the trust in any one or more of the following ways: directly to such beneficiary such amount as the Trustee may deem advisable as an allowance; to the guardian of such beneficiary; to a relative of such beneficiary upon the relative's agreement to spend such sum solely for the beneficiary's benefit; or by spending such sums directly for the benefit of such beneficiary.

7. I name and appoint ...., whose address is ...., as Trustee of this Trust, to act without bond, with full powers as heretofore mentioned. If such Trustee shall predecease me, or be unwilling or unable to act, or shall die before the termination of the Trust, I name and appoint ...., whose address is ...., as Trustee of this Trust, to act without bond, with full powers as heretofore mentioned. (And if such second Trustee shall predecease me, or be unwilling or unable to act, or shall die before the termination of the Trust, I name and appoint ....,

whose address is ...., as Trustee of this Trust, to act without bond, with full powers as heretofore mentioned.)

ARTICLE V

In the event my wife shall predecease me, or not survive me for 60 days, and all of my children shall have, at the time of my death, attained the age at which their share of the trust was to be distributed, then I direct that my residuary estate be divided into as many parts or shares as there are children surviving me, or lawful descendants of a deceased child, per stirpes, and that one part or share thereof be paid over and distributed to each child, or lawful descendants, per stirpes.

ARTICLE VI

If my wife predeceases me, or shall not survive me for 60 days, and none of my descendants shall survive me, then I give, devise, and bequeath my residuary estate as follows: (use applicable line).

___1. One half to ....
___2. One half to ....
___3. Other ....
....

ARTICLE VII

I appoint as (Executor) (Executrix), to serve without bond, the following:

___1. My wife
___2. Other ....

I give my (Executor) (Executrix) the fullest power and authority in all matters and questions, including complete authority to sell at public or private sale, for cash or credit, with or without security, invest, reinvest, mortgage, to compromise and settle claims, lease, pledge, and dispose of all property, at such times upon such terms and conditions as he or she may determine, all without court order.

ARTICLE VIII

If the person named in Article VII shall predecease me, or be unable or unwilling to serve, then I appoint ...., whose address is ...., as Executor without bond, with full powers as heretofore described. (And if the foregoing person shall predecease me, or be unable or unwilling to serve, then I appoint

....

whose address is ...., as Executor without bond, with full powers as heretofore described.)

ARTICLE IX

If my wife shall predecease me, or shall be unable or unwilling to serve as guardian of my children or of any beneficiaries under this will who are minors or incapacitated at the time of my death, then I appoint ...., as guardian of the person and estate of such children and beneficiaries, to serve without bond, with full powers as heretofore described in Article IV. (And if said guardian shall predecease me, or be unable or unwilling to serve, then I appoint ...., as said guardian without bond, with the same powers.)

ARTICLE X

No payment required or authorized to be made, and no property required or authorized to be distributed by this will or the trust, shall be subject to anticipation, hypothecation, or alienation, or to attachment, garnishment, seizure, levy of execution, or by creditors through any legal process.

ARTICLE XI

If any beneficiary shall be a minor at the time he or she becomes entitled to distribution, then the payment of such share shall be deferred until the minor reaches the age of 21 years; and in the meantime, such share shall be held by my Trustee, in trust, subject to the provisions and conditions of this will; provided, however, the trusts shall terminate not later than 21 years after the death of the last survivor of myself and all beneficiaries hereunder living at the time of my death.

IN WITNESS WHEREOF, I hereby sign, seal, and declare this as my Last Will and Testament this .... day of ....
19............

.... (SEAL)
Signature

The foregoing instrument, consisting of .... pages, this included, the first pages bearing on the left-hand margin the signature of the Testator, was this .... day of .... 19............, signed, sealed and declared by the Testator as and for his Last Will and Testament in the presence of us, who at his request, in his presence, and in the presence of each other, have subscribed our names as witnesses thereto.

....   residing at ....
....   residing at ....
....   residing at ....

Form 2

LAST WILL AND TESTAMENT

[For Married Man with No Children; No Estate Tax Problems]

I, ..., a resident of the City of ....,
County of ...., State of ...., do make,
publish, and declare this to be my Last Will and Testament, and hereby
revoke all former wills and codicils made by me.

ARTICLE I

I direct that all my legal and enforceable debts, including funeral
expenses (and including the cost of a suitable monument at my grave),
expenses of last illness, and the expense of the administration of my
estate, be paid by my (Executor) (Executrix) hereinafter named, or (his)
(her) successor, as soon after my decease as may be practical.

ARTICLE II

I give and bequeath the following: (for use when applicable)
1. To ...., that certain property described as: ....
2. To ...., that certain property described as: ....

ARTICLE III

All the rest, residue, and remainder of my property, real, personal,
and mixed, at whatever time acquired by me, and wheresoever situated
(hereinafter called my residuary estate), including all property over
which I have testamentary power of disposition or appointment, I give,
devise and bequeath to my wife, ..., to the exclusion
of any child or children now or hereafter born or adopted, provided that
my wife shall survive me for 60 days. The proceeds of any insurance
on my life, payable to my estate or to my executors and administrators,
shall be considered a part of my residuary estate, and are hereby specifically bequeathed as part of said residuary estate.

ARTICLE IV

If my wife predeceases me, or shall not survive me for 60 days, then
I give, devise, and bequeath my residuary estate as follows: (use applicable line)
___1. One half to ....
___2. One half to ....
___3. Other ....
....

ARTICLE V

I appoint as (Executor) (Executrix), to serve without bond, the following:
___1. My wife
___2. Other ....
I give my (Executor) (Executrix) the fullest power and authority in all

matters and questions, including complete authority to sell at public or private sale, for cash or credit, with or without security, invest, reinvest, mortgage, to compromise and settle claims, lease, pledge, and dispose of all property, at such times and upon such terms and conditions as he or she may determine, all without court order.

ARTICLE VI

If the person named in Article V shall predecease me, or be unable or unwilling to serve, then I appoint ...., whose address is ...., as Executor without bond, with full powers as heretofore described. (And if the foregoing person shall predecease me, or be unable or unwilling to serve, then I appoint ...., whose address is ...., as Executor without bond, with full powers as heretofore described.)

IN WITNESS WHEREOF, I hereby sign, seal, and declare this as my Last Will and Testament this ....day of .... 19............

.... (SEAL)
Signature

The foregoing instrument, consisting of .... pages, this included, the first page(s) bearing on the left-hand margin the signature of the Testator, was this .... day of .... 19............, signed, sealed and declared by the Testator as and for his Last Will and Testament in the presence of us, who at his request, in his presence, and in the presence of each other, have subscribed our names as witnesses thereto.

.... residing at ....
.... residing at ....
.... residing at ....

Form 3

LAST WILL AND TESTAMENT

[For Married Man with Grown Children; No Estate Tax Problems; No Trust Provision Desired]

I, ..., a resident of the City of ...., County of ....:., State of ...., do make, publish, and declare this to be my Last Will and Testament, and hereby revoke all former wills and codicils made by me.

ARTICLE I

I direct that all my legal and enforceable debts, including funeral expenses (and including the cost of a suitable monument at my grave), expenses of last illness, and the expense of the administration of my estate, be paid by my (Executor) (Executrix) hereinafter named, or (his) (her) successor, as soon after my decease as may be practical.

ARTICLE II

I give and bequeath the following: (for use when applicable)

1. To ...., that certain property described as:

....

2. To ...., that certain property described as:

....

ARTICLE III

All the rest, residue, and remainder of my property, real, personal, and mixed, at whatever time acquired by me, and wheresoever situated (hereinafter called my residuary estate), including all property over which I have testamentary power of disposition or appointment, I give, devise and bequeath to my wife, ..., to the exclusion of any child or children now or hereafter born or adopted, provided that my wife shall survive me for 60 days. The proceeds of any insurance on my life, payable to my estate or to my executors and administrators, shall be considered a part of my residuary estate, and are hereby specifically bequeathed as a part of said residuary estate.

ARTICLE IV

If my wife predeceases me, or shall not survive me for 60 days, then I give, devise and bequeath my residuary estate equally to my children, share and share alike. If any or all of my children shall predecease me, or die simultaneously with me, then I give, devise and bequeath the share of such deceased child to the lawful descendants of such deceased child, per stirpes.

ARTICLE V

If my wife predeceases me, or shall not survive me for 60 days, and none of my descendants shall survive me, then I give, devise and bequeath my residuary estate as follows (use applicable line):

__1. One half to ....

__2. One half to ....

__3. Other ....

....

ARTICLE VI

I appoint as (Executor) (Executrix), to serve without bond, the following:

__1. My wife

__2. Other ....

I give my (Executor) (Executrix) the fullest power and authority in all matters and questions, including complete authority to sell at public or private sale, for cash or credit, with or without security, invest, reinvest, mortgage, to compromise and settle claims, lease, pledge, and dispose of all property, at such times and upon such terms and conditions as he or she may determine, all without court order.

ARTICLE VII

If the person named in Article VI shall predecease me, or be unable or unwilling to serve, then I appoint ...., whose address is ...., as Executor without bond, with full powers as heretofore described. (And if the foregoing person shall predecease me, or be unable or unwilling to serve, then I appoint ...., whose address is ...., as Executor without bond, with full powers as heretofore described.)

IN WITNESS WHEREOF, I hereby sign, seal, and declare this as my Last Will and Testament this .... day of .... 19............

.... (SEAL)
Signature

The foregoing instrument, consisting of .... pages, this included, the first pages bearing on the left-hand margin the signature of the Testator, was this .... day of .... 19............, signed, sealed and declared by the Testator as and for his Last Will and Testament in the presence of us, who at his request, in his presence, and in the presence of each other, have subscribed our names as witnesses thereto.

.... residing at ....
.... residing at ....
.... residing at ....

Form 4

CODICIL TO WILL

[To Be Used When Minor Changes Are Desired]

I, ..., a resident of the City of ...., County of ...., State of ...., do make, publish, and declare this to be a Codicil to my Last Will and Testament.

ARTICLE I

I hereby revoke Article II of my said Will, and direct that the property described therein shall go to ....

ARTICLE II

I hereby revoke the appointment of ...., as Trustee under my said Will, and appoint, in his place, ..., whose address is ...., to serve with the same powers and authority.

ARTICLE III

In all other respects, I hereby ratify and confirm the provisions of my said Will, except as revoked or modified by this Codicil.

IN WITNESS WHEREOF, I hereby sign, seal, and declare this as a Codicil to my Last Will and Testament (under date of the .... day

of .... 19............) this .... day of
.... 19............

.... (SEAL)

Signature

The foregoing instrument, consisting of this page, was this ....
day of .... 19............, signed, sealed and declared by
the Testator as and for a Codicil to his Last Will and Testament dated
the .... day of .... 19............, in the presence of
us, who at his request, in his presence, and in the presence of each
other, have subscribed our names as witnesses thereto.

....   residing at ....
....   residing at ....
....   residing at ....

CHAPTER 6

So You're Going Into Business

ONCE UPON A TIME, LONG, LONG AGO, WHEN A MAN WANTED TO open a business, he put up a sign, rolled up his sleeves, and went to work. There were no licenses, taxes, financing, lease-back agreements, franchises, pension plans, anti-trust laws, or profit-sharing. There were no collapsible corporations, capital gains, labor strikes, workmen's compensation, or preferred stock issues.

Those days are gone forever. So that now, if you're going into business, it's not enough to know your product, or to be a good salesman, or a specialist in your field. You have to know something about the rules of the game: tax exposure, liability problems, and what legal form your business should take.

A. Should You Incorporate?

One of the first questions to decide is: should you incorporate? Before you can really answer, you need to have some idea of the advantages and disadvantages of the various ways of carrying on a business.

The basic method, of course, is the sole proprietorship—the one-man operation. Even in our jet-age society, this form of business still thrives, and can be practical and economic in many situations.

Let's look at it more closely. Here are some of the reasons it remains popular:

169

1. It's not subject to as many regulations, reporting requirements and red tape as a corporation.

2. It's less expensive to start (you don't have to pay the costs and fees that usually are part of a corporation's initial operations).

3. You can be in charge without having to clear your decisions through a board of directors or partners.

4. You're not subject to the "double tax" that corporations are vulnerable to (one on the corporation's profits, and another on any dividends paid to the stockholders).

5. Losses and other deductions can be offset directly against other personal income (this can sometimes be true with a corporation, but not in all cases).

6. Less formality.

But there are drawbacks. Some of them are:

1. The owner is liable, personally, for all debts of the business. This is probably the single biggest disadvantage (in a corporation, the liability is generally limited only to your investment).

2. If the owner dies or is incapacitated, the business often comes to a standstill.

3. All of the profits are taxable income to the owner.

4. He doesn't have the full tax benefit of pension plans allowed to corporate employees.

As a rule, if your risk of loss is small, you should consider operating as a sole proprietorship. But if you're in a business where you buy a sizable amount of merchandise or supplies, and there's a chance, say, that a bad season can put you out of commission, you'll want to seriously think about incorporating. If you're a sole proprietor and you owe money, you can be sued personally, and most of your assets would be subject to a judgment (for exceptions to this rule, see Chapter 7).

Here are some typical situations:

1. Suppose you plan to buy or open a hardware store, and expect to carry a big inventory. At various times, you'll owe several suppliers substantial sums of money. What should you do? By incorporating, you'd limit your liability to just what you invest in the store. If the business folds, your personal assets wouldn't be gobbled up with it.

2. Now let's assume you're a plumber, with not a particularly large supply of parts or materials. Your business depends on your service and the time you spend. On any given day, you don't have much money invested. In this case, you probably wouldn't be too worried about limiting your liability, and a corporation may not be much advantage to you. One caution, though: you'll need to carry liability insurance, protecting you in the event you're sued for damage you cause. If you can't get that kind of insurance, then the picture changes, and a corporation might be advisable, to at least give you some protection against a big judgment.

What if you plan to have one or more persons associated with you in your venture? Should you incorporate or should you work as partners?

Basically, a partnership is an arrangement between two or more people to carry on a business. But it's a special breed of legal cat, and you should know something about its characteristics.

The most significant feature of a partnership is that each member can legally bind and obligate the others. This means that the actions or conduct of one of the partners can make you personally responsible. Obviously, if you have any doubt about the integrity or capability of a prospective partner, you shouldn't set up a partnership (or, for that matter, any other business with him).

Are there advantages to a partnership? Like the sole owner business, there's less formality than a corporation. In addition, the "double tax" and many of the statutory regulations imposed on a corporation are avoided.

How about the disadvantages? Again, as with the sole proprietorship, there's unlimited personal liability. And even worse, you're now on the hook for obligations of the business even if they're incurred without your knowledge by one of your partners (there are certain duties of "contribution" by the members, but you can't always count on this to soften the impact too much).

Another difficulty is that the death or withdrawal of any of the members can cause the partnership to be dissolved. With proper planning, this obstacle can be overcome (see page 194, for discussion of buy-and-sell agreements). Sadly, too many partnerships are set up without any thought given to death or disability.

We've been looking at sole proprietorships and partnerships. But how about the corporation itself? Here's what you should know about it:

To begin with, a corporation is a legal "being," separate and apart from its stockholders. It can sue and be sued, and can enter into contracts. The corporation receives its breath of life from a charter, or articles of incorporation, filed with the state.

Why should you incorporate? Some of the reasons are:

1. Your liability is limited, except in rare cases, to the amount you put in for your share or part of the corporation.

2. You can quickly transfer your ownership interest, represented by your shares of stock, without the corporation dissolving.

3. The corporation continues to exist despite the death or incapacity of a stockholder.

4. There can be flexibility in operation, particularly in large businesses (such as through the use of voting and nonvoting stock, preferred shares, profit-sharing and pension plans, stock options, etc.).

5. The corporation's capital can be expanded by issuing and selling additional shares of stock.

6. The corporation has various tax options available to it, and in many cases can even choose to be taxed as a partnership (a corporation adopting this option is referred to as a "small business corporation" or a "Chapter S" corporation).

7. Shares of corporation stock can be used for estate and family planning.

8. The corporation, by accumulating its earnings, rather than distributing them, can ease the tax burden of its stockholders (this can sometimes work as a drawback, though, with the corporation "locking in" its earnings, so that stockholders are not able to get dividends).

Conversely, there are some problems and dangers with the incorporated form of business. For example, if earnings or profits are allowed to accumulate unreasonably, or if a large portion of the earnings is from incorporating personal talents (such as a movie star), or from investment income, the corporation can be hit with a large special tax.

There can also be expenses of several hundred dollars, right at the outset, just to set up the corporation (see Section B).

The limited liability of the company can also boomerang. Many suppliers and businesses are reluctant to sell on open account, or to extend credit, to a corporation—especially one that's just been formed—unless the officers or stockholders personally guarantee the debt.

Another difficulty can arise over the easy transfer of stock. It's possible that you, as a stockholder, can find yourself stuck with some unpleasant or unsavory associates who weren't there the day before. There's a way around this: at the beginning, insist on a "buy-and-sell" agreement, prohibiting the sale of stock to outsiders unless the shares are first offered to the other holders. See Section I.

If you're a minority stockholder in a corporation, you'll often find you don't have much say-so in what goes on. The majority holder of the stock generally controls the board of directors—and also the corporation. Unless you can show fraud or mismanagement, which is tough to do, you're out of luck.

Very often two people will set up a business, each putting in substantially the same amount of money and energy, but one will get 51% of the stock, for any one of a number of reasons (such as the company was "his" idea; or he'll be the president; or even because he happens to be older). If you're about to accept 49% of the stock, hold on a minute. You'll find yourself in a weak position later. So if you're putting in approximately half of the money in a new corporation, insist on having half the stock. That way, you'll have an effective "veto," if necessary, of the corporation's actions; and in many states, you could force a liquidation of the company if it became essential to protect your rights. (Actually, some kind of agreement to arbitrate would be preferable to liquidating.) But at any rate, don't paint yourself into a corner by accepting 49%, unless it's absolutely necessary to carry out the deal.

How, then, do you actually decide whether to incorporate? Here are the main considerations, in the typical case:

1. Limitation of your personal liability. You'll need to decide how important this is to you in your situation, and what your chances are of being financially ruined if the business goes sour. The corporation gives you the most protection.

2. Tax considerations. In many businesses, the name of the game is taxes. For instance, in a situation where you're fairly positive

you'll have large income from other sources during the coming year, and you also expect the new company to show a profit; by incorporating, the earnings could be retained in the business—although not "unreasonably"—so that they wouldn't be taxable to you right away. (But be on the lookout for the opposite result: if you expect the business to show a loss the first year, you might get a tax break by remaining unincorporated. The idea here is to write off the business's loss against other personal income that you have. Or if you have losses in other ventures you're in, but you expect the new business to make money the first year, your other losses could be used to offset the profit, if you don't incorporate. If any of these factors will be present in your case, you should look into the requirements necessary to qualify as a "small business corporation." This allows you to get the advantages of incorporation, and yet the shareholders can elect to be taxed as individuals.)

3. Continuity of the business if one or more of the principals dies or withdraws. The corporation has the advantage here.

4. Ability to do business in more than one state and to cross state lines. A corporation is supposed to "qualify" in each state where it operates—pay certain fees and file a copy of its charter; an unincorporated business can move about more freely.

5. Privacy. Most states require annual reports by corporations, listing officers, directors, and other information; unincorporated businesses are usually exempt from such regulation, although a few states do require partnership papers to be filed.

6. The type of income earned. If it's almost all "investment income," as defined by government regulations, the Revenue Service will call your corporation a "holding company," and you'll be whacked with a large tax penalty.

7. Tax consequences when you liquidate or dissolve the business. With a corporation, the stockholders are generally taxed at the time of liquidation; with a partnership, the tax is put off until the assets are sold. In certain situations, where early liquidation is expected, this factor can influence your decision to incorporate or not.

8. The number of owners the business will have. Usually, with a large number, a corporation is more convenient and practical because of the issuance and transferability of shares, centralized

management, and protection from liability for the acts of other members.

9. The advisability of establishing pension and profit-sharing plans. The corporation is the answer here.

In short, there are a wide range of conditions you'll need to weigh and balance before deciding on a corporation. But once you understand the advantages and disadvantages, you should be better able to make the decision.

B. How Much Will It Cost?

In every state, the corporation charter, or articles of incorporation, has to be sent to the appropriate state office—traditionally, the Secretary of State—for his acceptance. There are certain fees you're charged for this approval. In most places, the expense depends on how many shares of stock are authorized and the value of the shares. For a small corporation, you'd probably expect this fee to run somewhere between $50 and $500, on the average. If you're working out a complicated financial structure, with different classes of stock, you can expect a larger expense.

You'll also want a "corporation kit," consisting of the corporation seal, stock certificates (see Section F), a book for the minutes of the meetings, and a stock book to keep a record of the shareholders. Many stationery stores or printing shops carry these. There are also several companies that do an extensive mail-order business for these kits. One is State Seal & Certificate Co., Rt. 1, Box 80, Morriston, FL 32668. You can get such a kit for as little as $35 in some cities, but they usually cost about $40 to $75.

The corporation seal, which is included in the kit, is a mark, or impression used to identify the company on legal documents. The printer or stationery store will make the seal for you, either in a desk model, or a smaller "pocket size," which is more convenient.

Most lawyers are able to prepare incorporation papers. They'll usually spend some time with you, first, discussing whether a corporation is advisable for your purposes. Then they'll ask for some required information about the names and addresses of the stockholders, officers and directors; the principal purpose of the business; and the amount of money you'll be starting with. Sometimes an accountant is consulted, so that the tax impact can be evaluated. The actual preparation of the papers is not particularly complicated. A form is usually followed, and appropriate information is filled in.

The basic document is the corporate charter (articles of incorporation). A typical charter for a small corporation is shown in Form 1 at the end of this chapter. This will be suitable in most cases for the average business.

If the Secretary of State where you're incorporating requires any additional details, he'll return the papers to you, and ask that you add the information.

A corporation ordinarily has by-laws. These are rules that are somewhat more specific than the charter, designed to govern the inner workings of the company, and to set out, in detail, various duties and regulations. It's usually not necessary to file the by-laws with the Secretary of State, but they're prepared at the same time as the corporate charter. A typical form of by-laws for use in the average case is shown as Form 2 at the end of this chapter.

As soon as the corporation is approved by the designated state official, you would customarily have an initial meeting of the incorporators. You'd ordinarily know in advance what's to be decided at the first meeting; and it's not uncommon to have the minutes of the meeting typed up ahead of time, when the other papers are prepared. A form for such minutes is reprinted at the conclusion of this chapter as Form 3.

There might be other documents you'll use: promissory notes (see Section F, for advantages of lending money to the corporation, instead of buying stock); deeds; buy-and-sell agreements (Section I); and leases.

A lawyer's charge for these services is often a flat fee. You can expect the charge to start from a low of $150, to a high of about $500, for the "ordinary" corporation. The more typical range is probably $200 to $350, depending on the locality you're in. If your corporation has some unusual problems, or some complicated stock gimmicks (voting and nonvoting, preferred stock, etc.), the fee will be more.

C. Can You Own All the Stock?

There are probably more "family" corporations in the United States than any other kind. This type of business typically consists of the small, independent owner, whose wife helps out part-time and whose children or relatives also contribute some services. It's sometimes spoken of as a "close corporation," although that term is actually a little broader.

It's true that most families find the formalities of a corporation unattractive (annual meetings, filing requirements), but the limited liability feature is normally enough to offset those disadvantages. And it's now increasingly common to find the local retail merchant, and even the individual craftsman, setting up a corporation.

Let's say you've now decided to incorporate. How should you issue the stock? Does the wife have to hold "one share"?

If you've actually set up a bona fide corporation, it's not really necessary that there be more than one stockholder. You can legally own all of the shares, if you want to, just about all over. Yet the notion persists that somebody else has to own one share.

Some of this stems from the requirement in many states, that there be three incorporators, and usually they agree to "subscribe" to the corporation's stock. But there's generally nothing that prevents them from transferring all their stock to one person as soon as the corporation is approved. In fact, this is a standard practice in many jurisdictions.

A few courts in the past—notably Kentucky and Maryland—have ruled that by holding all the stock, you could cause the suspension of a corporation's powers; but even in those places, the court would then allow you to transfer the stock to others if anyone objected to your sole ownership.

There are also cases where a "one-man" corporation is set up purposely to defraud creditors, or where the sole owner uses the company's assets interchangeably with his, and mixes the corporation's money with his own. In these situations, it's possible for a court to "pierce" the corporation, and make the one-owner stockholder liable for the company's debts. But this would be true even if the wife owned some stock.

Just be sure that the corporation keeps separate books and records, its own bank account, has regular meetings, and operates as a true corporation. If you do this, then it's legally permissible to hold all the stock in your own name. Of course, if you (or your wife) will be happier letting her have one share, don't fight it. But it isn't necessary.

D. Other Factors to Consider

Once you've made up your mind to incorporate, there are a few other decisions you'll need to make. Most of these are routine, in the ordinary case, but there can be varying elements that can influence you.

For instance, you'll have to decide what state to incorporate in. It may sound fairly elementary that you'd choose the place where you live, or where the company's principal business will be. But not always. Occasionally, there are reasons for incorporating in another state. Some areas, for example, have burdensome restrictions that might drive you to another locale (although there are only a handful of such states). If this happens, you might prefer one of the more "liberal" states (Delaware and Nevada have been popular in recent years). A few jurisdictions impose some extra liability on stockholders for certain claims—such as for unpaid wages—but this wouldn't normally be a reason for going to another state (unless you were looking for a way to cheat a whole block of workers before you even got started). There are also differences from state to state on dividends and on corporate indebtedness, but in the standard corporation, this shouldn't affect you.

So unless you know of some special overriding reason for setting up shop out-of-state, you'd ordinarily stick to where you'll be doing most of your business.

Next, you'll need a name for the corporation. You might think it would be nice to use a catchy little moniker like General Motors Auto Sales, or A. T. & T. Plumbers. Don't. You can't use a name that's too similar to an existing name in your state. Sometimes, though, if you change it just enough so that the public won't be confused, you can get by. The Secretary of State is the official that will usually pass on the name you pick. But watch out: even if he says O.K., his approval can be challenged in court if the name is too similar.

Let's assume you're starting business in Jacksonville, Florida, and you decide on the name Atomic Cleaners Corporation. But you're told that in Miami—about 360 miles away—there's already a company with the same name. In the past, Florida law would allow you to incorporate if you added some differentiating geographical phrase—such as Atomic Cleaners Corporation *of Jacksonville*. You may not get by with this type of minor change in other states, but you should check with your Secretary of State. The risk, of course, is that the original corporation could still sue you. Also, if your business eventually expanded to other cities—and you found yourself actually operating in the territory of the other corporation—there would be almost certain litigation.

A story that made the rounds several years back was that an enterprising merchant opened a small department store in Miami Beach under the name "Macy's." According to the story, the real Macy's in New York sued him to stop using the name, even though he was over a thousand miles from New York. Ingeniously, he changed his sign, putting up a new name. But in large letters underneath, he put "FORMERLY KNOWN AS MACY'S DEPARTMENT STORE." It was a nice try, but he wasn't able to do it.

Before you decide on the name you'll use, see if it's available by calling or writing the Secretary of State. Do this before you run up any expense for printing stationery, stock certificates, or other papers, in case your first choice is already taken. Also, think of a second and third alternative and have them ready for clearance with the Secretary of State to avoid delay.

The name you pick will have to include some identifying word to show you're a corporation, such as "incorporated," "corporation," or "company." An abbreviation of one of these is acceptable, too. For many years, New York has required more than the word "company," so you'll need to find out from the state corporation office how far you have to go.

Once you've chosen the name, you'll need to decide on the types of stock to issue (see Section F, as to par and nonpar). If all the investors are more or less on an equal basis, you'll usually issue only one class of shares, spoken of as "common stock." Some of the members may have more shares than the others, but each share would carry with it voting and dividend rights.

On a few occasions, you'll want the stock divided into more than one class, and you might decide to issue "preferred stock." The holders of such shares are given first crack at payment of earnings, and are paid before any of the "common" stockholders. Normally, the preferred shareholders have no voting rights, but they're often given the right to exchange their shares for common stock. There are all kinds of possible combinations, some of them quite exotic, but these are beyond the scope of this book, and are not ordinarily used in a small corporation. If you feel that your circumstances justify such an arrangement, you'll need to have a lawyer help you.

The primary purpose of the corporation should be described in the corporation charter (such as: "to sell shoes and accessories"; or "to build, remodel, or repair houses, buildings, and other structures"). It's customary, though, to give the corporation fairly broad powers and authority so as not to restrict its operations. Otherwise, its right to act could be questioned at some later time.

E. What Happens If You're Sued?

Like all of us, a corporation can have its financial problems. Suppose you're the president of your corporation, and one dark and gloomy day the sheriff hands you a shiny summons. The corporation has been sued.

In many states, a corporation isn't allowed to defend itself in court without a lawyer (the theory being that if a stockholder or officer tries to represent the company, he's engaging in the unauthorized practice of law). If the suit is properly prepared, the corporation will be sued as a separate entity, in its company name. If the person suing (the plaintiff) wins, a judgment is entered against the corporation, but not against the stockholders, directors, or officers (except in rare cases of actual fraud or criminal activity). If the company doesn't pay, then any of its assets can be seized, or "levied upon," by the sheriff or constable, and sold at public sale, to pay the judgment.

Suppose, though, that instead of the corporation being named as the defendant, the suit is against you, personally, rather than as a representative of the company. This happens, at times, through ignorance or mistake by the plaintiff (he may not know or remember that your business is incorporated). Once in a while, it's done deliberately by a plaintiff who prefers to get a judgment against you, individually—thinking his collection chances are better—and he hopes that you won't raise any objection.

When this happens, the corporation's existence must be called to the court's attention by an affidavit or motion. If the judge is satisfied that your corporation is properly registered, the suit against you will be dropped, and will continue against the company.

Every now and then, the opposing side will attempt to show that the debt is actually yours, personally, and not the corporation's, or that you've used the corporation as a vehicle to defraud creditors. If this occurs, you're getting into deep water, and you better get a lawyer before you get in over your head.

A corporation is subject to a variety of possible lawsuits. It can be sued not only for breaking a contract or failing to pay a bill, but for what the law calls "torts" (damages from accidents, improper work, and even intentional wrongs—slander, false arrest, assault and battery). You should carry broad liability insurance, if at all possible, to cover these tort actions. The expense is well worth it.

F. Stockholders and Directors

The stockholders are the owners of a corporation. The business, when it incorporates, issues shares of ownership in the form of stock certificates. These are paid for either by money, property, or services.

In theory, the stockholders don't control the policies of the company (although in actual practice, they often do). The stockholders choose the directors, who, in turn, are responsible for managing the business and establishing its actions and conduct. Ordinarily, the corporate charter doesn't impose any restriction on who can be a stockholder, except in special situations.

Before the corporation begins its operations, it's customary for the organizers (sometimes spoken of as the "promoters") to decide how much stock will be authorized, the amount of money or other consideration to be paid for the shares, and how much stock will be issued. Most states require a corporation to start business with a minimum amount of money (such as $500), but the actual sum will be agreed upon by the incorporators.

If several people are starting the corporation and putting in equal amounts, it's probable that each will get the same number of shares of stock (although this isn't required). A "share" is merely a unit, or part, of the total value of the company. If the corporation is worth $10,000, and there are 100 shares, then each one would be worth $100.

In a small corporation, it isn't necessary to authorize a large number of shares. In fact, since many states charge a filing fee based on the number of shares, it's smarter to issue only a limited number. In the average case, 100 shares, or even as few as 50, will be adequate. It's also a good idea not to issue all of the authorized stock. Leave at least a third to a half of the shares unissued (spoken of as "treasury stock"). That way, if you want to take in additional investors later, or would like to reward an employee with stock, you'll have some, in reserve. If you've issued all the stock to start with, then you'd have to amend the corporation charter, which is an extra cost that will put a dent in your pocketbook.

Each holder of stock will be issued a stock certificate, showing his name and the number of shares he owns. The certificates are usually printed up in advance, and are numbered in sequence. In the ordinary case, 25 certificates should do the job nicely.

Prior to World War II, it was customary for most corporations to issue "par value" stock. This meant that each share had a stated value on its face, such as $5.00, which supposedly represented the amount contributed by the shareholder. But since the value of a share of stock can fluctuate greatly, depending on the overall worth of the corporation, the "par value" of the stock becomes misleading. There were also problems when the actual worth dropped below the par value; several courts have held that in those situations a creditor of the corporation could compel a stockholder to ante up the difference between the par value and the reduced worth.

To avoid these difficulties, another type of stock became increasingly used after the war: the "nonpar" stock. Under this device, the certificate of stock has no stated value, but merely indicates so many shares of "no par value." The actual value will depend on what an investor is willing to pay for it anyway, based on a variety of factors. Merely because the share says "$5.00 par value" is no indication of its worth.

At times, though, there can be valid reasons for issuing par value shares. They might be easier to sell, in some cases, and there might even be a certain psychological impetus to seeing a stated value on a certificate. But despite these reasons, the no-par shares are being issued more and more, and they are legal in all states (except Nebraska, by a curious constitutional restriction).

Several legal writers still favor the issuance of par value stock, but at a very low or "nominal" value, such as a dollar a share. They claim that these low par shares really serve the same purpose as no-par stock, and can result in savings in some parts of the country (this comes about because of the way a number of states determine the value of no-par shares in setting filing fees and yearly taxes; these states will automatically give an arbitrary assessment to each no-par share—say $100—and charge a fee on that basis, even though the actual value may be less).

Your best choice, then, in the usual situation, will be either a low par value or no-par. If you're able to, find out from a lawyer, or from the Secretary of State's office, which method will be cheaper, and how much the two choices will cost you for filing fees and corporation taxes.

The type of stock to be issued isn't the only decision you'll have. Even more basic is the question of how best to turn over the money and other property to the corporation, so that it can get off the ground. This is more complicated than it sounds. The simple way, obviously, is to deliver an agreed sum or consideration, such as $1,000, to the corporation, and receive shares of stock in exchange. But there's a better way to handle it in a small or family corporation: lend part of the $1,000 to the corporation, say $500. Instead of getting $1,000 worth of stock certificates, you get half that amount, and you have the corporation give you a promissory note for the money you're lending. The company still winds up with the same amount of dollars, but you get a tax break. It works like this: when the corporation has some profits or earnings to distribute later, you can get your "loan" paid back to you, tax-free. It won't be "income," or a dividend to you, but merely a repayment of your loan. So you don't pay personal income tax on it.

What happens if you do it the other way, and buy $1,000 worth of stock certificates without the loan? You'd have a different tax set-up; now, if you draw out your $500 from the profits, it's considered a dividend to you, and you're taxed on it.

Then why not call the whole thousand dollars a loan, or $999 of it, so that you can get back your entire investment without paying any taxes? It's been tried; but the government recognizes this possibility too. It's called "thin incorporation," and refers to putting in a top-heavy loan investment in a corporation, and too little for shares of stock. If Uncle Sam thinks your capital is too "thin," the whole scheme gets thrown out, and *all* of the investment will be considered as payment for shares of stock.

You have to walk a narrow line to pass the test. As long as the ratio of loans to stock-capitalization is no more than three to one (two to one is safer still), you should be on firm ground. In fact, higher ratios have been approved, but they're risky. You might have to show that the loans are legitimate. To cover yourself here, be sure that an actual promissory note is issued, with a definite payment date (for example, on or before 24 months). Avoid making it payable on "demand," or in too short or too long a period of time. For instance, in one case, a payment date of 99 years was considered unrealistic, and was disallowed by the court. Have the note provide for interest payments, and specify what can happen on default. Be careful about continually renewing the debt; if you do it as a regular practice, the Treasury Department may balk and say it's not genuine. The interest, incidentally, can be deducted by the corporation, although *you'll* have to pay personal income tax on it.

A form of promissory note is shown as Form 4 at the end of this chapter.

You can't go overboard, though, with these "stockholder loans." If the books show the corporation owes too much, you might have trouble getting outside credit, particularly from a bank. One possibility is to "subordinate" your loan to the bank; that is, to agree that you won't get repaid until the bank does. This can be hazardous, though; if you make a habit of it, you run the risk of the Treasury boys again looking over your shoulder and hollering that you haven't made a real loan—that it's just payment for stock, after all. Moral: don't "subordinate," unless you have to.

There have been other reasons cited for "lending" some of your investment to the corporation. For one thing, if the corporation becomes insolvent, you might be able to be paid back along with other creditors (stockholders come last). Another reason, in the past, was that—if the corporation went under—you could deduct the loss on the loan on your income tax return (this is still true), while a loss on a stock investment wasn't fully deductible; it was subject to special "capital loss" limitations under the Internal Revenue Code. This rule has been softened somewhat, though. In a small corporation, you can issue stock—called "Section 1244" stock—that lets you deduct your loss from stock investment, up to a certain maximum, if the corporation goes defunct. There are no disadvantages if you're eligible (most small companies are), and the tax benefits are well worth it. It's best to have a corporate resolution authorizing the "1244" stock, even though the law no longer requires a written plan. A form of resolution is shown at the end of the chapter (Form 5).

The stockholders in a small corporation will normally be the directors. But they don't have to be. The directors can include "outsiders," such as the corporation's lawyer, its accountant, and some of its key personnel, who might not be stockholders.

Be a little careful here, though. While it's true that the stock-holders technically control the directors, you can get caught in a squeeze—possibly from a family quarrel—where you, as the majority stockholder, are outvoted by the other directors. To avoid this, you should provide in the by-laws that the controlling stock-holder (or, more properly, the holders of a majority of the stock) can remove the directors at any time.

The directors, by law, are required to act in good faith, and as a "prudent man." But they're not liable for mistakes of judgment unless it's shown that they failed to use diligence or reasonable care. The directors are supposed to meet at least once a year, formally; as a practical matter, though, in most family or small corporations, this isn't done. The directors merely decide on a course of action, either over the telephone or informally, and carry it out. However, to stay in the good graces of the various governmental authorities, you better plan to have a meeting once a year. Generally, all you need to do is select the officers—who more often than not, will be the same from year to year—and write up a set of "form" minutes, as shown at the end of this chapter (Form 6). If you're declaring any dividends, or have any other business—such as approving a new lease or okaying a major purchase—this should also be shown.

The minutes are important as a record of what's been done in the past, and will sometimes help to avoid misunderstandings (and, hopefully, lawsuits).

If your corporation deals with a bank or a lending institution, you might be asked to furnish a "corporate resolution" approving a certain course of action. To illustrate: if you open a new checking account for the company, the bank will want a copy of the resolution, with the corporate seal. Don't get nervous. Most banks have their own form, or you can use the one at the end of this chapter (Form 7). If the corporation is borrowing money, you'll need to show that the directors authorized the loan. Use the type of resolution shown as Form 8.

You should keep these resolutions, and the minutes of meetings, in the "minute book." A loose-leaf notebook is generally best for this (it's usually furnished as part of the corporation kit described in Section B). You can also keep the other corporation papers in it. You'll find it helpful to put gummed labels on the edges of the appropriate pages, to show "certificate of incorporation," "by-laws," "minutes," and "special resolutions."

The minutes won't reflect every important decision the corporation makes. But it's proper to list such matters as salaries for the officers; authorization to enter into certain contracts; and sale or purchase of real estate.

The secretary of the corporation will keep the minutes, which don't have to be in any special format. He (or she) will take notes of what's said, and then type them up. (It's not illegal, of course, to keep them in long-hand.) Don't write down every word spoken; it's not necessary and will waste time. Also, it's not essential for the secretary to list the name of the person proposing a motion or resolution, unless there's a distinct reason to do so. And it's generally not required that you list the pro's and con's of a discussion, except when somebody requests it.

If a matter comes up during the year, needing quick action of the directors, it's common practice to call a special meeting. Remember, though, that proper notice has to be given to the directors, unless they waive this—which is often done.

G. Collection Problems

Let's move past the incorporation procedure. You've now opened your doors and are in business. But whether you're running a shoe store, a grocery, or a dress shop, you're going to have some collection problems.

So what do you do when the guy down the block doesn't pay his bill? Should you sue?

In the first place, it depends somewhat on who it is that owes you the money. If it's a corporation, you'll recall that it isn't the officers, directors or stockholders who owe the debt (except in unusual cases). Your claim is against the company itself. If the corporation has no assets, or has already closed its doors, you'll have a rough time salvaging anything. If it's a going business, or has property, than a judgment should be collectible.

When you sell to a new corporation, be cautious about extending unlimited credit. It's easy to get stung. Unless you're familiar with the company's financial structure, you should try to get a personal guarantee of the debt, in writing, from one or more of the officers. This might dampen your relations with them, and can even queer the deal, but you run a risk when you give credit to an untested corporation. An alternative is to sell C.O.D. for a period of time, until you can see that the corporation is on its feet.

When your claim is against a sole proprietorship or a partnership (see Section A), you're in a different boat. The owners or partners are now vulnerable, personally, for the whole debt. This doesn't always mean you'll be paid (see Chapter 7), but you can go against the individual assets of the debtor or each partner. On occasion, you'll run into the argument, from a partnership, that the obligation wasn't authorized by the rest of the partners. It doesn't have to be. As long as the transaction is within the scope of the partnership business, and you haven't been alerted to the contrary, you have the right to assume it's authorized. There are exceptions, of course. If a partner in a neighborhood grocery store orders a $5,000 piano from you, you probably have a duty to check the order with the other partners, since it's out of the ordinary field of their business.

If your debtor is a minor or a married woman, you can have some troubles. You can try to collect from the man of the family, but he's only legally liable for "necessities"—usually food, clothing, shelter and medical care. And if the husband can show he gives the wife adequate money for support, you might even have a problem suing him for "necessities."

So the best policy here is to be cautious on credit sales to married women and minors. You should know, though, that recent laws have indicated that discrimination against married women can be illegal.

Be careful about collection tactics that can make you vulnerable to a lawsuit. There's nothing wrong with calling the debtor, or writing him a letter. But watch your step if you're planning to call his boss. A great number of creditors use this strategy regularly, but you're laying yourself wide open to legal action, if you do. It's becoming fashionable to file suits against overzealous bill collectors who adopt this tactic, charging them with slander, libel, or invasion of privacy, just for phoning the man's employer. So stay away from this.

If you've been getting the runaround from one or more of your accounts, and have nothing but a fistful of promises, you may have to sue him. But before you do, make one final effort. Don't call him on the phone, though. He's probably used to that by now. Instead, write him a tough letter, showing him you're not kidding, and that you mean business. In the letter, give him a firm deadline, and let him know that suit will be filed. A suggested format for such a letter is illustrated as Form 9.

Suppose he still doesn't pay. In many states, if the debt is under a few hundred dollars, you can handle the lawsuit without a lawyer, in a "small claims court." The jurisdiction of these courts is usually limited to between $500 and $2,500, but in some places it's as high as $5,000. You'll pay a nominal court filing fee—around $20 to $50—and the clerk of the court will help you prepare the papers.

If your claim is too high for the small claims court, you'll need a lawyer to handle it for you. Most attorneys will take on collections for a percentage of what they collect, with the fee ranging from 25% to 33⅓%. The lawyer will probably ask you to give him a deposit to cover court costs. In addition, it's not out of line—depending on the prospects of collection—to ask you for a retainer, or down payment on the fee. This retainer will be credited on the final fee, but if he can't collect anything for you, then you won't get the retainer back. This amount will depend on the size of your claim, the difficulties in the case, and the estimated time involved. On a five hundred dollar collection, a typical retainer might be $100 to $150. If your claim is around $2,000, you can figure a retainer of maybe $200 to $350. The higher you go, the higher the retainer. On a $5,000 collection, you might have to pay about $750. You'll still pay a percentage, but the retainer will be applied against it.

Try to get the lawyer to handle the case without a retainer. If it's a valid claim, with a good chance of collection, he might be willing to pass up the retainer. If the prospects of getting any money from the defendant look dim to the lawyer, though, then don't expect him to sue without the retainer.

In all states, if you win the case, the judge will add the court costs to the amount of the judgment—these include filing fee, sheriff's charges for serving the papers, witness fees, etc. But there's a joker in the deck: in most jurisdictions, the attorney's fee is not considered one of the costs of court, and you can't get the defendant to pay it. (In a few special situations, the lawyer's fees are recoverable, but usually they're not). There's one way to get your legal expenses, though: if the debtor has agreed, in writing, to pay them (such as in a promissory note, or a written contract). Without such an agreement, you're generally out of luck. Unfortunately, most claims on open account, or for sales of merchandise, are based on invoices or purchase orders, rather than on promissory notes or contracts, and there's rarely a provision for attorney's fees.

If you sell on open account, or extend credit to a customer, you should add to, or have printed on your sales slips or invoices, something like this: *"By acceptance of the merchandise described in this paper, the buyer agrees to pay the amounts due; and agrees to pay all costs, including a reasonable attorney's fee, whether suit be brought or not, if an attorney is employed to collect the amounts due."*

This language may not be completely acceptable in all states, but it will hold up in most places, and allow you to collect your legal fees. Very few buyers will object to the provision; if they do, you should explain that it's standard practice (and, in fact, similar language is used in most bank notes and commercial mortgages).

In addition to court costs (and attorney's fees, when applicable), you will ordinarily be entitled to interest on the debt, computed from the time the money became due. This will be added to the amount of the judgment.

Just because you sue and are awarded a judgment, though, doesn't mean you have your money. Your troubles may just be starting. The judgment is merely a finding by the court that a certain amount of money is legally owing to you. But collecting it is up to you. For some of the problems, see Chapter 7. In most areas, you're entitled to a special document from the court called a "writ of execution," which directs the sheriff or constable to seize ("levy upon") the property of the defendant, and sell it to satisfy your judgment. You'll need to take the writ of execution to the sheriff and file it with him.

You should also record a copy of the judgment in the local recorder's office where deeds and other papers are filed. (In some states, the judgment is recorded automatically, but in others, it isn't.) Once it's on record, the judgment acts as a "lien" against any real estate of the defendant.

All of this sounds simple enough, and you might be wondering how the defendant can get out of paying when you have a judgment. As a starter, certain property is exempt from the execution and judgment (see Chapter 7, Section C). And most sheriffs won't go out looking for property to levy on; they expect you to give them detailed instructions, and descriptions of the debtor's assets. What's more, you'll probably have to put up a healthy deposit for the sheriff's expenses.

If you know that the defendant has a bank account, you can try to attach (or "garnishee") the money. This is fairly technical, and the procedure varies from state to state. Try to get assistance from the clerk of the court; if he won't help you, you'll have to contact a lawyer to handle it for you.

You can also attach or garnishee a debtor's wages in most states (a notable exception is Texas; Pennsylvania also prohibits such attachments except for support, board, and educational loans). In some places, you can tie up 10% of a person's wages; in others, a higher percentage. Florida has a strange "all-or-nothing" law: if the defendant is head of a family, his entire salary is exempt (even if he makes $50,000 a year as a corporation executive); but if he doesn't support a family, the law permits his *entire* salary to be attached. However, there's now a federal garnishment law, that takes priority over state statutes, and that permits some minimum exemptions.

If the defendant has an automobile, that's often a good starting point for enforcing your judgment. You can write to the Department of Motor Vehicles in your state to find out if a car is registered in his name, and whether there are any liens or mortgages against it. Then check with the holder of the lien—usually a bank or finance company—to find out how much is still owing. If the balance is almost equal to the car's value, don't waste any more time with it. But if he only owes a small amount, you should consider having the sheriff levy on the car.

In most states, after judgment, there are "discovery" procedures to force a defendant to disclose his assets. This can cost you money, though, and you shouldn't be disappointed if you don't turn up anything of real value.

Sometimes, even when you don't know of any assets that the debtor has, you can be successful by writing a "bluff" letter to the sheriff requesting that he seize all of the defendant's property within a short period—usually five or seven days—if the judgment isn't paid. The key to this tactic is to send a copy of the letter to your debtor. You're really shooting in the dark, since you'll generally have no idea of what the defendant has, if anything. And the sheriff isn't about to start fishing around to find some assets without your telling him exactly what to look for and where to find it. But most defendants don't know this. So the strategy of this kind of letter is to scare the debtor, and smoke him out, so that he'll come up with payment. A suggested form is reproduced as Form 10.

As you'll readily see, there are problems in collecting, even after you have a judgment. As a matter of fact, if you can settle your claim without going to court—even if you have to accept a little less than the amount owing—do it. Certainly, there are some exceptions to this advice: when you *know* a judgment is fully collectible; or when you can get attorney's fees; or maybe where there's a "principle" involved—although you'll soon find that very few principles are really worth the aggravation and expense of a lawsuit. But generally speaking, you'll find that a settlement will save you time, inconvenience, and probably money.

Be on your guard about giving a release in exchange for a personal check. Wait until the check clears, or insist on a bank check, money order, or cash.

Every so often, you'll receive a check for less than you're owed, and you'll find scrawled on it, "payment in full." Should you disregard the notation and cash the check? This is one of those situations where you can get trapped. Here's the law that controls: if your claim is a definite and certain amount, not disputed, and is presently due and owing, then—in theory—you don't waive your rights by cashing the check. In other words, merely marking "paid in full" for such a debt *doesn't* wipe it out. But this theoretical analysis may not hold water in actual practice. Why not? Because often there *is* some dispute over the amount, or an argument about the quality of your merchandise or services. If there really is a disagreement, and you accept the check, you're stuck. The law considers this a compromise (an "accord and satisfaction"), and the debt is discharged. It wouldn't even do you any good, in that case, to cross out the "paid in full" portion, or to tell the maker of the check that although you're cashing it, you're not accepting it as full payment.

If you aren't satisfied with the amount of the "paid in full" check, then you should send it back without delay. If you keep it too long, the court might decide that you accepted it in full satisfaction of the claim.

H. Partnerships

We've previously looked at some of the advantages and disadvantages of a partnership. You should also be aware of the basic procedures involved in establishing one.

Many partnerships exist without any formal written agreement; the parties trust each other and understand their relationship. But if one of them died or became disabled, the survivor would be tangled in a web of legal problems. It's better to have a written partnership contract, and to plan in advance for future uncertainties.

In a partnership agreement, it's customary to decide on a name for the business. More often than not, the partners use a variation of their own names—like "Smith and Jones, Plumbers." But they can use a fictitious or "trade" name, such as "Ace Plumbers." Watch out for using a name that's similar to somebody else's. You can end up being sued (see discussion on the use of corporate names in Section D). If you decide to use a "trade" name, you'll probably have to register it with the local recording office, or Secretary of State—depending on your state's statutes.

The partnership papers should set out the type of business activity to be carried on; the length of time the business will operate, if a specific term has been agreed on; how much each partner will contribute, and in what form (cash, property, or services); whether any loans will be made; agreements as to salary or drawing accounts; and the method of dividing profits and losses.

Usually the partners will share equally in the profits and losses, but this doesn't have to be true. If one of the parties puts up the bulk of the money, or is the "brains" of the business, the agreement could provide for a larger share of the profits to him. Note, though, that if the partners decide not to "draw out" all the profits, they'll still be taxed as though they did. Each partner pays taxes on his part of the business income—and deducts a proportionate share of losses regardless of whether the partnership distributes the income or not.

The partnership agreement might also cover the duties of the partners—who's supposed to do what. It's customary to also specify where the books and records will be kept (generally at the principal place of business), and that each partner can inspect the books at all reasonable times.

Although many partnership contracts neglect to provide for the death or incapacity of a partner, you should see that these points are covered. If you expect to continue the business after one of the partners dies or drops out, then spell it out in the papers. Consider working out a buy-and-sell agreement (page 197), so that the remaining parties can carry on the operations. Without such a provision, the business is legally dissolved, and there can be snarls in liquidating the assets and closing out the business.

A form of partnership agreement is shown as Form 11.

There's another type of partnership, useful in special situations, called a "limited partnership." Its main purpose is to allow people to invest in a business or enterprise without becoming personally liable for the debts. In exchange for this limited liability, the investor (or "limited partner") has no voice in the management of the partnership, and no control of the business. In effect, he's an inactive or "silent" partner. He shares, though, in the profits.

This type of arrangement can work out well when one or more "general partners" are in a position to run the show, but are looking for financial backing. In several parts of the country, limited partnerships are formed to buy real estate and to build apartments or other structures. The general partners do the work, but bring in several investors as limited partners. This method is often preferred to incorporation, because of some tax advantages for the members, and retention of control by the general partners.

To organize a limited partnership, you have to observe certain formalities required by statute, and you need to file the partnership papers with the State.

Remember, though, that if you put in your money as a limited partner, don't start making policy decisions and getting actively involved. If you do, a court might say you're really a general partner and subject to unlimited liability.

I. Buy-and-Sell Agreements

In most carefully planned partnership agreements and small corporations, the parties try to insure the continuation of the business if one of the members withdraws or passes on. The recommended way of doing it is through a buy-and-sell agreement.

With a corporation, the agreement will usually restrict the right of a stockholder to sell his shares to outsiders, unless the company, or the members remaining, are given first right of refusal, based on the predetermined price. This restriction should also be marked on the stock certificate itself. If you try, though, to use an *absolute* restriction against selling to outsiders, under *any* circumstances, the provision will probably be invalid.

The agreement will also have language requiring the corporation, or the survivors, to buy the shares or interest of a deceased stockholder. Sometimes the provision is in the form of an option to purchase, rather than a binding obligation. But in most cases, a *requirement* to buy and sell will be more in keeping with the intent of the agreement.

With the corporation buy-and-sell agreement, you'll need to decide whether the individual stockholders will be buying the shares of the deceased member (called a "cross purchase"), or whether the corporation, itself, will buy them, and "retire" its stock. In some states, a corporation can only purchase its stock from its "surplus," and in other states, only from "earned surplus." So you could conceivably find that these prohibitions will block the sale, if you've determined that the company will be doing the buying. To avoid this obstacle, you could give the corporation a first right of refusal, and then permit the stockholders, individually, to purchase, if the corporation can't or won't exercise its right to buy.

How do you decide, though, whether there should be a "cross purchase"—by the stockholders—or "stock retirement," with the corporation buying its own shares? There are two sides to the question, and not all lawyers agree on which is better. Some of the reasons given for having the "stock retirement" by the corporation, include:

1. You can use the corporation's funds, which haven't been taxed to you yet; while under the cross-purchase plan, you may have to use your own money. This reason isn't too persuasive, though, if you're counting on life insurance proceeds to pay for the stock (see page 197).

2. If you're planning on life insurance funds, the stock retirement method is simpler. The corporation can take out one policy on each stockholder, name itself as beneficiary, and keep continuous ownership. But in the cross purchase plan, each stockholder would have to carry insurance on the lives of all the others. With more than three stockholders, this could get out of hand.

3. The life insurance policies are assets of the corporation, and can be cashed or used as collateral in an emergency.

Some of the claimed advantages of the cross purchase by the stockholders, include:

1. There are fewer tax problems.

2. There may be tax benefits if the surviving stockholders plan to

liquidate the corporation or sell their shares in the near future. For example, the "cost basis" at which you bought your original stock stays the same if the corporation retires its shares, but the value would now be greater because there are fewer shares out. So if you were to sell or liquidate, you'd have a taxable capital gain. But in the cross purchase, the result would be different. Although the "cost basis" on your original shares would stay the same, the "cost basis" for the new shares being purchased would be the amount you're now paying for them. If you sell or liquidate, the capital gains tax will be less than under the stock retirement method.

If you decide on the stock retirement plan, with the corporation buying the shares, you have to be alert to three possible dangers. One is the failure of the corporation to buy *all* the stock of the deceased shareholder (a partial purchase can lead to a taxable dividend to the deceased's estate). A second danger is if the original agreement calls for a cross purchase by the stockholders, but the corporation, instead, buys the shares (this can also lead to a dividend). A third risk is the possibility that by accumulating funds to redeem or retire stock, a corporation might be charged with "unreasonable accumulation of earnings" by Internal Revenue, and be socked with a tax penalty.

There are ways to get around each of these hazards, but they're complicated and intricate. If any of these situations might apply to your case, you should get expert help—either from a lawyer or an accountant, or both.

The hardest part of a buy-and-sell agreement is deciding on a selling price for the stock. There are several standard methods, but each of them has drawbacks.

Probably the most common is to set a price in the agreement itself, and provide for changing it from time to time—usually yearly—either by endorsing the back of the agreement, or by a separate memorandum. The real problem with this is that most people keep putting off the periodic reevaluation, and it's likely that when one of the parties dies several years later, you discover that the last price agreed upon—which may have been years before—would not be a fair valuation. Here's a possible way out of this: put in the agreement that if the reevaluation hasn't been made within a certain time before the death of a party (say, 12 months), then the value will be determined by the representative of the deceased stockholder and the buyer; and if they can't agree, then by an outside arbitrator or appraiser. This can take time, though, and be expensive. An alternative, instead of arbitration or appraisal, is to set the price by the "net worth" or "book value." You'll probably need to have this done by an accountant. The trouble with this method—even though it's a popular device—is that it won't show actual market value of assets, and may not include any proper valuation for such intangibles as good will.

Another method is based on "capitalization of earnings." This is an accounting procedure of averaging the net profits of a business at a specific rate, and coming up with a figure. You ordinarily wouldn't use this system for a small business.

After you decide on the method of setting the purchase price, you still have to figure out where the money will come from. In most businesses, there aren't enough liquid assets to be able to buy out a large stock interest. How do you swing it? The best solution, in the ordinary case, is to take out insurance on the lives of the stockholders or partners. The proceeds, at death, are then used to buy out the interest of the deceased member. If it turns out that the purchase price is greater than the insurance proceeds, it's customary to allow the balance to be paid in installments. The corporation (or stockholders) would sign a note for the amount still owing, payable over some reasonable period—such as three years—and would pledge the stock certificates as security for payment.

A form of buy-and-sell agreement for a corporation, with stock retirement provisions, and one for cross purchase, can be found at the end of the chapter. Most of the larger insurance companies also have forms of such agreements, which they'll give to you if you ask your agent.

In a partnership, the buy-and-sell agreement works on the same basic principle as with the corporation stockholders, and is frequently a part of the original partnership papers. The surviving partners will agree to buy out the interest of a deceased partner, and each partner binds his estate to sell. Be sure that the wives of the partners also sign the agreement; in many states, it's not enforceable without their joinder.

The agreement will cover the price to be paid, or the method of computing it; and when and how payment will be made (again, insurance is the logical way of raising the money).

You should know about one other aspect of the problem: will Internal Revenue accept, for tax purposes, the price that's set by the buy-and-sell agreement? Yes—if the following conditions are met:

1. The agreement is bona fide.
2. The price is reasonable at the time of the agreement.
3. The stock can't be sold, under the agreement, during the lifetime of the seller, without first offering it to the other parties at the price established by the agreement.

Since buy-and-sell agreements are so closely tied in with insurance (in most cases), you can expect your life insurance agent to encourage you to set up some sort of plan. Many agents have taken special courses, and are well read on the requirements. But be wary if they offer to draw up an agreement for you. Keep in mind that insurance, not law, is their specialty. This is a highly complex field, and no two situations are identical.

Form 1

FORM OF ARTICLES OF INCORPORATION

We, the undersigned, do hereby associate ourselves in order to form a corporation for the purpose hereinafter stated and do hereby certify as follows:

1. The name of this corporation shall be ....
2. The general nature of the business to be transacted by this corporation, together with, and in addition to, those powers conferred by the law of this state and the principles of common law upon corporations, is the following:

3. In furtherance, and not in limitation, of the general powers conferred by law and the objects and purposes herein set forth, this corporation shall also have the following powers:

a. To take, own, hold, deal in, mortgage or otherwise give liens against, and to lease, sell, exchange, transfer, or in any manner whatsoever buy or dispose of real property wherever situated.

b. To manufacture, purchase or acquire, and to hold, own, and in any manner dispose of and deal with goods, wares, merchandise and personal property wherever situated.

c. To enter into and perform contracts of every kind; to acquire and deal with its own stock, or stock in other corporations; to guarantee another's debts in furtherance of the lawful purposes of the corporation; to become a partner in any lawful business or venture.

d. To establish profit-sharing, pension and other employee plans.

e. To acquire the assets and good will of any person, firm or corporation, and to pay for such assets and good will in cash, stock of this corporation, or otherwise, or by undertaking any of the liabilities of the transferor; to hold or in any manner dispose of the property so acquired; to conduct in any lawful manner the whole or any part of any business so acquired, and to exercise all the powers necessary or convenient in and about the conduct and management of such business.

f. To apply for, purchase, register, or in any manner to acquire and dispose of patents, licenses, copyrights, trademarks, tradenames, inventions, or other rights; to work, operate, or develop the same; and to carry on any business which may directly or indirectly effectuate these objects.

g. Without limit as to amount, to draw, make, accept, endorse, discount, and issue notes, drafts, bills of exchange, bonds, debentures, and other negotiable instruments and evidences of indebtedness, to the maximum extent permitted by law.

h. To have one or more offices; to conduct its business and promote its objects within and without the state.

i. To carry on any other business in connection with the foregoing, and with all the powers conferred upon corporations by the laws and statutes of the state.

4. The aforesaid enumerated powers are to be construed both as purposes and powers, and shall not be limited or restricted by reference to or inference from the terms of any provision herein; nor shall the expression of one thing be deemed to exclude another, although it be of like nature.

5. The amount of the total authorized capital stock which may be issued by the corporation is .... shares of common stock of (check applicable line) (and preferred stock, if any)

___a. No par value.

___b. Par value of $............ per share.

___c. Preferred stock, as follows: ....
....

All or any part of said capital stock may be payable either in cash, property, labor or services at a just valuation to be fixed by the Board of Directors, and the judgment of such Directors as to the value shall, in the absence of fraud, be conclusive upon the stockholders and parties dealing with the corporation. The capital stock may be issued and paid for at such time or terms and conditions as the Directors may determine and the amount of the capital stock increased or decreased in the manner provided by law; provided, however, that the stock of the corporation shall be non-assessable.

6. The amount of capital with which this corporation shall begin business is $...............................

7. The existence of this corporation shall be perpetual.

8. The principal office of this corporation in the state is to be located at .... in the city of ...., and the agent in charge thereof shall be ....

9. The number of directors of this corporation shall be not less than: (Check applicable line.)

___a. Three

___b. Four

___c. Five

___d. Other: ....

10. The names and mailing addresses of the Board of Directors and Officers who, subject to the provisions of these Articles and the By-Laws to be adopted, shall hold office until their successors are elected and qualified are:

NAME	POSITION	ADDRESS

11. The names and mailing addresses of each subscriber to these Articles of Incorporation, and the number of shares of stock of this corporation which each agrees to take and to pay for are as follows:

NAME   NO. OF SHARES   ADDRESS

the proceeds of which shall amount to at least the sum stated in paragraph 6 of these Articles.

IN WITNESS WHEREOF, we, being all of the original subscribers to the capital stock of this corporation for the purpose of forming a corporation, do make and file these Articles, and accordingly set our hands and seals this the .... day of .... 19............

.... (SEAL)
.... (SEAL)
.... (SEAL)

STATE OF ....
COUNTY OF ....

Before me, the undersigned authority, personally appeared ...., each to me known and known to me to be the persons described in and who signed and executed the foregoing Articles of Incorporation, and they did acknowledge that they signed the foregoing and that the facts therein stated are true and correct.

IN WITNESS WHEREOF, I have set my hand and official seal this .... day of .... 19............

....
Notary Public, State and County aforesaid, My commission expires:

....
(Notarial Seal)

Form 2

CORPORATION BY-LAWS

ARTICLE I. NAME AND LOCATION. The name of this corporation shall be: .... Its principal office shall be located at .... in the City of ...., State of .... Other offices for the transaction of business shall be located at such other places as the Board of Directors may from time to time determine.

ARTICLE II. CAPITAL STOCK. The total authorized capital stock of this corporation shall be .... shares of common stock of: (check applicable line) (and preferred stock, if any)

__a. No par.
__b. Par value of $..............................

__c. Preferred stock, as follows: ....
....

All certificates of stock shall be signed by the President and the Secretary and shall be sealed with the corporate seal.

Treasury stock shall be held by the corporation subject to the disposal of the Board of Directors, and shall neither vote nor participate in dividends.

The corporation shall have a first lien on all the shares of its capital stock, and upon all dividends declared upon the same, for any indebtedness of the respective holders thereof to the corporation.

Transfers of stock shall be made only on the books of the corporation; and the old certificate, properly endorsed, shall be surrendered and cancelled before a new certificate is issued.

In case of loss or destruction of a certificate of stock, no new certificate shall be issued in lieu thereof except upon satisfactory proof to the Board of Directors of such loss or destruction; and upon the giving of satisfactory security against loss to the corporation; any such certificate shall be plainly marked "Duplicate" upon its face.

ARTICLE III. STOCKHOLDERS' MEETINGS. An annual meeting of the stockholders shall be held at .... o'clock ....M. on the .... day .... each year, commencing on the .... day of .... 19............, or if said date shall be a holiday, on the following day, at the principal office of the corporation. At such meeting the stockholders shall elect directors to serve until their successors are elected and qualified.

A special meeting of the stockholders, to be held at the same place as the annual meeting, may be called at any time whenever requested by stockholders holding a majority of the outstanding stock.

Unless prohibited by law, the stockholders holding a majority of the outstanding shares entitled to vote may, at any time, terminate the term of office of all or any of the directors, with or without cause, by a vote at any annual or special meeting, or by written statements, signed by the holders of a majority of such stock, and filed with the secretary or, in his absence, with any other officer. Such removal shall be effective immediately even if successors are not elected simultaneously, and the vacancies on the board of directors shall be filled only by the stockholders.

Notice of the time and place of all annual and special meetings shall be given 10 days before the date thereof, except that notice may be waived on consent of stockholders owning the following proportion of the outstanding stock: (Check applicable line.)

__a. A majority.
__b. Two-thirds majority.
__c. Three-fourths majority.
__d. Other: ....

The President, or in his absence, the Vice-President, shall preside at all meetings of the stockholders.

At every such meeting, each stockholder of common stock shall be entitled to cast one vote for each share of stock held in his name, which vote may be cast by him either in person, or by proxy. All proxies shall be in writing, and shall be filed with the Secretary and by him entered of record in the minutes of the meeting.

ARTICLE IV. DIRECTORS. The business and property of the corporation shall be managed by a board of not less than three or by an executive committee appointed by said board.

The regular meeting of the directors shall be held immediately after the adjournment of each annual stockholders' meeting. Special meetings of the board of directors may be called by the President.

Notice of all regular and special meetings shall be mailed to each director, by the Secretary, at least 10 days before such meeting, unless such notice is waived.

A quorum for the transaction of business at any meeting of the directors shall consist of a majority of the members of the board.

The directors shall elect the officers of the corporation and fix their salaries. Such election shall be held at the directors' meeting following each annual stockholders' meeting. Any officer may be removed, with or without cause, by vote of the directors at any regular or special meeting, unless such removal is prohibited by law.

Vacancies in the board of directors may be filled by the remaining directors at any regular or special meeting of the directors, except when such vacancy shall occur through removal by stockholders holding a majority of the outstanding shares, as hereinabove provided.

At each annual stockholders' meeting, the directors shall submit a statement of the business done during the preceding year, together with a report of the general financial condition of the corporation, and of the condition of its property.

ARTICLE V. OFFICERS. The officers of the corporation shall be a President, a Vice-President, a Secretary, and a Treasurer (and, in the discretion of the directors, an assistant secretary), who shall be elected for a term of one year, and shall hold office until their successors are elected and qualified.

The President shall preside at all directors' and stockholders' meetings; shall sign all stock certificates and written contracts and undertakings of the corporation; and shall perform all such other duties as are incident to his office. In case of disability, or absence from the city, of the President, his duties shall be performed by the Vice-President, who shall have equal and concurrent powers.

The Secretary shall issue notice of all directors' and stockholders' meetings; shall attend and keep the minutes of such meetings; and shall perform all such other duties as are incident to his office. In case of disability or absence, his duties shall be performed by the assistant secretary, if any.

The Treasurer shall have custody of all money and securities of the corporation. He shall keep regular books of account and shall submit them, together with all his vouchers, receipts, records and other papers, to the directors for their examination and approval as often as they may require; and shall perform all such other duties as are incident to his office.

ARTICLE VI. DIVIDENDS AND FINANCE. Dividends, to be paid out of the surplus earnings of the corporation, may be declared from time to time by resolution of the board of directors by vote of a majority thereof.

The funds of the corporation shall be deposited in such bank or banks as the directors shall designate, and shall be withdrawn only upon the check of the corporation, signed as the directors shall from time to time resolve.

ARTICLE VII. AMENDMENTS. Amendments to these By-Laws may be made by a vote of the stockholders holding a majority of the outstanding stock at any annual or special meeting, the notice of such special meeting to contain the nature of the proposed amendment.

We hereby adopt and ratify the foregoing By-Laws.

....

....

....

....

Form 3

MINUTES OF INITIAL MEETING OF INCORPORATORS AND SUBSCRIBERS

The initial meeting of the incorporators and subscribers to the capital stock of .... was held at

       (Name of Corporation)

.... in the city of .... at .... o'clock ....M., on the .... day of .... 19............ The following were present, being all of the incorporators and subscribers:

On motion duly made and carried, ... was elected temporary chairman, and .... was elected temporary secretary.

It was reported that the corporate charter heretofore filed with the Secretary of State had been approved. On motion duly made and carried, those certain By-Laws preceding these minutes were adopted and approved.

Thereupon, the incorporators and subscribers took the following action: (check applicable part)

__1. Announced that they had transferred and assigned their sub-scriptive rights to stock to ....

....

__2. Proposed that the following shares be issued:
NAME   CERT. NO.   NO. OF SHARES   CONSIDERATION

....

....

Thereupon, on motion duly made and carried, the following were ratified and elected as directors of this corporation for the following year, and until their successors are chosen:

Thereupon, on motion duly made and carried, the following resolution was passed:
RESOLVED: That the board of directors is hereby authorized to manage the affairs of the corporation and to exercise all powers vested in said board by the foregoing by-laws, the corporate charter, and the laws of the state.

Other business:

Whereupon, the meeting was adjourned.
The undersigned hereby waive notice of the foregoing meeting.

....
....

Form 4

CORPORATION PROMISSORY NOTE

Amount: $...................................   Date ....
                                               Place ....
FOR VALUE RECEIVED, the undersigned corporation promises to pay to the order of .... the principal sum of $ ...., together with interest at the rate of ....% per year, on or before 24 months from the date hereof.

We agree to pay all costs of collection, and reasonable attorneys' fees if this note is turned over to an attorney for collection, after default; and we hereby waive presentment, protest, notice of protest, and notice of dishonor.

                                               ....
                                               Name of the Corporation
                                       By ....
                                               Its President
                                       Attest: ....
                                               Its Secretary

(Corporate seal)

Form 5

MINUTES OF INITIAL MEETING OF DIRECTORS AUTHORIZING SECTION 1244 STOCK

The initial meeting of the board of directors of .... was held at ....in the city of .... at .... o'clock ....M., on the .... day of .... 19............ The following were present, being all of the directors:

On motion duly made and carried, the following were ratified and elected as officers of the corporation for the following year, and until their successors are chosen:

Thereupon, the following resolution was adopted:

WHEREAS, the board of directors deems it advisable to issue the common stock of this corporation in such manner that qualified holders may receive the benefits of Section 1244 of the Internal Revenue Code; and

WHEREAS, this corporation qualifies as a small business corporation as defined in Section 1244;

NOW, THEREFORE, BE IT RESOLVED that the board of directors are authorized and directed to issue the corporation's certificates of stock as follows:

NAME	CERT. NO.	NO. OF SHARES	CONSIDERATION

The aforesaid stock issuance is made subject to the following terms and conditions:

1. Such shares shall be issued so that such stock shall qualify as "Section 1244 Stock," as such term is used and defined in the Internal Revenue Code and the regulations issued thereunder.

2. Issuance of such stock shall take place on the .... day of .... 19............, and in no event shall such stock be issued after two years from the date of this resolution, or after the corporation shall make a subsequent offering of stock, whichever shall be sooner.

3. The maximum amount to be received by the corporation for the stock to be issued pursuant to this resolution and plan shall be $50,000.*

Whereupon, the meeting was adjourned.

....
Secretary

*The issuance is limited by law to $1,000,000, and the entire capitalization can't exceed that amount.

The undersigned directors hereby waive notice of the foregoing meeting.

....
....

Form 6

MINUTES OF DIRECTORS' ANNUAL MEETING

The annual meeting of directors of ....
                                                    (Name of Corporation)
was held at its office in the city of .... at .... o'clock
__M., on the .... day of .... 19............. The follow-
ing were present:

constituting __all__a majority (check applicable provision) of the directors.

The minutes of the annual meeting of the stockholders were read and approved.

On motion duly made and carried, the following were nominated and elected as officers of the corporation for the following year, and until their successors are chosen:

Other business:

Whereupon, the meeting was adjourned.

                                    ....
                                                    Secretary

Form 6B

WAIVER OF NOTICE OF DIRECTORS' MEETING

The undersigned, being the following proportion of the directors of the corporation:
    __1. All
    __2. Three-fourths majority.
    __3. Two-thirds majority.
    __4. Majority.
    __5. Other ....
do hereby waive notice of the foregoing meeting and consent to any and all action taken thereat, as evidenced by the foregoing minutes.

....
....

Form 6C

MINUTES OF STOCKHOLDERS' ANNUAL MEETING

The annual meeting of the stockholders of ....
(Name of Corp.)
was held at its office in the city of .... at .... o'clock
............M., on the .... day of .... 19............. The
following were present:
constituting __all __a majority (check applicable provision) of the stockholders.

The meeting was called to order by the President. The directors'
statement of the business done during the preceding year, and a report
of the general financial condition of the corporation, was submitted to
the stockholders and approved.

On motion duly made and carried, the following were nominated and
elected as directors of the corporation for the following year, and until
their successors are chosen:

Other business:

Whereupon, the meeting was adjourned.

....
Secretary

Form 6D

WAIVER OF NOTICE OF STOCKHOLDERS' MEETING

The undersigned, being the following proportion of the stockholders
of the corporation:
__1. All.
__2. Three-fourths majority.
__3. Two-thirds majority.
__4. Majority.
__5. Other ....
do hereby waive notice of the foregoing meeting and consent to any
and all action taken thereat, as evidenced by the foregoing minutes.

....
....

Form 7

RESOLUTION OF DIRECTORS AUTHORIZING DEPOSIT AND WITHDRAWAL OF FUNDS IN

.... (Name of Bank)

    I Certify that the following is a true copy of a certain resolution of the Board of Directors of ....

(Name of Corp. in full)

a Corporation duly organized and existing under the laws of

.... , having its principal place of

(Name of state where organized)

business in .... duly

(Name of City or Town and State)

adopted in accordance with the By-Laws, and recorded in the minutes of, a meeting of said Board held on ....,

(Date of meeting)

19............, and now in full force and effect;

RESOLVED:

    1. An account or accounts be opened for and in the name of this Corporation with .... (hereinafter referred to as the Bank), that the persons whose titles are listed below are authorized to sign and agree to the provisions of said Bank's customary corporation signature card, and that said Bank is hereby authorized to pay or otherwise honor any checks, drafts, or other orders issued from time to time, for debit to said account when signed by ....

....

(Please insert above titles [not names] of officers, for example: President, Treasurer, etc.; also, if more than one is inserted indicate whether they are to sign singly, any two, jointly or otherwise) including any such payable to or for the benefit of any signer thereof, or other officers, or employee, individually, without inquiry as to the circumstances of the issue or the disposition of the proceeds thereof.

    2. That the Bank is hereby authorized to accept for deposit for account of this Corporation, for credit, or for collection, or otherwise, any and all checks, drafts, and other instruments of any kind endorsed by any person, or by hand stamp impression, in the name of this Corporation, or without endorsement.

    3. The aforesaid officers of this Corporation, be and they hereby are authorized to act for this Corporation in all matters and transactions relating to any of its business with the Bank, including the withdrawal of property at any time held by the Bank for account of this Corporation.

    4. That the Secretary is directed to furnish the said Bank a certified copy of these resolutions, the names of all officers and other persons herein authorized to deal with said Bank, together with a specimen of

the signature of each, under the Seal of the Corporation, and that, until receipt by the Bank of notice to the contrary, in the form of a certificate signed by the Secretary, under the Corporate Seal, the Bank is authorized to rely upon all statements made or furnished in accordance herewith.

I FURTHER CERTIFY that the following are the officers of said Corporation, duly qualified and now acting as such:

NAME	TITLE OF OFFICE HELD
....	....
....	....
....	....
....	....
....	....
....	....
....	....
....	....

IN WITNESS WHEREOF, I have hereunto subscribed my name and affixed the seal of the said Corporation this .... day of ...., 19............

(Corporate Seal)

....
(Secretary)

Form 8

FORM OF RESOLUTION AUTHORIZING LOAN

RESOLVED: That ....:... is hereby
(Name of Corporation)
authorized and directed to borrow the sum of $............ from .... on the following terms and conditions:

and ...., as President of this corporation, is authorized and directed to execute a note, mortgage, and any and all necessary papers or instruments on behalf of said corporation, to carry out the loan.

....

I, ..., as secretary of the foregoing named corporation, do hereby certify that the above is a true and correct copy of a resolution adopted by the board of directors of said corporation on the .... day of .... 19............, and that such resolution is in full force and effect.

Dated this .... day of .... 19............

(Corporate Seal)

....
Secretary

Form 9

FORM OF COLLECTION LETTER

16 Squirrel Street
New York, N. Y.
Date_____

Mr. John Smith
123 Main Street
New York, N. Y.

Balance due: $_____

Dear Mr. Smith:

Your account with us is now long past due.

We are therefore obligated to take legal proceedings against you, unless some immediate arrangements are made for payment of your balance.

If we file suit, you will be charged with large additional expenses for court costs, interest, and attorney's fees. In addition, your credit rating will be seriously impaired.

Unless payment is in our hands within seven days after the date of this letter, legal action will be filed without further notice to you.

We trust this will not be necessary.

Sincerely yours,
XYZ COMPANY
By

FORM OF LETTER TO THE SHERIFF

16 Squirrel Street
New York, N. Y.
Date _____

Sheriff of _____County

_____
Address

_____
City and State

Re: Judgment and writ of execution against

_____
Name of Defendant

_____
Address

Case No. _____

Dear Sir:

Please seize, and levy against, all available assets and property of the above named defendant, within seven days after the date of this letter, pursuant to writ of execution issued by the court.

By a copy hereof, we are advising the defendant of our intentions. If payment is made to us in the meantime, we will promptly advise you.

Thank you.

Sincerely yours,
XYZ COMPANY
By

copy to:

_____
Name of Defendant

_____
Address

Form 11

PARTNERSHIP AGREEMENT

Date ....

THIS AGREEMENT, made between the following persons, on the terms and conditions set out below: (list of names of partners)

....

....

1. The parties agree to become partners under the name of ...., for the purpose of ....
....

2. The partnership business shall be conducted at ....
..............................., or wherever else the partners may agree, and shall commence business on ....

3. The partnership shall continue until dissolved or liquidated.

4. The capital and assets of the partnership shall be contributed as follows:

NAME OF PARTNER   PER CENT

and the partners shall contribute the following amounts, or services, to the partnership:

NAME OF PARTNER	CASH	SERVICES OR SKILLS	OTHER

5. The net profits shall be divided as follows:

NAME OF PARTNER   PER CENT

and net losses shall be borne by them in the same percentages.

6. The partners shall: (Check applicable line.)
__a. Be permitted drawing accounts each (week) (month) as follows:

NAME OF PARTNER   AMOUNT

__b. Be permitted drawing accounts as may be mutually agreed upon.

7. The partners shall: (Check applicable line.)
__a. Devote full time to the business.
__b. Devote such time as shall be necessary to the proper, efficient, and successful operation of the business.
__c. Other: ....

8. The partners shall have equal rights in the management and operation of the business, and all decisions shall: (Check applicable line.)
__a. Require consent of all the partners.
__b. Require a majority vote of the partners.

___c. Other: ....

9. The partnership books shall be kept at the principal place of business and shall be open at all times to the inspection of the partners. At the end of each: (Check one.)

___a. Month

___b. Three months

___c. Other: ....

the books shall be balanced and accurate operating information, showing the operations of the previous period, shall be made available to the partners. The books shall be audited at the end of each fiscal year and statements furnished to the partners.

10. All funds of the partnership shall be deposited in the .... Bank of ...., or such other banks as may be agreed upon, and all withdrawals and checks shall require the signature of: (Check applicable line.)

___a. All partners.

___b. Any two of the partners.

___c. Any one of the partners.

___d. Other: ....

11. When a partner is temporarily unable to devote his time to the partnership because of health or other reasons, he shall be entitled to such draws and shares of the profits as may be determined by: (Check applicable line.)

___a. A majority vote.

___b. All of the other partners.

___c. Other: ....

12. No partner, without the consent of all the others, shall borrow money or endorse any notes on behalf of the partnership; transfer partnership assets or his interest in the partnership; engage in any competitive business either directly or indirectly; assign, compromise, or release any debt due the partnership except upon full payment; or buy or agree to buy any property for the partnership other than the kind bought and sold in the regular course of its business.

13. (a) Any partner may retire from the partnership by giving the others .... days written notice of his intention to do so. The remaining partners shall have the right to terminate and liquidate the partnership, or to purchase the share of the retiring partner in the same proportion as their respective shares of the partnership. If the partners elect to purchase the interest of the retiring partner, they shall give written notice to him at or before the time his retirement becomes effective.

(b) If the remaining partners purchase the interest of the retiring partner, the purchase price shall be: (Check applicable line.)

___a. The amount of $.............................

___b. Equal to the book value of the retiring partner's interest, as reflected in the books of the partnership, and as determined by accepted accounting principles; provided, however, the partners may agree, in writing, at any time, upon a different valuation of a partner's share. If any such agreement of value shall have been executed more than 12 months before the date of purchase of such partner's interest, such agreement of value shall have no effect.

__c. Other: ....
....

(c) The purchase price for the interest of such retiring partner shall be paid as follows: (Check applicable lines.)

__a. In cash, within .... days after his retirement.

__b. By the remaining partners executing and delivering a promissory note for such price, payable within .... months thereafter,

    __(1) With interest of ....% per year

    __(2) Without interest

and being payable in equal installments

    __(1) Monthly

    __(2) Quarterly

    __(3) Yearly

    __(4) Other: ....

(d) Upon receipt of payment or the promissory note, the retiring partner shall sign any instruments necessary to transfer his interest in the partnership assets.

14. Upon the death or total incapacity of any partner ("total incapacity" being defined as the total physical or mental incapacity of a partner for a continuous period of __a. 30 days; __b. 60 days; __c. 90 days; __d. Other ....), the remaining partners shall purchase, and the estate of such deceased or incapacitated partner shall sell, the share of the deceased or incapacitated partner, at a price determined in accordance with paragraph 13. The purchase price for such share shall be paid in the same manner as set forth in paragraph 13, to wit:

__a. In cash, within .... days after the death or incapacity of such partner.

__b. By the remaining partners executing and delivering a promissory note for such price, payable within .... months thereafter,

    __(1) With interest of ....% per year

    __(2) Without interest

and being payable in equal installments

    __(1) Monthly

    __(2) Quarterly

    __(3) Yearly

    __(4) Other: ....

If book value shall be used to determine the purchase price, the book value shall be determined as of the close of the month immediately preceding death or incapacity.

15. This agreement shall terminate upon the occurrence of any one of the following events:

a. Cessation of the partnership business.

b. Bankruptcy, receivership, or dissolution of the partnership, or bankruptcy or receivership of any of the partners.

16. The continuing partners shall have the right to use the name of the partnership.

IN WITNESS WHEREOF, the parties have signed and sealed this agreement the date above stated.

.... (SEAL)

Signature of Partner

Witnesses: .... (SEAL)

....   Signature of Partner

.... (SEAL)

Signature of Partner
Joined by their respective wives*

.... (SEAL)

.... (SEAL)

.... (SEAL)

*Required in certain states

Form 12

STOCK RETIREMENT BUY-AND-SELL AGREEMENT
[With Price Set By Book Value]

Date ....

THIS AGREEMENT, made between ...., a corporation (hereinafter referred to as "the corporation"); and ....
.... (and ....),
(hereinafter referred to as "the stockholders).

WHEREAS, all the shares of the capital stock of the corporation, issued and outstanding, are owned by the above-named stockholders; and

WHEREAS, the parties hereto believe it to be in their mutual interests to provide for continuity of ownership and control of the corporation;

NOW, THEREFORE, in consideration of the mutual obligations and covenants herein, it is agreed as follows:

1. So long as this agreement shall remain in effect, none of the stockholders shall assign, encumber, or dispose of his shares of stock in the corporation, without the written consent of the corporation and of the other stockholders, unless he shall have first offered such shares to the corporation on the terms and conditions set forth hereinafter. Thereafter, the corporation shall have .... days after receipt of notice, to purchase such shares, at a price equal to book value, as described hereinafter. If the corporation fails to purchase such shares,

the stockholders shall have the right to purchase such shares, in proportion to their respective holdings, within .... days thereafter. If any stockholder elects not to purchase his full proportionate share of the stock, the remaining shares may be purchased by the other stockholders. If the stock is not purchased within the time specified, the stockholder desiring to sell shall have the right to sell to any other person, but shall not sell without giving the corporation and the remaining stockholders the right to purchase such stock at the price and on the terms offered to such other person.

2. Upon the death or total incapacity of one or more of the stockholders, the corporation shall purchase, and the estate of such stockholder shall sell, all of the shares of stock of the corporation owned by such stockholder at the time of his death or incapacity, at a price determined in accordance with paragraphs 3 and 4. The purchase price shall be paid by the corporation as follows: (Check applicable line.)

__a. In cash, within __(1) 30 days; __(2) 60 days; __(3) 90 days; __(4) Other period: ....
following notice of the death or total incapacity of such stockholder.

__b. At the option of the corporation, by execution and delivery, within __ days after notice of the death or total incapacity of such stockholder, of a note for the purchase price, payable in __ equal monthly installments, with interest at ....% per year. Said stock shall be pledged with the estate of such stockholder to secure full payment of said note. The note shall provide for a privilege of prepayment without penalty, and that a default in the payment of any installment shall cause all remaining principal and interest to become due and payable at the holder's option. While such stock is so held, and as long as the purchase is not in default, the purchaser shall be entitled to all voting rights with respect thereto.

3. The purchase price of the shares of stock shall be the "book value" of such shares, as of the close of business on the last day of the calendar month preceding the date of death or total incapacity. "Book value" shall be determined in accordance with sound accounting practice.

4. Notwithstanding the foregoing, the stockholders may at any time fix the value of the stock by endorsement, signed by the stockholders, on the back of this agreement, or by a certificate or memorandum of agreed value signed by each stockholder. If at any time when it becomes necessary to determine the book value of the stock, a certificate of agreed value has been executed less than 12 months before the date as of which the book value is to be determined, then the value set forth in such certificate, or endorsement hereto, shall be accepted as book value. The stockholders may at any time execute a new certificate of agreed value, or a new endorsement hereto, which shall automatically replace all prior valuations.

5. If at the time the corporation is required to make payment of the

purchase price for all the stock of a deceased stockholder, its surplus is insufficient for such purpose, then (a) the entire available surplus shall be used to purchase part of the stock of the decedent stockholder, and (b) the corporation and the stockholders shall promptly take all required action to reduce the capital stock of the corporation to the extent necessary for the redemption of the unpurchased stock. Payment of the stock so redeemed or retired shall be made as determined hereinabove. If the corporation shall nevertheless be unable to purchase the shares of stock of the decedent, either because prohibited by law, or otherwise, the obligation of the corporation shall be deemed assumed by the surviving stockholders, on the same terms and conditions stated in paragraphs 3 and 4.

6. The provisions requiring purchase of the stock of a deceased stockholder shall be of no effect if all the stockholders shall die within __ days of each other.

7. If the corporation shall receive any proceeds of any policy of insurance on the life of a deceased stockholder, such proceeds shall be paid by the corporation to the decedent's estate, to the extent of the purchase price of the decedent's stock, such payment to be deemed made on account of such purchase price.

8. If any of the stockholders shall become totally physically or mentally incapacitated (such incapacity being defined as the total physical or mental incapacity of a stockholder for a continuous period of __a. 30 days __b. 60 days __c. 90 days __d. Other: ....), then the corporation shall purchase, and the incapacitated stockholder shall sell, all of the shares of stock of the corporation owned by the incapacitated stockholder, on the same terms and conditions as set forth in paragraphs 2, 3, and 4. The stock certificates shall be endorsed and signed by the guardian, if any, of the incapacitated stockholder, or if none, then by his wife, and if none, then by one of the officers of the corporation, it being agreed by all the stockholders that such persons are hereby granted and given irrevocable authority to endorse and sign such certificates.

9. So long as any part of the purchase price of shares of stock sold in accordance with this agreement remains unpaid, the corporation shall not declare or pay dividends on its capital stock; reorganize its capital structure (except as necessary to reduce its capital as required by the foregoing provisions); merge or consolidate with any other corporation or sell any of its assets except in the regular course of business; or increase the salary of any officer or executive employee of the corporation. So long as any part of such purchase price shall remain unpaid, the transferor, or his representative, shall have the right to examine the books and records of the corporation at all reasonable times, and receive copies of all accounting reports and tax returns prepared for or on behalf of the corporation. If the corporation breaches any of its obligations under this paragraph, the transferor or his representative shall

have the right to declare the entire unpaid balance due and payable forthwith.

10. Each certificate representing shares of stock of the corporation now or hereafter held by the stockholders shall have written thereon a legend in substantially the following form: "The transfer of the shares of stock of this corporation is restricted under the terms of an agreement dated the .... day of .... 19............, a copy of which is on file at the office of the corporation."

11. This agreement shall terminate upon the occurrence of any one of the following events:

   a. Cessation of the corporation's business.

   b. Bankruptcy, receivership, or dissolution of the corporation.

   c. The voluntary agreement of all the parties who are then bound by the terms hereof.

12. The parties hereto agree to execute any instruments necessary or proper to carry out the purposes of this agreement.

13. Notwithstanding anything to the contrary herein, the stockholders shall have the right, at any time, to sell, assign, or transfer all or any part of their shares of capital stock to a wife, lawful descendants, or in trust for any of the foregoing; provided, however, that such transferees shall be fully bound by the terms and conditions of this agreement.

14. This agreement shall be binding on the heirs, personal representatives, assigns, and successors of the parties hereto.

IN WITNESS WHEREOF, we have hereunto set our hands and seals the date above stated.

....
Name of the Corporation

By ....
Its President

Attest: ....
Its Secretary

(Corporate Seal)   .... (SEAL)
                                 Stockholder

Witnesses:

                                 .... (SEAL)
                                 Stockholder

.... (SEAL)
                                 Stockholder

.... (SEAL)
                                 Stockholder

Form 13

CROSS-PURCHASE BUY-AND-SELL AGREEMENT
[With Price Set By Agreement]

Date ....

THIS AGREEMENT made between ....,
..............................., ..., and ....,
hereinafter referred to as "the stockholders."

WHEREAS, all the shares of the capital stock of ....
(name of corporation), issued and outstanding, are owned by the above-
named stockholders; and

WHEREAS, the stockholders hereto believe it to be in their mutual
interests to provide for continuity of ownership and control of the corporation;

NOW, THEREFORE, in consideration of the mutual obligations and
covenants herein, it is agreed as follows;

1. So long as this agreement shall remain in effect, none of the stockholders shall assign, encumber, or dispose of his shares of stock in the
corporation, without the written consent of the other stockholders, unless he shall have first offered such shares to the other stockholders
on the terms and conditions set forth hereinafter. The stockholders
shall have the right to purchase such shares in proportion to their respective holdings, within __ days thereafter. If any stockholder elects
not to purchase his full proportionate share of the stock, the remaining
shares may be purchased by the other stockholders. If the stock is not
purchased within the time specified, the stockholder desiring to sell
shall have the right to sell to any other person, but shall not sell without
giving the other stockholders the right to purchase such stock at the
price and on the terms offered to such other person.

2. The parties agree that the present value of each share of stock is
$............................. per share, and that their respective shares of stock
are valued at the following amounts:

NAME OF STOCKHOLDER   AMOUNT

Within 30 days after each fiscal year of the corporation, or as soon
thereafter as possible, the stockholders shall agree upon a redetermi-
nation of the value of the shares of stock and of their respective interests, and shall endorse such redetermined values, with their signatures,
on a schedule to be attached hereto, or by a separate certificate or
memorandum signed by the stockholders. If the stockholders fail to
redetermine such values for a particular year, the last determined values shall prevail; provided, however, if at the time of the exercise of the
right or obligation of purchase provided for in this agreement, the agreed
valuation shall have been made more than 12 months prior thereto,

then such valuation shall be of no effect in determining the purchase price; and in that event, the value shall be determined by the agreement of all the stockholders, including (where applicable under the provisions thereinafter stated) the representative of a deceased or incapacitated stockholder. If they fail to agree within .... days, on such valuation, then the value shall be determined as follows: (Check applicable line.)

__a. By arbitration; the selling stockholder (or his personal representative) shall select one arbitrator, and the remaining stockholders shall select one arbitrator. If the two arbitrators are unable to agree on the value, they shall appoint a third arbitrator, and the decision of the majority shall be binding on all parties. Instead of each side selecting one arbitrator, the parties may agree to select the American Arbitration Association to arbitrate.

__b. By "book value" of the shares, as of the close of business on the last day of the calendar month preceding the exercise of the right of purchase, or preceding the death or total incapacity of a stockholder, where applicable. "Book value" shall be determined in accordance with sound accounting practice.

3. Upon the death or total incapacity of one or more stockholders, the surviving stockholders shall buy, and the estate of the deceased or incapacitated stockholder shall sell, all of the shares of stock of the corporation owned by the deceased or incapacitated stockholder at the time of his death or incapacity, at a price determined in accordance with this agreement, and on the terms and conditions set forth herein.

4. The purchase price for the stock shall be paid as follows: (Check applicable line.)

__a. In cash, within __(1) 30 days __(2) 60 days __(3) 90 days __(4) Other period: .... following notice of the death or total incapacity of such stockholder.

__b. At the option of the buyers, by execution and delivery, within __ days after notice of the death or total incapacity of such stockholder, of a note or notes for the purchase price, payable in __ equal monthly installments, with interest at __% per year. Said stock shall be pledged with the estate of such stockholder to secure full payment of said note. The note shall provide for a privilege of prepayment without penalty, and that a default in the payment of any installment shall cause all remaining principal and interest to become due and payable at the holder's option. While such stock is so held, and as long as the purchaser is not in default, the purchaser shall be entitled to all voting rights with respect thereto.

5. The provisions requiring purchase of the stock of a deceased stockholder shall be of no effect if all the stockholders shall die within __ days of each other.

6. If any stockholder shall receive any proceeds of any policy of insurance on the life of a deceased stockholder, such proceeds shall be paid by the stockholder to the decedent's estate, to the extent of the

purchase price of the decedent's stock, such payment to be deemed made on account of such purchase price.

7. If any of the stockholders shall become totally physically or mentally incapacitated (such incapacity being defined as the total physical or mental incapacity of a stockholder for a continuous period of __a. 30 days __b. 60 days __c. 90 days __. Other: ....), then the surviving stockholders shall purchase, and the incapacitated stockholder shall sell, all of the shares of stock of the corporation owned by the incapacitated stockholder, on the same terms and conditions as set forth in paragraphs 2, 3 and 4. The stock certificates shall be endorsed and signed by the guardian, if any, of the incapacitated stockholder, or if none, then by his wife, and if none, then by one of the officers of the corporation, it being agreed by all the stockholders that such persons are hereby granted and given irrevocable authority to endorse and sign such certificates.

8. Each certificate representing shares of stock of the corporation now or hereafter held by the stockholders shall have written thereon a legend in substantially the following form: "The transfer of the shares of stock of this corporation is restricted under the terms of an agreement dated the .... day of .... 19............, a copy of which is on file at the office of the corporation."

9. This agreement shall terminate upon the occurrence of any one of the following events:
   a. Cessation of the corporation's business.
   b. Bankruptcy, receivership, or dissolution of the corporation.
   c. The voluntary agreement of all the parties who are then bound by the terms thereof.

10. Notwithstanding anything to the contrary herein, the stockholders shall have the right, at any time, to sell, assign, or transfer all or any part of their shares of capital stock to a wife, lawful descendants, or in trust for any of the foregoing; provided, however, that such transferees shall be fully bound by the terms and conditions of this agreement.

11. The parties hereto agree to execute any instruments necessary or proper to carry out the purposes of this agreement.

12. This agreement shall be binding on the heirs, personal representatives, assigns, and successors of the parties hereto.

IN WITNESS WHEREOF, we have hereunto set our hands and seals
the date above stated.

.... (SEAL)
Stockholder

.... (SEAL)
Stockholder

.... (SEAL)
Stockholder

Witnesses:

....

.... (SEAL)
Stockholder

CHAPTER 7

So You Owe Money And Can't Pay

IT'S BEEN SAID THAT MANKIND IS DIVIDED INTO TWO GROUPS; THOSE that owe money, and those that they owe it to. If you happen to be in the first group, or expect to be, you've no doubt heard all the myths and lore about what a creditor can do and what he can't, and what a debtor can do and what he can't.

And it's likely you've stored up a veritable wealth of misinformation.

Some jurisdictions are known as "debtor" states, because there are various protections and exemptions allowed by the law there. Other states favor the creditor, and make it uncomfortable on the bird who's behind in his payments. But there are certain rules and provisions, common to most places, that you should be acquainted with.

A. If You Pay a "Little," What Can They Do?

Let's assume that you're really down on your luck, and you've been laid off work. Your wife just had an operation, and the bills are piling up. The rent is due and the finance company is bellyaching about repossessing your car. In short, you owe money and can't pay.

If your payments are past due or your account is delinquent, a creditor has the legal right to sue you. Most contracts that allow you to make monthly payments contain an "acceleration" clause. This means that if you miss an installment, the creditor has the right to declare the entire balance due and payable. Once you get yourself in this unhappy position, he doesn't have to accept your back payments or allow you to catch up; he can rely strictly on the contract and demand it all. This can happen with the payments on a car, your house, or on most major appliances—TV, stereo, refrigerator, etc.

There's a persistent rumor that says if you pay a "little," the creditor has to accept it, and that he can't sue. This just "ain't so." Even if you pay all the late charges and collection fees, to try to bring the account current, there's no law that forces the creditor to take it. If he's tired of fooling with your account, or he's had collection problems with you in the past, don't be surprised if he stands firm and insists on the full balance.

But the picture isn't as black as it looks. The vast majority of creditors will usually go along with you on any reasonable proposal if you can send in *something* on a regular basis. Remember, though, that they don't *have* to accept it. But as a practical matter, the old adage of "half a loaf is better than none" is applicable in most cases. The company's credit department may fume and fuss and send you several "final" letters. They'll bully you by threatening to sue. But if you can bring them some money *each week*, and tell them—in a nice way—that you're doing the best you can at present, the chances are that they'll go along with you. They realize—probably more than you do—that it costs them time, effort and greenbacks to go to court. Naturally, they don't *want* to accept reduced payments, and they'll invariably try to scare you with threats; but it's generally just not good business for them to sue, except as a last resort. The key, though, is your regularity and dependability. If you say you'll send in ten bucks every Friday, then be sure you do it. If you don't, then you can't expect much leniency.

There are notable exceptions to this "pay-a-little" routine. If your payment record with this creditor has been consistently poor, or you've given him more than one bad check, you might find that they'll send your payment back, and give you a deadline to cough up the balance. If, in addition, the equipment or appliance that you're buying on time has a good resale value, it becomes more likely that the finance company or bank will repossess it. But if they threaten to do exactly that, don't make it easy for them. Don't turn it over without a court order. In most "time contracts" (called conditional sales, security agreements, or retain title contracts), a creditor can retake the equipment or merchandise without going to court if you voluntarily turn it over to him, or if you leave it where he can easily pick it up. But if you refuse—politely—to let him take it, then he's forced to go to court, as a rule. He can legally do this, all right, but it'll cost him money (sometimes as much as $500 for filing fees, sheriff's charges and legal costs). So if you stand your ground—but at the same time (and this is all-important) pay *some* money—the average creditor will go along, reluctantly. Or course, if you've tried the same dodge three or four times before, you can't expect to keep getting away with it. Sooner or later they'll decide they'd rather lay out the money for court costs than to keep dunning you.

But if you act honorably, and pay regularly—even a "little"— you have a better than 50-50 chance of preventing the lawsuit, and the potential damage to your credit rating.

Another tip: if you see a financial crisis looming on the horizon, and you know you won't be able to pay a bill when it comes due, don't bury your head in the sand and hope the creditor may forget about you, or that maybe he'll lose your card. You'll be in a much better position, psychologically, if *you* go to the creditor (or call him) to tell him about it. Do this *before* the account is delinquent, and before he has to write you a letter. Tell him, briefly, what your problem is (sickness, layoff from work, and so forth) and then tell him what you're able to do—that you'll either pay next week, or you'll send in half on Friday. Once *you* go to *him*—rather than vice versa—your prospects of getting sympathetic treatment jump considerably. But if you "lay low" and say nothing, and wait for him to contact *you*—which is inevitable—you'll start off with the proverbial two strikes.

Obviously, not every creditor will extend the time of payment if you're having troubles. But most of them will, if you're sincere and show you're making an honest effort to pay.

Suppose you pay a little and do it regularly as best you can. But Charlie Creditor, instead of playing ball and being understanding, sends your payment back, tells you he's not going to be a nursemaid, and that he's filing suit. Unfortunately, it's not always easy to tell whether he's bluffing. In 90% of the cases, though, you'll get a letter from a lawyer before suit is actually filed. If you decide you're really going to be sued, or if you feel you can't possibly raise the money, there's one final tactic you can try.

You write a courteous letter—this is much more effective than telephoning at this point—explaining that you have no alternative

than to file bankruptcy. This is the word that still strikes fear in the
hearts of every red-blooded collection manager. If they think you
may mean it, and if you make some proposal to send in at least
some payment (you tell them you're making the offer in a final effort
to avoid bankruptcy), the odds are in your favor that Charlie will
pull up his horse and slow down. A suggested form of letter is
shown at the end of this chapter (Form 1).

Whether filing bankruptcy is, in fact, what you should do, will
depend on several factors (see Section E). But your *threat* of doing
it may save you from *actually* doing it later on.

The mortgage on your home is in somewhat of a special category
(see Section H). The threat of bankruptcy may not worry the average mortgage company, because it can still foreclose and take the
house, although bankruptcy can usually delay the foreclosure; and
on V.A. and F.H.A. loans, the mortgage lender is especially un-
concerned, since it'll be paid most or all of its money by the federal
government, if you default.

So, in a nutshell, if you owe money and pay a "little," can
Charlie Creditor still sue you? You better believe he can. But if you
play your cards right, there's a good chance that he won't.

B. Can Your Wages Be Attached?

There are statutes in all states covering the attachment of wages—
usually called garnishment—to pay a debt. These laws vary from
place to place, and there's little uniformity.

In a majority of the states, a certain portion of your wage is
exempt from garnishment. The percentage is not the same all over,
but in general, it runs from 50% to 90%. Many of the statutes
require you to be the head of a family, though, before you can claim
the exemption. In Florida, if you meet this test, then 100% of your
wages are exempt, even if you're a high-salaried executive. In some
states, wages can't be attached, but they can lose their sheltered
status as soon as they're received by the wage earner. Some states
exempt all earnings from attachment, except to pay support, or for
room and board. Other states exempt wages only for laborers and
mechanics. A few states grant a flat exemption—ranging from as
little as $15 a week to $100 a week. A handful of places formerly
had no exemption at all if the debt was incurred for necessities.
And in a few sections, if you were not the head of a family, a

creditor could garnishee your entire salary under some conditions. Several places allow an exemption for wages earned within a certain period prior to the garnishment. But several years ago, a federal law made some sweeping garnishment changes, limiting garnishment to 25% of a worker's weekly take-home pay, and sometimes even less (although it can be more than 25% for court-ordered support, taxes, and some other court orders); but if the state law grants even more liberal exemptions, then the state law would apply. The federal law became effective July 1, 1970.

Even if you come under one of the exemptions or exceptions, you still have to take some affirmative steps to get the benefit of the law. You'll have to make some kind of affidavit or oath, as a rule, to get your pay released.

One of the harsh side-effects of garnishment is the bad taste it leaves with your employer. Some bosses are understanding, but others have, in the past, adopted a standing policy against garnishment; if an employee's wages were attached, out he went and he was canned. The federal law (known as the Consumer Credit Protection Act), changed this, and now bars the firing of an employee by reason of garnishment for "any one indebtedness." (If you're garnisheed by more than one creditor, then the law won't help you.) If you think there's a chance your creditor is going to garnishee your pay, you probably ought to talk it over with your supervisor or payroll department. Find out what the company policy is. If it's "one-time-and-you're-on-the-black-list," you'd better work out something fast with the creditor.

Sometimes you can arrange to have a certain amount of your salary held back, regularly, by your employer and paid to the creditor. If your boss agrees, most of the time this will head off a garnishment.

A particularly vicious practice, permitted in some states, is to allow garnishment of wages at the beginning of the lawsuit and even before the court has decided that you owe the money. The creditor has to put up a bond, and if it turns out he's not entitled to a judgment, you'd have a claim for damages. But it can be humiliating to have your wages attached when you didn't even know you'd been sued.

If your wages are garnisheed, you should either contact a lawyer or call the clerk of the court to find out what part of your pay is exempt and how you apply for the exemption. In many courts—particularly the "small claims" variety—the clerk will prepare the necessary affidavit of exemption for you, if you're eligible. But it's urgent that you take immediate action. The longer you wait, the longer your pay will be held up. It's also possible that by waiting too long, you might waive your rights.

If you're unmarried, or in a state that allows garnishment of your wages, you should contact the creditor or his attorney as soon as you can, and try to arrange some payment plan. You might get your employer to deduct a certain amount each payday; or pay a lump sum; or work out a schedule of reduced payments. Most creditors are not overly proud of their tying up your pay—it's a distasteful business at best—and they'll usually go along with some reasonable proposal.

When you're garnisheed, you should ask your employer to file— without delay—the necessary information or affidavit in court, as to how much pay you're due. The clerk of the court or a lawyer will do this for him. In some states, your boss is required to hold back, in the garnishment, all moneys you earn, from the time the legal papers are served, until he files an affidavit or statement in court. So he should move without delay in order that as little as possible will be caught in the garnishment.

For instance, in several states, here's what would happen: you're paid on Fridays, for a week's work. On Monday, your employer receives garnishment papers. If he waits until Friday to answer them, or to file his affidavit in court, he'll owe you a full week's pay again, and he'll have to hold it back (unless you're eligible for the exemption). On the other hand, if he answered immediately— on Monday—he'd owe you for only one day, and that's all that you'd lose. This isn't true in all places, though, and you'd need to know for sure how your state law reads. In addition, if the creditor caught only a day's pay in the garnishment, in some jurisdictions, he could try another garnishment the following week (probably filing it on Thursday this time). Luckily, this isn't true in all states, but the best thing to do is to try to work out a settlement before this happens.

A particularly vulnerable situation is when both the husband and wife work. If your state law gives an exemption to the wages earned by the head of the family, then your wife can be wide open to garnishment. Credit managers and collection lawyers are generally aware of this, and their first attack might be against the wife's wages. You can talk to the wife's employer, and try to arrange a payment plan with the creditor. Or if nothing works, you can consider bankruptcy (see Section E).

Your best way out of the garnishment predicament, is to hope that you fit into one of the exemption categories allowed by your state or by the 1970 federal law. Besides exemptions for heads of the family and others mentioned earlier, several states have other special classes of persons exempt, such as public employees and government workers. Seamen's wages have been exempt from garnishment for many years by act of Congress.

C. Can They Get Your Home Or Other Assets?

Let's assume that the worst has happened. You've tried reduced payments, promises, sweet-talk, and even threats of bankruptcy. Nothing works. The fatal day has come and you now have a judgment against you.

What can happen? In the first place, you should understand that they can't put you in jail. Actually, there *are* some cases where you *can* be imprisoned for debt, but these are situations where you either violate a court order—such as by not paying child support or alimony—or give a bad check for a bill. But these are the exceptions, and not the rule.

After the creditor gets a judgment against you, he's entitled to a document from the court, generally called a "writ of execution" (see Chapter 6, page 190). He can turn this over to the sheriff or similar court official with instructions to seize or attach your assets. The sheriff "levies" on your property, and sells it at public sale.

But don't despair. There's a ray of hope. Every state, by statute or constitution, allows certain exceptions against judgments and executions. The law, everywhere, gives a debtor a right to keep some of his property free from seizure and sale. The theory is to allow a person to retain at least part of his belongings, so as not to be a burden on the public.

In most states, your "homestead" is exempt from the typical claims of creditors. The homestead includes the dwelling house and surrounding grounds, although there's usually a limit to how much land you can have. To claim the exemption, some states require that you be the head of a family. But if you're single, or live in a house with grown children who aren't dependent on you, you might find you won't be eligible for the exemption. Note, though, that this immunity from creditors' claims is different from the *tax* exemption allowed by many states to homesteads; for that type of exemption, it's not usually necessary to be the head of a family.

A few claims *can* be enforced against your home, even if you'd customarily be entitled to the exemption. These exceptions include mortgage obligations, labor and material furnished to the house, and taxes.

In addition to the homestead exemption, almost every jurisdiction grants protection, in one form or another, to tools and implements used in the debtor's trade. To be exempt in most states, though, the items must be reasonably necessary, or customary, in your occupation. For example, if you're a barber, and you have an expensive photocopying machine, you'll probably have trouble claiming it's exempt. A few courts have taken a narrow view of the word "tools," and have ruled that it includes only small objects that can be held in the hand or operated by manual force. Most courts, though, have allowed a broader interpretation. In fact, in several cases, the question has been raised whether an automobile can be a "tool or implement" used in a trade or business. The decisions aren't consistent, but a number of courts have held that if the car is necessary in carrying on your occupation, then it's exempt. You can't count on this being true in every situation, though.

Other courts have ruled that the equipment, books and instruments of professional men are also immune from a judgment.

Furthermore, most statutes exempt household goods and personal effects from the claims of creditors. Sometimes specific items are listed in the law—such as beds or wearing apparel—but many of the states have provisions with wider application. In a number of statutes, the clothing exemption, though, is limited to those items that are "necessary." This doesn't mean you can keep only one dress or suit, but you can expect to run into opposition if you tried to hold on to an expensive mink coat. Even on this point, there are differences of opinion; in a New Jersey case, the court ruled that an expensive lace shawl was exempt. Some cases have even held that a gold ring and a watch were "wearing apparel."

In a few localities, motor vehicles are specifically exempt, and in several parts of the country, there are exemptions for horses and other domestic animals.

The majority of states protect the proceeds of life insurance policies, and the cash surrender value, from creditors. Some places have a limitation on the amount you can claim, but several don't. How about payments under disability or accident policies? Again, some states exempt these benefits, too, but not all of them do.

By state or federal statutes, most pensions and retirement benefits are exempt. This can be a little misleading, though. Suppose you get your pension money and deposit it in a bank. Still exempt? A few cases have said no. The better reasoned decisions (and the weight of authority), though, say yes.

If you're the head of your family, you'll be allowed an exemption, in a number of states, for personal property— regardless of its nature—up to a specific dollar amount. Historically, the exemption will be something like $1,000. You'd have the right to claim that amount, free from creditors' claims, whether in the form of a bank account, stocks, a car, or any combination of assets.

So, in summary, even though Charlie Creditor has his judgment entered against you, don't go slashing your wrists yet. A large portion of your property and income—and even all of it, in some cases—may be exempt.

D. Jointly-Owned Property

In a previous chapter (see page 44), we looked at some of the consequences of owning property with someone else. There are also some special rules applicable to this type of ownership when debts are involved. Suppose you and your wife have title to some real estate (other than your home), and now a bill collector gets a judgment, but only against *you*, not against the missus. Can he take the property away—or at least your "half"?

The answer would be no in several, but not all of the states recognizing "estates by the entireties" (see page 139, for a detailed discussion of such estates). This type of ownership, also called "tenancies" by the entireties, is a special kind of title, held by a husband and wife. In those states that permit it, all you have to do is take title like this: John Doe and Mary Doe, his wife. That's all there is to it. Then automatically, you have an estate by the entireties. (This may not be true in a few states, where it's apparently necessary to specifically indicate the intention to own the property as an estate by the entireties.)

You'll recall that if either you or your wife passes on, the survivor takes the entire title (see page 44). But there's an equally important feature in force in many of the states. Each of you is legally considered as owning *all* of the property, since the law there says a husband and wife are "one person." If you think that you each own *half* the property in those states, you're wrong. You both together, own the entire thing. This sounds like legal gobbledygook, you might say. What difference does it make? Plenty! Since each of you owns the whole pie, a creditor of only one of you is blocked from attaching the property, or any part of it. Only if a creditor has a judgment against *both of you* could he seize the property.

Let's put it this way. If your state permits this unique breed of estate by the entireties, and the judgment is against you alone, the creditor is out of luck. Your jointly-owned property is protected.

For a list of states that permit estates by the entireties, see the chart at the end of the chapter.

This "unity" of husband and wife seems to be losing favor, gradually, possibly because of the hostility of creditors, and possibly because of the passage of Married Women's Acts, emancipating women to a large degree. However, in many states, it's still a perfectly legal and proper way to hold title to property and assets. In those states, your creditor (unless he had a judgment against your wife as well) would have to hunt for something else to levy on.

Be careful, though, about having the title in the disjunctive; that is: John Doe *or* Mary Doe, his wife. In several states, this is not considered a true estate by the entireties. Many times, bank accounts and stock certificates are set up this way. Clearly, there's nothing wrong with having your accounts opened in that fashion. But if you want the property to be considered as an estate by the entireties, then you'd probably have to change it and see that it wasn't "or," but "and." A bank will be glad to put the account in any form you want it, but they might require two signatures—your's and your wife's—on each check. So you have to weigh the convenience of a single signature with the desirability, to you, of having a bona fide estate by the entireties. If you're not concerned with judgments, then the "or" on the account will be fine. You should also understand that once you're in debt or already have been sued, then it's usually too late to start worrying about changing the ownership to an estate by the entireties.

You'll also want to be on your guard for this: suppose a creditor has a judgment against you alone, and you and your wife own property by the entireties. Everything is in both names—checking account, real estate, car. You're safe, for now. But assume that a year or two later, your wife passes away. Now the property is all legally yours. And if Charlie Creditor finds out about it, you've got troubles. In fact, even if he doesn't find out about it, you'll generally have a problem giving clear title to real estate. (For the possibility of bankruptcy in this situation, see Section G.)

If you happen to be in a state that doesn't permit estates by the entireties, then a husband and wife would own property either "jointly" or "in common." In both cases, though, your creditor would then be in a position, in most places, to attach your interest in the property. Your wife would be considered as owning half the property (contrary to the result with an estate by the entireties), and the creditor could seize the other half that you own. He could then force a division, or partition, of the property.

This works the same way with joint ownership with persons other than your spouse. If you and your brother, for example, acquire a piece of property together, your half interest in it will ordinarily be vulnerable to your creditor's judgment.

A handful of states recognize "community property" of a husband and wife (see list at the end of this chapter). This is another form of joint ownership. The laws in these states are not uniform. Some permit a creditor of one of the spouses to attach the community property, but most don't.

E. Is Bankruptcy the Answer?

Thirty or forty years ago, bankruptcy was a nasty word that conjured up visions of immoral deadbeats cheating innocent creditors. Not anymore. Bankruptcy proceedings have become commonplace, if not fashionable, these days, and there's no longer the dreaded stigma that was once attached.

If you're way over your head in debt, and have been trying, unsuccessfully, to keep the wolf away, you've probably glanced furtively in the direction of a lawyer more than once, and wondered: is bankruptcy the answer?

Maybe. But you better know what it tastes like, before you bite.

Bankruptcy, basically, is a legal proceeding, filed in a federal district court, when a debtor doesn't have enough assets to pay his bills as they come due. The main purpose is to enable a debtor to "discharge," or wipe out, his debts. But at the same time, any nonexempt assets of the debtor are made available to creditors.

Bankruptcy can either be voluntary (you, as the debtor, file the petition), or involuntary (creditors bring the action). The involuntary proceeding is often spoken of as "throwing someone into bankruptcy." Actually, there isn't much chance of a creditor doing that to you nowadays, unless you run a large business, or have fraudulently or illegally given away your property (see Section F). Creditors realize that the expense of bankruptcy—administrative costs, legal fees, trustee's charges—eat up most of the assets that might be available, and they're very reluctant to push you into it.

The voluntary proceeding is by far the more common. You're required to file a multi-paged petition, in triplicate, under oath, listing all of your property and a schedule of your creditors, with the amount owed to each. (Many stationery stores and printers have the forms available for sale; they cost about ten dollars.) The schedule also has a section for you to list any exemptions allowed by law (see Section C). In addition, there's a required "statement of affairs," which is a detailed questionnaire, calling for financial information, type of business, conveyances made within a year, what payments you've made to creditors, and similar questions.

The papers are filed with the clerk of the U.S. Bankruptcy Court where you live, or where your principal place of business is, and notices are sent to each of the listed creditors, by the bankruptcy clerk. The notice explains that you've filed a petition, and sets a date, usually within 30 days, for a meeting of creditors. You're required to be at the meeting, and the creditors and court trustee are allowed to question you, and to look at your books and records.

The questions can be quite thorough and searching in a case where there's a large amount of money involved, or suspicion of fraud or concealment of assets. But if you're a typical wage-earner or small businessman who's simply up to his neck in hock, and you haven't done anything dishonest, the questions will be fairly brief and routine. You can expect to be asked about your bank accounts, other assets (if any), and property you've given away.

If you have no assets—other than property that's exempt under the law—the meeting will probably be over in less than an hour. A few months later, an order will be entered, "discharging" your debts and wiping the slate clean.

Sounds easy, right? You're ready to rush right down to file? Let's look first at some of the hazards.

To begin with, not all claims are discharged by bankruptcy. Like hardy weeds, several types survive the proceeding, and will still be around to harass you later on. So if your primary goal in going through bankruptcy is to knock out any of these particular debts, you better forget it. Those not discharged, under the law, are:

1. Any taxes, whether state, federal, or local.

2. Liability for obtaining property or money by false pretenses or representations. This could include giving a false financial statement, if you're a businessman.

3. Liability for willful and malicious injury, such as assaulting or slandering somebody. But not every injury is included here; the average automobile accident claim, and suits based on negligence, are not considered "willful and malicious," and therefore *would* be discharged by bankruptcy.

4. Alimony and support payments.

5. Liability for seduction and breach of promise.

6. Debts incurred through misappropriation while acting in some trust or fiduciary capacity.

7. Claims for wages earned by employees within three months before bankruptcy.

8. Moneys deposited by your employees as security.

9. Loans incurred for education.

On top of these, any debts that are not properly listed by you in the bankruptcy petition (spoken of as not "scheduled") won't be discharged. This means if you leave out a creditor, his debt is still enforceable (unless you can prove he had actual knowledge of the bankruptcy).

There are some other debts which, in theory, are discharged, and yet the bankruptcy might not be of any benefit to you. This arises primarily when you've given a creditor a lien, or mortgage, or other security interest in property. To illustrate, say you've bought a car, a refrigerator, and a washing machine, all "on time." It's almost certain you've signed contracts, giving the finance company or seller a lien, or right to take the property if you don't pay. So now you're in default on these three accounts, and you'd like to jump into bankruptcy and get a clean bill of health. You can, but there's one catch. Although your personal liability *will* be discharged, the creditor might still be able to reclaim his merchandise, or repossess it.

If you're willing to give up those items, that's fine. But don't count on bankruptcy to keep them.

Suppose you'd like to retain the car, and you feel you could manage the one payment if the rest of your bills were cleared. In some cases, you can make a new agreement, or ratify the old one, after you file bankruptcy, and keep paying on the car. The creditor will be delighted to go along with you. But there's a fly in the ointment. You have to list the car, in your schedule of assets. As we'll see later, you're required to turn over all of your nonexempt properties and possessions to a court trustee. He then sells what he can and gives the net proceeds to the creditors. So in many cases, it wouldn't do you much good to keep up the payments on the car. But you have an ace in the hole if you can claim the car as an exemption under your state law (see Section C) or under the federal statute, which exempts a portion of your car's value, plus various other items, such as part of the equity in your home, a certain specified amount of household furnishings, wearing apparel and jewelry, and other belongings. Unfortunately, most states have opted not to follow the federal guidelines; instead, the majority of them only allow the exemptions permitted by their own statutes.

When it comes to liens and mortgages, you have to watch for another booby trap. Many finance companies, when they lend you money, will routinely have you sign a mortgage on *all* your household furniture. Then several months later, when you think that bankruptcy will free you from the loan, you find that they're threatening to pick up your furniture. The law now gives some protection from such liens, if the loan wasn't used to buy the furniture. But you should check the copies of your loan agreements. If your furniture is mortgaged or pledged, bear in mind that your creditor may try to enforce his lien, even in bankruptcy. If your furniture isn't worth saving, then this might not be much of a worry to you. In fact, it might be more of a headache to the finance company, than to you. As a general proposition—unless your furniture has unusual value—the creditor won't want to get involved with disposing of used furniture. It may be valuable to you and your family, but it won't bring much on the open market. Often a whole houseful of used furniture won't sell for over $150. So the creditor has a dilemma; he wants to salvage part of his money, but he'll be shot down in the bankruptcy proceeding. Yet it'll cost him $150 or more, in the typical case, to enforce his mortgage and just to pick up your old furniture. (Remember—don't turn it over voluntarily. See Section A.) So it's a good bet that the average creditor, in the typical family bankruptcy, won't bother your furniture, even though he has a lien or mortgage on it. He'll probably prefer to just write off the debt, especially if it's in the $150 to $400 range. Don't forget though, that he doesn't *have* to do this. If you have costly items—color TV, piano, a big stereo—or precious antiques of special value, then you're vulnerable. But if you have the run-of-the-mill load of tables, beds and chairs with nothing of any earth-shaking significance, your prospects are good that they'll leave you alone.

Another problem with loan companies is the possibility that you may have given them an incorrect financial statement. If you've left out some bills, or overstated your assets, the creditor might be able to keep his debt "alive" and have it survive the bankruptcy. So if you're ever in the position of having to borrow money from a loan company or bank, and you're asked to list your debts, make sure you put down all of them. Don't be gullible enough to believe the loan officer's insinuation that you just have to list "some of them, so that we'll have some idea of the kind of people you owe money to." Some finance companies probably do this unintentionally, but you'll have a hard time explaining, in a bankruptcy proceeding, your failure to list all your bills in any financial statement you've previously given.

O.K. Now you've carefully gone over your debts. You owe exactly 15 creditors a total of say $7,500. You feel there's just no other solution than bankruptcy. But what about your assets? Don't lose sight of the fact that everything over your exemptions goes into the "pot," and is available to creditors. If this causes you to squirm, then bankruptcy may not be best for you. Take a case where you've decided you'd like to claim the exemptions under the new federal law. You quickly add up your possessions, and you tick off $500 that you have in the bank, a car worth $700, personal effects and furniture worth not over $300, $7900 equity in your house, and a boat worth $1100, for total assets of about $10,500. If you filed bankruptcy, then depending on your state, maybe about $1600 of your assets would go to the creditors. If you're willing to do this, fine and dandy, and bankruptcy may be practical for you. But there are a few alternatives that you should consider first (for a discussion of these, see page 239).

There are some other drawbacks to bankruptcy. You have to submit to questioning (see page 235), and if you have anything to hide, you better pass it up. Moreover, bankruptcy is a fairly expensive procedure. The court filing fees run about $90, and a lawyer will charge somewhere between $200 to $500, in the normal case, and in *advance*. His fee will be greater in a complicated case or where there may be some kind of contest.

You should also consider the long range effect of bankruptcy. Your credit rating will come out fairly well-scarred (although, surprisingly not completely destroyed). It'll usually take several months before you can expect to buy regularly on credit, even if some companies are ready to trust you almost immediately. Keep in mind, too, that you can't file successive bankruptcies. You have to wait six years before you're eligible to go through it again.

What are the alternatives to bankruptcy? There are a few procedures set out in the Bankruptcy Law, itself, allowing you to continue working, or to stay in business under some plan, approved by the Court, to pay off gradually, or at reduced amounts. These provisions are somewhat technical, though, and you might need a lawyer to carry you through. A major disadvantage is the expense.

There's another alternative, outside of bankruptcy, that sometimes works, if you're really interested in straightening out your woes and paying your debts. The idea is to prepare a form letter—usually mimeographed or photocopied—sending it to all the creditors, laying on the line exactly what your financial picture is. You summarize your debts, how much your assets are, what your income is, and the amount of your monthly payments and expenses. And then comes the crux of the plan. You explain what you feel you're able to do. This will take one of two approaches: you either ask for a moratorium, or delay, in making any payments, or you propose a schedule of reduced payments.

If you ask for a delay, it can only be for a relatively short time. Probably about 120 days is the most that a creditor would consider. You'll need a reasonable justification for the delay, and some persuasive argument as to why you think you'll be better able to pay after the moratorium. This plan is practical if there's been prolonged illness, and you're just going back to work; or maybe you've recently changed jobs; or possibly your wife had a baby, but she'll be working again in three months or so. In other words, you have to do a selling job and convince the creditors that your excuse is legitimate and that your prospects will improve if they string along with you.

The second approach is to offer lower payments. This is more appealing to the creditors than the moratorium plan. Again, though, you have to give a convincing presentation of your situation, or the creditors' immediate reaction will be a loud "no." If you propose too small an amount, they'll turn you down. About the lowest you can hope to get by with is a third of the usual payment. But you'll have to be in pretty rough shape for a creditor to accept that. Somewhere around 50% is the amount you have the best chance with.

It's important to assure the creditors that you're serious about the plan, but you must point out that if they're not willing to go along, then you have no alternative than to file bankruptcy. Send an extra copy of the letter to each creditor, and ask him to sign and return it to you, if he approves.

For this "non-bankruptcy" method to work, it's practically essential that *all* the creditors approve. If one or two won't agree, then it's likely they'll sue you, and the whole proposal will be knocked out of whack. Occasionally you can get by with one or two dissenting creditors, if you're able to keep paying them. If the others find out, though, the plan will generally fall apart.

If you're wondering what on earth would make a creditor even *consider* accepting reduced payments, or permitting a moratorium, the answer is plain business practicality. It costs them money and time to go to court, plus they have no assurance they'll get anything even with a judgment. And don't overlook the power of the threat of bankruptcy. Creditors are well aware of their dim collection prospects when you actually go through with it.

So if you really feel that you'd like to pay off your creditors, and you think you can do it with a little breathing room, try the "non-bankruptcy" letter proposal. The worst that can happen is that they tell you to jump in the lake.

A form you can adapt to your use is shown at the end of the chapter.

Watch out for one danger, though, if you're dealing with finance companies or "high-interest" lenders. If they accept a reduced payment plan, such as 50%, you may end up paying *all* interest and nothing on the principal. For example, in some states, a small loan company can legally charge as much as 3% per month on your unpaid balance. If you owe $300, this would be $9 a month for interest alone. If your regular payment of $18 is reduced in half, to $9, then all you'd be paying is interest. What you'd have to do is get them to agree to a reduced interest rate. Most of them will go along with this, rather than see you file bankruptcy.

Another alternative to bankruptcy—and really the most common—is the "do-nothing" approach; you take no action at all, and allow the creditors to sue you and have judgments entered. Although this is not actually a solution, it may be that you're "judgment-proof" (see Section G), and that a creditor wouldn't be able to get anything from you.

Many small corporations adopt this attitude, and won't even defend a lawsuit, since they feel they're "judgment-proof." If they're not able to meet their obligations, they usually sell as much of their inventory or stock-in-trade as they can, and let the creditors sue. Since there generally isn't any personal liability (see page 244), the corporation just goes "defunct" and closes it doors.

But there can be at least two reasons for a corporation to go into bankruptcy. The first is to avoid personal liability on taxes. If your corporation owes certain moneys to the government, such as for back withholding taxes or social security on employees, the officers and directors can be held personally liable, in some cases, if the company goes under. Even though you might be able to walk away from the average creditor, you can't always do it to Uncle Sam. So if the corporation has any assets that can be sold by the bankruptcy trustee, you might be able to at least get the tax collector off your back. In bankruptcy, the delinquent taxes are a "priority claim," and get paid before general creditors. Without going through bankruptcy, it's likely that a long-suffering creditor could sue the corporation, get a judgment, and seize ("levy on") all the company's assets. Before you know it, the corporation would be drained dry, and you'd still be holding the bag for the tax money. But through bankruptcy, if there are any assets, they can be applied to pay the government.

A second reason for a corporation to consider bankruptcy is so that you can recoup a few dollars, yourself. Let's say that you, as a stockholder or officer, have made legitimate loans to your corporation over the past couple of years (see page 184). The company owes you $3,000, and you have bona fide promissory notes to prove it. If you try to repay yourself ahead of the creditors—when the corporation isn't able to pay its bills—then you're making an improper and voidable "preference" to yourself. So that's out. But if you allow the corporation to be sued, and judgments entered, then the available remaining assets will be seized and sold by the sheriff, for the benefit of the judgment-creditor. *You* end up with nothing, and your promissory notes are worthless. On the other hand, if the corporation goes into bankruptcy, you'd be entitled to file a claim, along with the other creditors, and you'd share in the net proceeds with them. Here's how it would work. If the corporation owed general creditors $30,000, including the $3,000 note to you, you'd be entitled to 10% of any net proceeds ($3,000 being 10% of the total debts). If, after expenses and costs, the trustee's sale of the corporate assets brought in $5,000, you'd get 10%, or $500.

If you do decide on bankruptcy, there are a few other points you should know about. If, within a year of bankruptcy, you've made any transfers of your property without getting fair value in return, it's possible these will be set aside, if you were insolvent at the time, or did it to defraud creditors. If it was done in good faith, or for adequate consideration, it'll probably stand up.

The bankruptcy law also prohibits you from "preferring" one creditor over another, within ninety days of bankruptcy. This type of "preference" will ordinarily be voided; also, if you repay a debt to yourself or an "insider" within a year of bankruptcy, there's a good chance it'll be set aside.

As we've seen (page 234), the primary purpose of going into voluntary bankruptcy is to be discharged from your debts. So before you file, you need to be sure you're eligible for discharge. There are several grounds for being denied relief:

1. Committing a bankruptcy offense punishable by imprisonment (the most common are concealment and making a false oath).

2. Failure to keep or preserve books or records. But you don't always have to keep such records; the test is whether a complete disclosure of your financial condition depends on keeping such records. If your business is the kind in which records aren't usually kept, then this won't bar your discharge.

3. Obtaining credit through a false written financial statement. This only applies to someone in business; if you're a wage earner and give a false financial statement, this might keep that particular debt from being wiped out, but it won't stop your discharge from other bills.

4. Fraudulent conveyances or concealment within a year of filing bankruptcy.

5. A previous discharge, or similar proceeding, in bankruptcy within six years.

6. Refusal to obey a lawful order, or answer any material question approved by the court.

7. Failure to satisfactorily explain any loss or deficiency of assets.

In short, a discharge in bankruptcy is available to an honest debtor, who's kept reasonable records, cooperated with the court, and hasn't been through bankruptcy within the past six years. If you're going to run afoul of any of the above grounds, you better save your money and not file.

F. Can You Legally Hide Your Property?

Your creditors are breathing down your neck and screaming about filing suit. You have some assets—maybe a car and a little money in the bank—but you don't want the creditors to get it. How far can you go in "hiding" your property or transferring it to your wife or relatives?

The answer is: not very far.

When you're not insolvent—that is, when you're able to pay your bills as they come due—you can do just about whatever you want with your property, even give it away. But when you owe money, the rules change drastically. If you transfer property then, without adequate consideration, the law presumes you're doing it to gyp creditors.

You might be able to show, in defense, that you were really paying back a past debt by putting the property, say, in your Uncle George's name. But the courts will look closely at such transfers, and if there's any odor to it at all, it'll be set aside. If you make the conveyance after a judgment is entered against you, or even after the suit has been filed, you won't stand a chance. If you do it *before* the suit, you're still on pretty thin ice, but it might be harder for a creditor to find out about it, or to prove you were insolvent. Remember, though, that in most states, you can be made to submit to questioning after a judgment, and you can be asked about transfers of your property.

So if you think all you need to do is sign over the car to Uncle George, and that you'll be protected, you better wise up. You won't get away with it.

Many gun-shy businessmen, either through past misfortune or

from hearing about others' experience, automatically put everything in their wife's name. If you do this before you're indebted, it's probably legal, all right. But if your wife is jointly obligated on a debt with you (such as when the finance company makes her sign a note with you), this usually won't do you much good. (Also, there's the classic case of the guy who transfers a million dollars to his wife, to keep it from creditors, and then she divorces him.)

Then, too, there can be disadvantages to putting certain property in a wife's name. For instance, almost all states exempt a homestead from creditors' claims, when the house is owned by the "head of the family" (see Section C). Suppose, though, that you don't know this, and you try to outsmart your creditor by placing the house in your wife's name. If your wife happens to be jointly obligated on any debt with you, you could wind up losing the house, since she won't be entitled to claim the homestead exemption (only you—as the head of the family—can claim it, in most places).

G. How Good Is a Judgment?

It's been noted, in another chapter, that getting a judgment doesn't insure payment for a creditor (see page 190). In fact, if you don't have any money to pay bills, you may be what collection managers call—in polite society—judgment-proof. As we've seen, this means you have nothing tangible that a creditor can latch onto, or attach. You'll recall that there are exemptions permitted in all states (see Section C); in addition, wages are at least partially protected (Section B).

So if you don't have anything, is there a danger in allowing a judgment to be entered against you? Why should you consider going into bankruptcy (see Section E) if you have no assets anyway?

There are a few possible reasons and factors to consider.

1. To begin with, some creditors don't give up. It's true that the majority of them, after getting a judgment and finding you don't have much, just write it off and forget it. But a small handful will keep harassing you, writing letters, calling you and your employer, and otherwise making your life miserable. If this happens with more than one creditor, and you can't "shake them," then bankruptcy may be the way to get rid of them. Before you spend money

to file, though, try writing a get-tough letter to the creditor. A form is shown at the end of this chapter, as Form 5.

2. Another reason is if your wife works, or plans to. She may be vulnerable to garnishment of her wages (see Section B), since in many states, only wages earned by the family-head are exempt, and this would normally refer to the husband. It might be better, then, to file bankruptcy for both of you, so that her future wages will be protected. Be careful, though, for a possible danger here: if you happen to file bankruptcy just before her pay day, the court trustee will technically have the right to demand her "accrued" pay. Let's say she gets paid twice a month—$350 on the 15th, and the same amount on the 30th. If you file bankruptcy on the 14th, then her accrued pay for the past 14 days could be an asset that would be available to the trustee. How do you handle this? By filing on the second day of the month, after pay day. There would then be only one day's pay accrued, and this small amount would be waived by the creditors in the ordinary case. If you filed on the 2nd, you'd theoretically have to account for the money received the day before, but if you claim it went for day-to-day living expenses, such as groceries, rent, electricity, and so forth—as it probably did—there's generally very little objection.

3. A third problem with a judgment is that it remains on record as a claim against you for a long time, as much as 7 to 20 years. If this doesn't bother you, or you're planning to move to another county or state, then there's "no sweat." But if you expect to inherit any money in a few years, or to acquire property, then it may be advisable to consider bankruptcy (unless, of course, it's your intention to pay off the judgment some day).

4. A fourth reason might arise if the judgment is against you alone, but your wife has property, or you own it jointly with her, as an estate by the entireties (see Section D). You, yourself, may be immune to a judgment, at present, since the estate by the entireties is not generally susceptible to attachment for your debts, alone. But what happens if your wife dies? In most cases, the property would revert to you, as survivor, and the creditor could then jump in and enforce the judgment. So if the claim against you is a big one—even though you're "judgment-proof" today—give some thought to bankruptcy, if you own any "joint" assets or your wife has property.

H. Foreclosing On Your House

What can you do when the mortgage company is getting ready to foreclose on your house? The best weapon you have, if you're not able to make your mortgage payments, is *time*. Most mortgage companies are slow in gearing up for a foreclosure. They'll usually wait until you're at least two months behind—in most cases—before they'll start writing you. And if you still don't pay, it generally takes another month or so before their attorney is ready to file suit. In the vast majority of cases, they'll allow you to catch up the back payments if you're able to do so, since they're ordinarily not overly-anxious to have your house on their hands. You'll probably have to pay an attorney's fee to their lawyer, and some collection charges, but you'll be given a reasonable time to do it. Bear in mind, though, that there are exceptions. Some mortgage companies are notoriously tough, especially if you have a history of being in default.

A few mortgagees will allow you to catch up the back payments on a "double-up" basis. In other words, if you're four months behind, with monthly payments of $300, they'll let you pay $600 a month until you're current. You may have trouble doing this on F.H.A. or V.A. mortgages, though, because some lenders figure why should they "mess around" with you when they can get their money back from Uncle Sam (see Section A). But propose it anyway, if you can.

If the mortgage is held by a private investor, or is not a government-insured or government-guaranteed loan, you might be able to get a moratorium or extension for a few months (see Section E), or an agreement to reduce the payments. It's worth trying this before you throw in the towel.

There's another possibility: under bankruptcy (or a "Chapter 13" wage-earner plan), the foreclosure can be delayed for up to several months while you try to come up with the money you owe.

When you've gotten too far behind in your payments to be granted any more extensions, the lender will foreclose. The procedure varies from state to state, but there either has to be a judicial proceeding, or a public sale of the property. Even after suit is filed, you're given a certain period of time to "redeem" the property, if you're able to, by paying the full balance, plus costs. Sometimes you might be able to refinance the property and get a mortgage from a new lender, during the "redemption" period.

In most states, the foreclosure involves a public sale of your house by an officer of the court. If the amount that's bid is more than you owe, then you get the difference. But in actual practice, there's normally no bidder except the holder of the mortgage.

In a few jurisdictions, a judicial proceeding isn't required, and the mortgage company itself sells the property at a public sale, after advertising it. In some of the New England states, there's no sale at all, but after filing the necessary papers in court, the mortgage holder can take possession of the house.

What happens if the proceeds of the foreclosure sale are less than the mortgage balance? In most localities, the mortgagee can legally apply for a "deficiency," or personal judgment against you. As a practical matter, this isn't always easy to do, and many courts are reluctant to award a deficiency. If a mortgage company tries to get one against you, you'd ordinarily have the right to show what the "fair market value" of the property is, since the deficiency is limited to the difference between the mortgage balance and the fair market value, in most places.

If you know you'll lose the house and there's no way of saving it, you should consider the possibility of deeding the property to the mortgagee, in place of foreclosure. This will save them the expense and delay of a foreclosure. The advantage to you is that it won't look quite as bad on your credit rating. The mortgage company might even be willing to allow you to stay in the house for a few more weeks, in exchange for your signing the deed, since it'll take them at least two months to foreclose, in the average case— and often longer. You'll need to be sure, though, that they'll accept the deed as a complete release of the mortgage and won't try for a deficiency or other claims against you. Get this in writing either before or at the same time you sign the deed.

Be on the lookout for offers by any strangers who say they'll take over your mortgage and catch up the back payments, if you'll sign over the house to them. There are roving real estate operators, known as "equity skinners," who thrive on homeowners who are delinquent in their payments. Several schemes are used. One is for the equity skinner, after you move out, to rent the house, without making any mortgage payments. Since it often takes several months for the foreclosure to be completed, he pockets the rent as clear profit. Most of the time he won't even record the deed you gave him. So when the mortgage company gets around to foreclosing, *you're* the one that's named as a defendant, and it's *your* credit that's jeopardized. In other cases, the equity skinner offers you a house in a less expensive neighborhood, if you sign over the deed to him. But then he tells you the other house "fell through." To protect yourself, make sure that the delinquent mortgage payments are paid when you sign the deed. Either get a cashier's check from the buyer, payable to the mortgage company, or go to the mortgagee's office with the "stranger," to be certain he makes the payments.

I. Military Personnel

If you're in the armed forces of the United States, there are some special laws that help you if you're indebted. The main one is a federal statute called the Soldiers' and Sailors' Civil Relief Act.

One of its sections prevents a judgment from being entered against a serviceman, unless he's represented by a lawyer. So if you're sued and don't have an attorney, the judge will appoint one for you. The lawyer will write to you, or call you, and present any defense you might have.

Another part of the law grants an extension of time for payment of debts, if your entry into service has affected your ability to pay. For example: you're an electrician, making $1,500 a month, and you've recently bought a car and some applicances. Total installment payments: $600 a month. Now you're called up for military duty, and your military pay is too small for you to keep up the payments. Don't go off the deep end. You're entitled to relief under the law. You can also get an extension on your mortgage payments during your military service. It's likely that you'll be asked to pay only interest on the mortgage, and the taxes and insurance. If even these are too much for you, then you can probably get greater reductions, where warranted. Warning: these extensions and reductions apply only if your induction comes *after* you incur the debt. If you're already in the military, and you obligate yourself, then this section of the statute won't help you.

Many servicemen are particularly vulnerable to collection tactics of creditors. Typically, the serviceman is threatened with a letter to his commanding officer if the bill isn't paid. The armed forces aren't collection agencies, but you'll find it embarrassing if your commander keeps receiving letters saying you're a deadbeat. You can expect to be called into the commander's office and given a lecture about meeting your obligations. Explain to your superior that you're doing the best you can and that you're trying to pay—unless, of course, you don't agree that you owe the money. You might also consider writing a letter to the creditor, threatening him with a suit for invasion of privacy if he keeps writing your commanding officer. This will usually stop him. A suggested form of such a letter is at the end of this chapter.

J. What About Bad Checks?

Every state has laws making it a crime to give a worthless check. The penalty and the language differ from place to place, but basically these statutes prohibit you from knowingly giving a check that will bounce. If the check is dishonored, there's generally a presumption that you intended to defraud, and that you had knowledge it was a bad check. You'd then have the burden of showing a mistake, or other defense.

If you pay a bill by check, make sure you always have enough money in the bank to cover it. If your check bounces, most creditors will call you and allow you to make it good. But a few can play rough, especially if they've had collection problems with you in the past. They're likely to swear out a criminal warrant, charging you with giving a worthless check. This is really a form of legal blackmail, since they're not interested in having you locked up; they figure this is an effective club over your head to make you come up with the money. And they're right. In most places, the charge is dropped after you redeem the check, although you might have to pay some court costs. Technically, redeeming the check isn't a defense to the criminal charge, but unless you've gone all over town issuing bad checks, there's usually no one that objects to the dismissal of the warrant.

Suppose you can show that you didn't intentionally try to swindle anyone; that you made a subtraction error in your check book. It still is a nerve-wracking experience to have to appear before a criminal judge, justice of the peace or magistrate. And it's expensive if you hire a lawyer.

So don't give a check if there's any danger it'll bounce. Never give a check, which you've dated today, expecting to make it good tomorrow, when you deposit some funds to cover it. If you get sick in between, or can't get the money to the bank for some reason or other, you're susceptible to prosecution when the check bounces.

And don't let a creditor talk you into giving him a check "to hold." This is a trick used by some collection managers and bill collectors. They'll tell you they won't deposit it until you give them an "all-clear." But here's the catch: they hold it a few days and then deposit it, without your approval or knowledge. It bounces ten stories high. And they then swear out a warrant, charging you with issuing a worthless check. You'd have a good defense in court if you can prove what happened, but it'll cost you aggravation and loss of time, at best, and a criminal conviction if the judge doesn't believe your story.

If your creditor insists on "holding" your check, or if you're absolutely certain you can make it good by a certain date, you might get by with a post-dated check. If the check bounces later, you ordinarily wouldn't be vulnerable to prosecution. This is because the post-dated check is like giving a note or promise to pay in the future; if you don't pay on the "due date," you can be sued, but you haven't committed any crime. Post-dated checks are legal in most places, but there are a few quirks in some of the states, and you might have to call your lawyer or banker before you can be sure you're safe. But if you do use a post-dated check, see to it that you mark plainly on it: "This is a post-dated check." Why? Because if the check bounces when the date arrives, you'll have proof that it *was* post-dated. Otherwise, a disreputable creditor can claim you gave it to him on the date appearing on the check—and that he didn't know it was worthless.

In brief, be careful when you pay by check. If you owe money to a store or creditor, they can't put you in jail. But once you write your name on a rubber check, they can. So make sure you can always cover every check you write.

Form 1

LETTER TO CREDITOR, SUGGESTING BANKRUPTCY

16 Squirrel Street
New York, N. Y.

Date _____

Atomic Loan Company
123 Main Street
New York, N. Y.

Gentlemen:

I have carefully gone over my finances, and I can see no possible way for me to pay my bills at this time.

Therefore, I have reluctantly concluded that the most practical solution for me is to file bankruptcy.

However, in one final effort to avoid this, I am prepared to pay you $_____ per (week) (month) until I'm able to get back on my feet financially. If you are willing to accept this, please sign the enclosed copy of this letter, and return it to me. My first payment will be made on _____.

If you're not agreeable to this, or if I don't hear from you within 7 days, then I will plan to file bankruptcy proceedings, without further notice to you.

I'm sorry to have to take this action, and I still hope it won't be necessary.

Please let me hear from you. Thank you for your cooperation.

Sincerely yours,

John Doe

Form 2

STATES RECOGNIZING ESTATES BY THE ENTIRETIES AND COMMUNITY PROPERTY

	Recognizes Estates by Entireties	Doesn't Recognize Estates by Entireties	Recognizes Only For Real Estate	Community Property State
Alabama		X		
Alaska	X			
Arizona				X
Arkansas	X			
California				X
Colorado		X		
Connecticut		X		
Delaware	X			
D.C.	X			
Florida	X			
Georgia		X		
Hawaii	X			
Idaho				X
Illinois		X		
Indiana			X	
Iowa		X		
Kansas		X		
Kentucky	X			
Louisiana				X
Maine		X		
Maryland	X			
Massachusetts	X			
Michigan	Xa		X	
Minnesota		X		
Mississippi	X			
Missouri	X			
Montana		X		

	Recognizes Estates by Entireties	Doesn't Recognize Estates by Entireties	Recognizes Only For Real Estate	Community Property State
Nebraska		X		
Nevada				X
New Hampshire		X		
New Jersey			X	
New Mexico				X
New York			X	
North Carolina			X	
North Dakota		X		
Ohio			X	
Oklahoma	X			
Oregon			X	
Pennsylvania	X			
Rhode Island	X			
South Carolina		X		
South Dakota		X		
Tennessee	X			
Texas				X
Utah b				
Vermont	X			
Virginia	X			
Washington				X
West Virginia			X	
Wisconsin				Xc
Wyoming	X			

a For some personal property, but not all.
b No statutory provision.
c Some modifications.

Form 3

FORM LETTER TO ALL CREDITORS PROPOSING REDUCED PAYMENTS

16 Squirrel Street
New York, N. Y.
Date _____

TO: All my creditors

As you are no doubt aware, I am heavily in debt, and not able to meet my financial obligations. It appears that bankruptcy will be necessary; and if I take such action, I feel that my creditors would receive nothing.

However, in a final attempt to avoid bankruptcy, and in an effort to work out my problems, I am writing to all my creditors in the hope that you will go along with a proposed schedule of reduced payments.

My gross income, from all sources, is $_____, and my net "take-home" pay (including my wife's income) is $_____. My rock-bottom monthly expenditures for necessities are as follows:

House payment or rent	$_____
Gas, lights, water and garbage	_____
Telephone	_____
Food and groceries	_____
Household supplies (soaps, toothpaste, etc.)	_____
Fuel	_____
Clothing	_____
Transportation and insurance	_____
Laundry and dry cleaning	_____
Medical	_____
Car payment	_____
Other	_____
_____	_____
	_____
TOTAL	$_____

This leaves me approximately $_____ as a maximum available to pay off past-due accounts. My unpaid debts are as follows:

NAME OF CRED.   APPROX. BALANCE DUE PER MONTH

1.
2.
3.
4.
5.
6.

As you can see, it's impossible for me to pay my bills on my income. I have no savings. Therefore, subject to the approval of all of the creditors, I am willing to pay a total of $_____ to all of my creditors, each month, on a pro rata basis. This would mean paying each of you _____ % of your regular monthly payment, until the obligations are paid off, or until I am able to get back on my feet.

The proposed payment schedule is as follows:

> NAME OF CREDITOR   AMOUNT PER MONTH

1.
2.
3.
4.
5.
6.

If you are willing to accept this proposal, please let me know immediately, by signing the enclosed copy of this letter, and sending it to me by return mail with an up-to-date statement of the balance owed to you.

Unless *all* the creditors approve, the proposal will not work, and I'll be obligated to reluctantly file bankruptcy. I hope I won't have to do this, since I sincerely want to pay off my obligations, if I'm permitted to do so.

Incidentally, in order that the principal balances on my accounts be reduced with reasonable speed, I would also need an agreement from those creditors who are charging me interest, that you will reduce the interest, proportionately, during this period of reduced payments.

Please let me hear from you as soon as possible, and in no event later than _____.*

Thank you very much for your patience and understanding.

Sincerely yours,

John Doe

We agree to the foregoing.
NAME OF CREDITOR: _____
By _____
BALANCE: _____.
Interest will be adjusted as follows: _____

(*Insert a date 5 to 10 days away.)

Form 4

FORM LETTER TO ALL CREDITORS PROPOSING MORA-TORIUM

16 Squirrel Street
New York, N. Y.
Date _____

TO: All my creditors

As you are no doubt aware, I am heavily in debt, and not able to meet my financial obligations. It appears that bankruptcy will be necessary; and if I take such action, I feel that my creditors would receive nothing.

However, in a final attempt to avoid bankruptcy, and in an effort to work out my problems, I am writing to all my creditors in the hope that you will go along with my proposal.

As you may know, I've been out of work for the last _____weeks, because of my accident.* This has caused a tremendous hardship on me, and has made it impossible for me to pay my bills. But I feel that I'll be able to straighten myself out in the next few months, since I'm now going back to work.**

Therefore, I respectfully ask that you and the other creditors listed in this letter allow me a moratorium, or extension, for _____days,*** during which no payments would be made. By the end of that time, I feel sure I can again start making regular payments.

My gross income, from all sources, is $_____, and my net "take-home" pay (including my wife's income) is $_____. My rock-bottom monthly expenditures for necessities are as follows:

House payment or rent	$_____
Gas, lights, water and garbage	_____
Telephone	_____
Food and groceries	_____
Household supplies (soaps, toothpaste, etc.)	_____
Fuel	_____
Clothing	_____
Transportation and insurance	_____
Laundry and dry cleaning	_____
Medical	_____

(*Or list other reason for nonpayment, such as:
1. My wife had a baby, and our income was drastically reduced.
2. My wife has been seriously ill, and we've incurred enormous medical bills.
3. I've been laid off work.
**Or state other reason why you feel prospects will improve, such as:
Since my wife will be able to go back to work in 3 months, and resume her income.
***Usually 60 to 120 days, depending on your circumstances.)

Car payment   _____
Other   _____
_____

                                                     _____
                              TOTAL $_____

My outstanding debts, for which I ask a moratorium and extension,
are as follows:

NAME OF CRED.   APPROX. BALANCE DUE PER MONTH
  1.
  2.
  3.
  4.
  5.
  6.

I have no savings.

I had hoped I could offer you some reduced payment per month, for
the next few months, but this isn't possible, and I can only ask that you
allow me the extension.

If you are agreeable to my request, please let me know immediately,
by signing the enclosed copy of this letter, and sending it to me by
return mail.

Unless *all* the creditors approve, the proposal will not work, and I'll
be obligated to reluctantly file bankruptcy. I hope I won't have to do
this, since I sincerely want to pay off my obligations, if I'm permitted to
do so.

Please let me hear from you as soon as possible, and in no event
later than _____.****   Thank you very much for your patience
and understanding.

                                                     Sincerely yours,

                                                     John Doe

We agree to the foregoing.
NAME OF CREDITOR: _____
By _____

(****Insert a date 5 to 10 days away.)

Form 5

THREATENING LETTER TO CREDITOR

16 Squirrel Street
New York, N. Y.
Date _____

Atomic Loan Company
123 Main Street
New York, N. Y.

Gentlemen:

You have, in the last several days, called me a number of times about my account, and have contacted my employer.*

Please consider this as my formal notice to you to immediately stop such tactics. I fully understand my legal rights, and if you see fit to continue to harass me and to call or write my employer,* I will be obligated to bring legal proceedings against you for invasion of privacy and defamation of character.

I am doing the best I can to take care of my obligations, and I hope to pay you as soon as possible. But I am not willing to be subjected to your company's collection techniques.

Any further calls will result in a damage suit promptly filed against you.

Sincerely yours,

John Doe

(*Or commmanding officer, for military personnel)

CHAPTER 8

So You're Going To Be A Witness

THE COUPLE NEXT DOOR HAS BEEN SCREAMING AT EACH OTHER for weeks. A few times, when you've gone over to borrow a cup of sugar, you've heard a few choice profanities from the man of the house, and you found the little woman crying. But now, the commotion has subsided, and you learn that the husband has moved out. You breathe a sign of relief. Then one evening, a few weeks later, the wife asks you to become a witness in her divorce.

You're minding your own business, peacefully driving a few comfortable car lengths behind a sleek new convertible. Suddenly a station wagon zips into the intersection and crashes into the side of the convertible. You stop, offer to help, and you wait around for the police. Several days later, you're called by a lawyer and told that you might have to testify in court.

Most people prefer not getting involved in a lawsuit, especially someone else's. There's often somewhat of a reluctance—and even a fear—in having to be a witness. And an appearance in court can take up several hours of your time.

If you'd like to help your neighbor in her divorce case, you might decide you'll appear, voluntarily, without anybody ordering you or forcing you to be there. This is quite common, particularly if you're friendly with one of the parties to the case.

But suppose you don't want to be a witness. You're busy, and you can't see getting involved in somebody else's problems. Maybe you've been planning a trip out of town, or you just don't feel you know enough about the case to be of any help. Then what?

A. You're Served with a Subpoena

A subpoena is a document, issued by a court or other legal authority, commanding you to appear at a specified time and place to give testimony. It's usually delivered, or "served," by a deputy sheriff or constable, but in many states it can be served by a lawyer or other person. Once you receive one, you don't have much alternative about whether you'd prefer staying home. If you don't show up, you can be arrested or held in contempt of court. So unless you have a really good excuse (serious illness, death in the family, or some other emergency), you better be there.

If you do have a valid reason why you can't attend, you ought to immediately notify the judge or the clerk of the court. Don't wait until the last minute, though. As a courtesy, you should also call the lawyer who's handling the case—if you know his name. But you probably shouldn't rely entirely on *his* notifying the court for you. You need to do that yourself, to avoid being subjected to contempt.

The ordinary subpoena merely directs you to testify. You're not required to bring anything with you. But sometimes you'll be served with a "subpoena duces tecum." This is a fancy Latin term which tells you, in effect, to bring certain books or papers to court. For instance, if you're an accountant or banker, and have custody of some records that will be material to the case, it's not out of the ordinary for you to receive a subpoena duces tecum.

Even if you've told one of the lawyers that you'll appear voluntarily as a witness, don't be insulted if you're subpoenaed anyway. Many attorneys feel that a subpoenaed witness will appear more impartial to a jury, even if he's not. Furthermore, if you didn't show up, the lawyer's in a better position to get a delay in the trial, than if you weren't subpoenaed.

As a subpoenaed witness, you're generally entitled to a fee for coming to court. In most states, the amount is small, such as $10.00 per day—barely enough to cover your mileage expenses in some cases. If you have to come a long distance, though, you might be able to get more.

An "expert" witness is entitled to additional pay. If you're a doctor, engineer, appraiser, or are specially trained in another field, the court will allow you an extra fee. The exact amount will depend on your qualifications, the length of time your testimony takes, and the prevailing practice of the area. But you're not limited, in most cases, to the fee allowed by the judge. Make advance arrangements with the attorney or party calling you as a witness, so that they'll know what your estimated charges will be.

Most attorneys will try to give an expert witness an approximate hour to appear in court, so that you won't have to wait around all day. Unfortunately, it's hard to pinpoint the exact course of a trial, and it's possible you might have to sit in court for a while. If you're fairly close to the courthouse, ask that the lawyer permit you to remain in your office or place of business, until about half an hour before he needs you. Many lawyers will agree to this, and will telephone when they're ready.

If you're not an expert, it's less likely that the lawyer will be so accommodating. You'll probably be summoned to appear at the opening of the trial, and it's not unusual to have to wait around all day, or even several days, before you're called. To avoid this, try to contact the attorney in charge of the case, two or three days before the trial. Ask him if he can give you some estimate as to when he thinks he'll need you. He won't know exactly, but he might at least be able to tell you to come after lunch, or some other approximate time of day. If he can't give you any idea at all, and insists you be there when court opens, you better plan to bring along a magazine or other reading matter to occupy your time while you wait (in many cases, you won't be allowed in the courtroom until it's your turn to testify).

When your testimony is important to the case, the lawyer may want to talk to you before the trial. There's nothing unlawful or improper about this, but you're not legally obligated to talk to him, unless you want to. If you don't have anything to hide, there's generally little reason to refuse to see him. The only way, though, that you can be *required* to discuss the case in advance of the trial is by being subpoenaed, usually for a pre-trial proceeding called a deposition (see Section B). Many lawyers and insurance companies, realizing you won't be too receptive to taking off time from work just to discuss the case, will offer to pay you for your lost time. Again, there's nothing improper or immoral about this, but watch out for too high a payment. Don't put yourself in the position of being "paid" to testify.

B. What's a Deposition?

Occasionally, you'll be summoned or requested to appear for a deposition. This is a question and answer session that takes place before the trial, without the jury or the judge being present. The lawyers for both sides usually attend, and a court reporter records what is said.

The basic purpose is to allow the attorneys to ask you what you know about the case, so that they'll be better prepared for the trial. Sometimes they're "fishing" for information; other times they know more or less what you'll say, but they're trying to commit you to your story, under oath, so that you won't change it later.

The testimony given at the deposition is generally typed up afterwards, and is available during the trial. It can be used to contradict or "impeach" you, if you testify differently later in court. It can also be used if you can't appear for the trial because of sickness, absence from the state, or other similar reason.

The deposition is much more informal than the actual trial. It customarily takes place at the office of the court reporter or one of the lawyers, although in some communities it's taken at the courthouse. You're usually permitted to smoke, and the atmosphere is fairly casual. But despite this, don't get the idea that it's an unimportant part of the case. It isn't the time to crack jokes or be overly-chummy with the lawyers.

C. What Should You Say?

You'll be sworn to tell the truth—probably by the court reporter—and asked to identify yourself. From that point on, one of the lawyers will question you about the case. The procedure is seldom like what you see on television or in the movies. It's rare that one of the lawyers will try to embarrass you or "break you down."

Remember, you know what happened better than any of the attorneys, and they're only trying to find it out. There's no reason to be nervous or afraid. Be polite and pleasant, and try to act natural.

When you're asked something, just answer that particular question. Don't wander all over the block or volunteer information that you haven't been asked. For instance, if the lawyer wants to know how long you've lived at your present address, just tell him that. But don't go into a long dissertation about where you were before that, and how you happened to move, and that it rained the day the movers came. If he wants to know all of your fascinating background, he'll no doubt ask you.

Don't answer a question unless you understand it. That sounds pretty basic, but too many witnesses will answer when they're not positive what it means. If the question is involved or complicated, or you aren't able to follow it, don't hesitate to ask that it be repeated. Or tell the lawyer you didn't understand it. Be especially attentive to questions with double meanings, or that assume you've testified to a certain fact, when you haven't.

If you're able to answer a question in one word, such as "yes" or "no," that's usually the best answer to give. Don't feel, though, that you're required to answer yes or no when you can't. Obviously, you're not always able to do this, but be as brief as you can. If you have to explain an answer, do it. But don't give the history of western civilization in doing it.

Don't be evasive or a smart-aleck. Just tell what you know in a straightforward manner, and don't try to be clever.

If you're not sure about an answer, say so. There's nothing wrong with testifying that you don't know, or you can't remember. Some witnesses think they've got to have an answer for every question asked. Nobody expects you to know every minute detail; you'll get caught if you testify to something you're really not sure of. And don't be pinned down to giving precise figures about speed, distance or dates, when you're really not certain. If you think you can give a good estimate, you're allowed to do so. But tell the questioner it's your best estimate.

On occasion, you'll be asked what someone else told you or said. This is technically called "hearsay evidence," and in a trial, it's not permitted. But a much wider latitude is allowed in a deposition (remember, there's no judge there to give a ruling), and you'll be expected to answer. In fact, unless you're specifically instructed not to answer by one of the lawyers, you're generally required to answer all the questions. If you're asked something that might tend to incriminate you, or you're asked to disclose some secret process, you can refuse to answer. But this will happen less than one time out of a thousand, so don't worry about it.

Try not to memorize your story. Just tell what happened to the best of your ability. And stick to the facts, without exaggerating or constantly giving your opinion, unless you're asked for it. You don't have to rush your answer; there's no jury to impress, so you can take as much time as you need.

Above all else, tell the truth.

D. The Courtroom

Eventually, if the case isn't settled, it'll be tried. A few types of litigation are heard in the judge's chambers, without a jury. The majority, though, take place in the courtroom. If you've never been in a courtroom, you'll probably feel more at ease when you testify, if you plan to visit it a day or two before the trial.

In some cases, you'll be allowed to remain in the courtroom and listen to the evidence until it's your turn to testify. But don't be disappointed if you're instructed to remain outside until you're called. This is to prevent you from being influenced or swayed by the other testimony in the case. It's also common for the judge to instruct the witnesses not to discuss their testimony with anyone else, except the lawyers in the case.

When you're finally called to testify, you'll be directed to the bailiff or clerk, who will administer the witness's oath. You'll then take your seat in the "witness stand," which is more often than not, located to one side of where the judge sits. The acoustics in most courtrooms are poor, so you'll need to speak out loudly and clearly. Don't mumble or keep your hands near your mouth.

It's natural to be a little nervous, especially if this is your first time in court. Just remember there's really nothing to be scared of; everybody is just as anxious as you are to get out of the place and go home. So relax. You're only expected to tell what you know, and if you don't know something, you can say so. Don't be afraid to look at the jury when you testify. Most jurors are sympathetic to a witness. So don't think of them as enemies; they're not. Neither is the judge.

If the case has been in litigation for several months, or even years, and you've given your deposition a long time ago (see Section B), it may be helpful for you to review what you said, before the trial starts. The lawyer for the side calling you will have a copy of the deposition, or can get one. You might also want to look over any exhibits or documents that relate to your testimony.

Once you're on the witness stand, you should keep in mind the same suggestions as for giving your deposition (Section B). When you're being cross-examined, try not to look for "help" or a "signal" from the lawyer who called you as a witness. The jurors are quick to spot this, and will think you're being coached.

Traditionally, you'll be questioned first by the side that subpoenaed you. This is called "direct examination." It's probable that some of the questions will be objected to by the opposing attorney; if this happens, wait for a ruling by the judge before you answer.

When the direct examination is over, the other lawyer has the right to question you (cross-examination). Think before answering; don't spit out your answer before you digest the question. This also gives the attorney for your side a chance to object to any improper question. By the same token, don't go overboard in the other direction, and wait too long, every time, before you give an answer. It's all right to think, and you should do so, by all means; but if you constantly wait half a minute before answering, the jury is going to finally conclude that you don't know what you're talking about.

E. How To Dress

Some courts have no particular rule about the kind of clothing a witness has to wear in court. Other courts, though, are extremely particular, and will insist on a man wearing a coat and tie, and a woman wearing a dress. A few judges even keep a supply of jackets and ties available for the uninformed witness. To save embarrassment, check with the clerk of the court, the judge's secretary, or the lawyer for one of the parties, ahead of time.

What if you're required to come directly from work? You're dirty and grimy, and there's no possible way to change clothes in time. Better call one of the same people, and get a clearance. In such a situation, you'll usually be able to testify.

Try not to wear any flashy or loud clothing. A trial is serious business and the judge won't appreciate your overdressing. A woman can wear a hat, but it shouldn't be too distracting. She should stay away from any ultra-short skirts, and use cosmetics and jewelry discreetly.

F. The "Smart" Lawyer

You may not believe it, but most lawyers are fair and polite in court. You don't see too much of the fist-pounding, arm-waving type of attorney anymore. But occasionally, a lawyer can be sarcastic or belligerent with you. What do you do with the "smart" lawyer? How should you handle yourself?

In the first place, don't talk back or argue. You may have a terrible temptation to lash out at that cocky little so-and-so, and tell him not to point his finger at you, and who does he think he is to raise his voice at you. Don't do it. Swallow hard, and answer courteously. Don't lose your temper, even if it's a struggle. If you try to out-shout or out-smart him, you're a dead duck (unless you happen to be an expert in the field that he's questioning you about). You may be the best debater in your P.T.A. group, and be glib with a wisecrack, but you're out of your class if you try to butt heads with an experienced trial lawyer on his home ground. So keep your "cool" and don't fight him. The best weapon you have is mildness and courtesy.

If he gives you a question dripping with sarcasm, such as "You-mean-to-sit-there-and-tell-this-jury-that-you- don't-know-how-many-feet-my-client's-car-was-from-the-intersection? Is-that-what-you-want-us-to-believe?" Resist the temptation to answer with, "I've told you once; how many times do you want me to say it?" A simple "Yes, sir" is the proper answer.

Don't let him get you into an argument with him. You just stay with your story, if it's true. The sarcastic lawyer can make you feel uncomfortable and ready to argue. But this is all part of his strategy. Once you lose your temper, you're liable to say something that isn't correct, or you're likely to exaggerate. This is exactly what he wants. And worse yet, the jurors, who are usually on your side, lose their sympathy. So remember, keep your answers pleasant and well-mannered, even though it may not be easy to do.

Probably more common nowadays than the argumentative lawyer—and really more dangerous—is the overly sugary and solicitous lawyer. He can lead you on, with a series of innocent questions that you can easily answer with "yes." All the while he's nodding his head studiously, agreeing with you every inch of the way. And then when you least expect it, he has you calmly agreeing that you really didn't know what you were talking about when you said a certain fact was true. So be on your guard against letting him water down your testimony by putting words in your mouth.

Here's how that happens:

> "Q. Mr. Jones, you said you thought my client's car must have been doing about 70 miles an hour.
>
> "A. Yes, sir.
>
> "Q. Of course, it's possible that it could have been a little bit more or a little less, isn't that right?
>
> "A. I imagine so.
>
> "Q. And naturally you didn't have a speedometer to measure it exactly.
>
> "A. No.
>
> "Q. It's just your best estimate, to the best of your ability, isn't that right?"
>
> "A. Yes.
>
> "Q. And naturally you didn't have a chance to notice my client's car until just a second or two before the accident, isn't that true?
>
> "A. That's right.
>
> "Q. Just about at the time of impact.
>
> "A. A second or two before.
>
> "Q. So of course you weren't really watching for any long period of time.
>
> "A. No.
>
> "Q. So really and truly, to be perfectly fair, Mr. Jones, isn't it a fact that you can't swear *how* fast my client's car was traveling?
>
> "A. I guess not exactly."

The witness's answers were all proper until the last one. But then he weakened. He was *too* agreeable. At that point, a suggested answer to the question might have been something like this:

> "Q. So really and truly, to be perfectly fair, Mr. Jones, isn't it a fact that you can't swear exactly *how* fast my client's car was traveling?
>
> "A. I would say 70 miles an hour."

The lawyer's strategy, as you'll note, consists of a number of "isn't it true" or "isn't that a fact" types of questions. If you're not paying attention, you'll be trapped out on the limb, while the lawyer deftly saws it off behind you. So listen carefully to each question. And just because the lawyer is smiling pleasantly, don't drop your guard; watch out for the saw in his back pocket.

If you're in the habit of using expressions such as "I believe," or "I think," when you testify, a lawyer may try to catch you by getting you to admit that "you're really not sure." He might go a step further, with this sort of approach:

"Q. Are you willing to swear, Mr. Jones, that what you say is exactly the way it happened?"

Don't let this upset you. Remember, you were sworn to tell the truth at the very beginning of your testimony. You can remind the lawyer, gently, that you're swearing to all the answers you've given.

Part of the power of cross-examination consists of the lawyer's right to ask "leading questions." These are questions that suggest the desired answer. For instance, on direct examination, where leading questions are ordinarily not permitted, a lawyer might ask:

"Q. How far away was the other automobile when you heard the horn?" [Note: this question assumes that you have already testified that you did, in fact, hear a horn.]

But on cross-examination, he could "lead," and ask:

"Q. The other automobile was a car-length away when you heard the horn, isn't that true?"

There are a few trick questions lawyers sometimes ask, that you need to be leery of. One is, "Who have you discussed this case with?" The inference here is that you've gone all around town broadcasting your story. A witness instinctively reacts to this by trying to cover up, and might answer, "Nobody." This is obviously not true, since he's almost certainly talked to the other lawyer, at least, and probably his family. If you're asked this question, answer it truthfully. "I've talked to Mr. Smith's attorney. I also mentioned it to my wife, and to my supervisor when I told him I had to come to court."

You can also get backed into a corner if anything in your deposition (see Section B) differs from your courtroom testimony. You might feel there's not too much chance of that, but it happens with amazing frequency, sometimes even over immaterial matters. And once the cross-examiner catches you in a contradiction, you can look awfully foolish unless you know how to answer.

It can go something like this:

> "Q. Mr. Jones, isn't it true that you didn't notice what color the traffic light was until after the cars collided?
>
> "A. No, that's not correct.
>
> "Q. You saw the light before?
>
> "A. Well, right at the same time as the impact.
>
> "Q. At the exact same time?
>
> "A. Right."

(He's laid the trap. Then he refers to the deposition.)

> "Q. Mr. Jones, do you remember testifying at your deposition last December 15th, in the Loophole Building?
>
> "A. Yes.
>
> "Q. And the other lawyer, Mr. Brown, and the court reporter were there, and I asked you questions?
>
> "A. I remember.
>
> "Q. And you swore to tell the truth?
>
> "A. (Now getting a little nervous) Yes.
>
> "Q. And do you remember my asking you these questions on page 10, and your giving these answers:
>
>> 'Q. When did you notice the traffic light?
>>
>> 'A. Well, right after the crash.
>>
>> 'Q. You didn't notice the color until after the cars collided?
>>
>> 'A. That's right. They crashed, then I looked at the light.'
>
> "Q. Do you remember that, Mr. Jones?
>
> "A. I guess so.
>
> "Q. We're not here to guess, Mr. Jones. At the time of your deposition, you said you didn't see the light until *after* the crash.
>
> "A. Well—
>
> "Q. And today you tell us that's not correct.
>
> "A. Well, it all happened pretty fast.

"Q. Were you lying then, Mr. Jones, or are you lying now?"

This can be fairly devastating to an unprepared witness. There isn't any perfect way out. About the best you can do is to answer something like this:

"A. I wasn't lying either time. The accident happened. I saw the light. If any time passed, it was a fraction of a second."

Sometimes your answer will be materially different from what you said at the deposition, or from an earlier written statement you may have given. You may be tempted to deny entirely that you made the earlier statement; but this would be a mistake. The opposing lawyer will usually be able to prove that you did, in fact, make the statement. He'll either call the court reporter to testify from his notes, or put in other proof. If you're certain you couldn't possibly have said it—and this is rare—you can deny it. But normally your best approach is to say something like this, if the previous statement now seems wrong to you: "It's possible I did say that, but I must have misunderstood you." Or if you couldn't have misunderstood under any circumstances (such as where the original question was repeated two or three times), you might try: "I believe I might have said that, but if I did, I was mistaken." This makes you vulnerable to being discredited, but you don't have much alternative. You might be able to add something like: "I've thought about this quite a bit since then [or "I've gone over this several times since"] and I'm sure now that it happened as I've just said."

The opposing lawyer won't give up easily on this. He might ask:

"Q. But you know you were under oath when you made the statement at your deposition, isn't that right? And now you say you really weren't telling the truth?"

(Again, you have to make the best of a bad situation. Your answer might be:)

"A. I was telling the truth to the best of my ability. But I believe now that I was mistaken."

What should you do when just the opposite situation occurs? (That is, you've just testified to a certain fact, but your attention is unceremoniously called to an earlier contradiction; and you quickly realize your prior statement was probably correct.) Your answer would follow these lines:

> "A. I'm sorry. I believe my earlier statement was correct."

G. Things Not To Say Or Do

Even the best and most articulate witness will sometimes give the wrong answer or contradict himself. So you can't expect to get by without some mistakes. But there are certain things you should try to avoid when testifying, if at all possible.

In an accident case, don't mention insurance. Most drivers, of course, are insured; but in the overwhelming majority of American courts, this fact isn't permitted to be called to the jury's attention. Why? Because the courts feel that this could influence the jurors to bring in an improper verdict, basing it not on the evidence, but on the theory that "the insurance company can afford to pay it." Many judges will declare a mistrial if any reference to insurance is discussed in the jury's presence. So stay away from mentioning it, and don't refer to an insurance agent or adjuster.

Try not to testify about what someone else said or told you unless you're asked. This "hearsay evidence" (see Section C) is ordinarily not proper testimony, except in special circumstances. One major exception is that you can testify what was said by one of the parties to the case. But don't say what some third person told you.

Avoid being put in the position of calling anybody a liar, even if your testimony is exactly the opposite to what another witness has said. You'll find that what you remember can be quite different from what another witness recalls about the same event. You might even be contradicting what a policeman says about the case. The opposing lawyer will stare at you coldly, and may ask:

> "Q. Mr. Jones, you've just testified the light was green. But the policeman said, under oath, it was red. Are you saying he's a liar, Mr. Jones?"

(You should answer, to this effect:)

"A. No, sir. But I think he must be mistaken here, because the light was green."

Don't be pinned into saying:

"A. Well, he sure must be lying if he says it was red."

Once you get talked into accusing someone of lying, then your value as a witness is materially reduced. The jury, in fact, may have believed the other witness; or they may feel that they now have to decide between "you and him." This is an unhealthy situation. Don't allow yourself to be dragged into it.

Try not to make jokes on the witness stand. You may be the life of the party, and a regular panic at the bowling alley. But restrain yourself. The courtroom isn't the place for wisecracks by witnesses.

Don't chew gum. And never respond to a question by shaking your head; always give an audible answer.

Unless the question is specifically asked, don't mention that anybody was arrested. A ticket may have been given to one of the drivers in an accident, but this doesn't necessarily mean he's guilty, and you shouldn't voluntarily bring up the ticket or the arrest. In fact, even if the driver was found guilty, this might not always be admissible against him in a claim for damages.

Don't let your answers ramble or become a "narration." Answer the question that's asked; then stop.

Don't offer your opinion unless you're asked for it. The general rule—except for expert witnesses—is that opinions aren't allowed. In some circumstances, they're permitted, such as when testifying about distances, time, speed, drunkenness, or mental condition. But basically, you should confine your answer to facts—what you saw or know.

Try not to answer a question by saying to the cross-examiner, "I don't think that's any of your business." If he's hitting around on confidential matters, you have the right to turn to the judge and ask if you're required to answer. But don't do this unless it's absolutely necessary. And don't answer a question *with* a question, unless you weren't sure what was asked.

At times, you'll feel you'd like to make some notes of what you'll say at the trial, or you'd like to bring some kind of memorandum with you. Basically, there's nothing illegal about this. You're usually allowed to refresh your recollection from any kind of document. But don't just *read* from the paper or keep referring to it constantly. If you do, you can expect an objection. In some cases, if you have no independent memory of an event, a written record might be admissible. But certain special prerequisites have to be met.

Sometimes you'll be asked, on cross-examination, whether you've been paid to come to court to testify. This is a trick question. It's asked with an obvious insinuation that you're being paid for your testimony. If you've received compensation, either as an expert, or because you had to miss work, your answer may sound like you've been bought—and this is exactly the implication that's intended. But don't lie about it. You should answer truthfully, without saying you've been "paid to testify." Say, instead, that you're being paid for your time in court, and for the time you've lost from work.

If you happen to be friendly to one of the parties to the case, the opposing counsel may try to infer that you're slanting the truth to help your friend. It's probable that you'll be asked how long you've known him, and how well. But watch out for the baited question:

"Q. And of course, you want to see him win."

If you answer "yes," your effectiveness is diminished. If you say "no," the jury knows you're lying. Your answer may be corny, but it's about the only one you can give. It'll be something like:

"A. I only want to see that the truth is told and that justice is done."

H. "Perry Mason"

Movies, plays and TV have glamourized courtroom trials so that each case seems sensational and suspenseful. But only a handful of cases are that dramatic in real life. The day-to-day trial docket of a court consists of breach of contract suits, routine automobile accidents, collection of debts, and other ordinary legal matters.

And if you picture every trial lawyer as a Perry Mason—brilliant, smooth, quick-witted, a master of courtroom strategy and tactics, armed with a warehouse of information on every witness, from his conception to his bathroom habits—you're in for a letdown. There are, unfortunately, very few Perry Masons. From time to time, you'll read about spectacular victories by famous, flamboyant lawyers. But these are the rare exceptions. The average trial will match hardworking and conscientious lawyers, but you'll find that they're human. They lose cases, and they make errors.

So don't be overawed by the courtroom. If you're going to be a witness, it'll be an interesting experience for you. Be natural and don't be afraid. Try to be yourself. Answer the question that's asked. Tell the truth. And don't worry. Chances are, you'll do fine.

CHAPTER 9

So The State Wants Your Property

THE RIGHT TO HOLD PRIVATE PROPERTY IS GENERALLY CONSIDERED "basic" in our society. As long as you don't bother or annoy the fellow next door, you're supposed to be able to do just about anything you want to with your property. Suppose, in reliance on this, you buy a piece of land, build your dream house, and move in. You plan to spend the rest of your days there, contentedly rocking away on the front porch, peacefully minding your own business. And no power on earth can make you move.

No power, that is, except the government. If you happen to be in the way of a proposed new super highway, or you're smack in the middle of a planned school, then your days are numbered. No matter how long you've been living there (subject to unusual exceptions in a few states), or how much money you've invested, if a "public use" is involved, and the state wants your property, you can be made to move.

How can this happen? Through one of the oldest and most fundamental powers of government—the right of eminent domain.

A. Eminent Domain: What Is It?

Eminent domain is the right of the state, or other governmental body, to take private property for a public use. It's also called "condemnation," although that term sometimes is used in a much narrower sense to cover situations where a piece of property fails to meet health or building requirements. The power is said to be inherent in government, and has been in existence for centuries. In fact, the ancient Romans built their roads and aqueducts by taking private property.

With the beginning of modern times, the rights of the individual grew in importance, but they still yielded to the paramount right of the state. Under our present federal and state constitutions, though, when property is taken, the owner must be paid "just compensation" for it, and the taking must be done through "due process of law."

What is "just compensation"? This means the owner is entitled to adequate payment, usually measured by the fair market value of the property. This sounds simple enough, but it isn't. For instance, do you have to value the property based on its present use, or can you consider other more profitable prospects? The general rule is that the "highest and best use" of the property can be considered, as long as there's a likelihood it can be used within a reasonable time. But the courts won't allow you to completely speculate. Take a vacant tract of land, that you're not making any use of at all. But you feel that it could be subdivided and adapted for home sites. How do you value it? If, in fact, there are homes fairly near you, and it's reasonable that you could develop the property for houses, you'd probably be entitled to value it for that purpose, but as a whole tract. On the other hand, you haven't actually divided the land, or done anything to establish a subdivision. So you wouldn't be permitted to show the value of *each lot* in the proposed subdivision. The courts say that would be going too far, and such evidence would be considered speculative.

Eminent domain must also take place through "due process of law." This requires a fair procedure, with a reasonable opportunity to be heard and to present evidence. There are basically two methods by which your property can be taken. The first is by the vote or resolution of some administrative board or "condemning authority," who then files the appropriate papers with the county recording office or registry of deeds. At the same time, the condemning authority offers to pay the owner a specified value for the property, or deposits the amount in court. Through this system, there's no actual court proceeding, unless you decide you're unhappy with the amount, or you challenge the board's right to take your property. In that case, you'd bring an action to contest it.

The second, and more common method of eminent domain, is by judicial proceeding. A petition is filed in court by the condemning body, requesting that the court determine the right to take the property, and the compensation to be paid. Everybody that has an interest in the property is notified. There's a hearing, before the judge, to decide whether the property can be legally taken. The procedure isn't the same in all states, but the valuation is then determined by appraisers, commissioners, or by a jury, appointed for that purpose.

B. Can You Stop Them from Taking Your Property?

It's not only the "state" that can take your property. By statute in most places, various agencies of the government are given the power of eminent domain—school boards, cities, highway departments, and others. In fact, under special conditions, even certain private corporations, such as utilities and railroads, are given the power to take private property. So somewhere along the way, there's a good chance that your property, or part of it, will be taken by "condemnation."

Can you do anything about it, to stop it? Every once in a while, you'll read an article in the paper about some hardy soul who tried to hold off the might of an entire state with a shotgun, and refused to leave his homestead. But sooner or later, he has to give in. As long as the condemnation is for a "public purpose," then the state's rights are superior.

Suppose, though, that you don't agree it's a public purpose at all, or you feel the state has picked a bad spot for its new road. What can you do?

Several years back, the traditional concept of a public use was fairly narrow; it had to be for a structure or facility open to the general public, or for carrying on a governmental purpose—such as a post-office, courthouse, road, or school. But lately, in many places, there's a trend toward a broader definition, so that the power of eminent domain is now used for "community betterment," or for developing public resources, for conservation, or for "public improvement."

If you feel that your property won't meet even these liberal tests, or won't be used for a legitimate public purpose, you still have the right to dispute it in court. If the court finds that a genuine public purpose is being served, condemnation will be upheld. For instance, slum clearance has been approved as a proper project for eminent domain, as long as the proposed taking and improvements have a direct connection with public health or safety. But in one case in Massachusetts, the court wouldn't approve an attempt to condemn a large tract of vacant land outside a densely populated city, to be used to sell low-cost building sites to workers. Even though the buyers would be leaving overcrowded city tenements, the court felt that any public benefit was too indirect.

Historically, parks, public buildings and harbors have been considered proper uses for eminent domain. To illustrate how times change, let's consider the case of a library. Although there wouldn't be too much question nowadays that it's for a public purpose, in at least one old case, a court found that a library wasn't a necessary public building, and rejected condemnation for such use.

In recent years, eminent domain for public electricity and water uses has been approved. Drainage and filling of wet and swampy lands that are a danger to community health, have also been upheld. Most places, in addition, allow flood control and irrigation projects as "public uses."

In fact, the purposes that have been permitted are practically endless. You'll have a formidable task convincing a court, these days, that the proposed use isn't a public one. But if you really feel it isn't, then you have the right to litigate it in court.

Don't confuse "public use," though, with the question of whether the use is a wise one, or practical, or even whether it's essential. On these issues, the modern courts usually draw a line, and won't get themselves involved. Once the purpose is found to be a "public" one, the judge ordinarily won't be concerned with the wisdom or desirability of it.

The situation could come up this way. Say the state built a highway a few years ago, about a mile from you. Now they decide to build another road, running parallel with the first one, right across your property. You holler that they don't need a new highway; that the spot they're picking is plain stupid; and that the whole project is a waste of taxpayers' money. Save your breath. You won't have a chance. Your only real hope is to convince the state road department, or whoever is in charge of the project, that they're making a mistake. But once the decision is made, the court will almost always go along with it, since a public purpose is present.

C. Should You Take What You're Offered?

Either before the formal condemnation proceeding starts, or after it's voted upon—depending on the procedure used—you'll be offered a sum of money for your property. If you feel the amount is fair, then you'll accept it. But the main point to know is that you don't have to take what you're offered.

Remember that according to the law you're entitled to be fairly compensated. Just because some representative of the state says they'll pay you $3,000 for your property doesn't mean that's a fair price, or that you should jump at it without a second thought. You have the right to have the value determined as provided by the law of your state.

In several jurisdictions, a jury will decide the question of ''just compensation.'' In Florida, for example, a jury of 12 persons determines all disputes about the value of the property (the number of jurors is particularly significant, and is a recognition of the importance of condemnation in Florida, since in all other jury cases in that state—except those punishable by death—only six jurors are used). Not every state, though, requires a jury trial. In many places, it's customary to have property valued by three or more commissioners, ''viewers,'' or appraisers. There are certain procedural safeguards that have to be followed, but in the states adopting this method, a jury trial isn't used. Doesn't the U. S. Constitution guarantee a trial by jury in all cases? Contrary to popular opinion, the answer is no. The rule is that a state can't cut off the right to a jury trial if that right existed when a state's constitution was adopted. But many states didn't provide for a jury in condemnation cases when their constitutions were passed; so in those places, the value will be decided by the commissioners or appraisers.

This doesn't mean, though, that you're stopped from submitting evidence of the true value of your property. In every state, you have the right to show the damage you've suffered.

How do you do this? Principally through the testimony and opinions of witnesses. You'd ordinarily rely on persons who are experts in real estate values, and are used to dealing with property—such as realtors, tax assessors, and land appraisers.

But in most states, you're not limited to this kind of testimony. Many courts allow nonexpert witnesses to testify, if they live nearby or work in the vicinity and are familiar with property values in the area. As a matter of fact, in some cases, the best witness you can get will be a longtime resident of the neighborhood, who thoroughly knows the section and its physical surroundings, and is well acquainted with land values there.

In the majority of situations, the owner of the land is also entitled to give his opinion of the value. Sometime this won't carry much weight, but if you're a sincere witness, and can testify about the characteristics and improvements on your property, you might be able to get substantially more than the first offer. Let's say you have an old house, being acquired for a road right-of-way. It might even look like all the other houses in the neighborhood; but if you know that you recently put in new bathroom fixtures, panelling in the den, and central heating, and just finished painting the entire inside, you're in a good position to convince the jury or commissioners that your property is worth much more than the average house on the block.

D. Do You Need an Appraisal?

What should you do when you really don't have the slightest idea how much your mansion is worth? Maybe you've lived there for years, gradually improved the house, and carefully kept it repaired. The state now tells you it's worth $50,000 and they offer you that figure. But how do you really know whether that's fair? In the typical case, you don't. You'll need to talk to a real estate broker or appraiser. Many realtors are qualified to give you a fair valuation of your property. Find out, first, though, what they'll charge you for this advice. You'll find, sad to say, that most of them aren't really used to appearing as witnesses, or testifying in court. So right at the start you ought to check to see if they'd agree to give testimony at the trial or hearing. If they won't, or if they tell you that they seldom do, then you'll need to look further.

In most parts of the country, you'll be able to contact professional real estate appraisers. These are people who are specially trained to value property. Most of them have taken courses in appraising techniques and principles, and have several years of practical experience, in valuing properties for estates, banks, and governmental bodies. Ordinarily, they're members of one of the national appraising organizations, such as the Society of Real Estate Appraisers (S.R.E.A.), American Society of Appraisers (A.S.A.), or Member, American Institute of Real Estate Appraisers (M.A.I.).

In addition, most of these appraisers are veterans of the courtroom. They're frequently called as witnesses, and know how to present and document their opinions. If you're able to hire one of these appraisers to help you, do it.

A typical appraiser's checklist is shown at the end of the chapter.

But look out for one sticky problem. If you're not familiar with an appraiser's fees, you can end up with a hefty charge and not even get any real benefit out of it. Suppose, for example, you're trying to decide whether the state's $50,000 offer is fair. You hire an appraiser. He studiously measures your house and grounds, inspects the attic, checks under the house, meticulously compares other sale prices in the neighborhood. He takes several photographs, scrupulously analyzes market conditions, and presents you with a scholarly written report of several pages. His conclusion: take the $50,000.

And then he hands you his bill, which can run anywhere from $150 to several hundred bucks. Obviously, he's earned his fee. But you'll probably never use the appraisal, and you'll have difficulty getting reimbursed by the state (although you have an outside chance at it; see Section G). How do you protect yourself? Simply by asking the appraiser to first give you a preliminary or tentative valuation, in oral form. Most appraisers will be willing to let you have a "rough" verbal estimate, for a nominal fee (usually about $75; some won't even charge at all), to let you know the probable range of their valuation. If their opinion turns out close to the state's offer, then you won't need any formal or detailed report, and you're out of pocket only the seventy-five dollars or so. On the other hand, if the appraiser tells you his estimate would probably run around $60,000 or more, then you'd undoubtedly tell him to go ahead with his final report (again, though, find out what his charge will be).

Be leery of the so-called expert appraiser who tells you his fee will depend on the outcome of the case, or how much more he can get for you. This may sound all right in theory, but a reputable appraiser won't accept the case this way (except in very unusual circumstances), so steer clear of this approach.

Once you get the appraiser's opinion, if it's helpful to you, you ordinarily won't be interested in getting a second one. But if there's a great deal of money involved, and the state's estimate is way out of line, you might be willing to invest in another appraisal. This is frequently done with valuable commercial property.

When you have the appraisal, what's the next step? If the figure is close to the state's offer—within a few hundred dollars or thereabouts—you might be able to negotiate a little with the condemning agency. Most of the state's agents will claim that they're not allowed to haggle, but in many cases they're given at least a 10% leeway for bargaining, and often more. This may not be enough in your particular case, but if you're willing to settle for an additional 10%, you can probably get it. You'll find that the state's agent generally has some margin to negotiate because he knows it'll cost them money to fight in court.

If you're too far apart, you're probably not going to get any place bargaining, and you'll need to let the jury or commissioners decide.

In some jurisdictions, there's another tactic that can help you. Ask the state's representative to furnish you with a copy of their appraisal. In several states, you won't be allowed to look at it, but a number of places permit you to have a copy. This can be of invaluable help to you and your appraiser; and can supply you with key information in court, as a starting point, to challenge the state's offer. Otherwise, without the government's appraisal, you're stabbing in the dark, and it's harder to discredit their valuation.

E. What Damages Can You Claim?

In theory, you're entitled to all the damages you incur from the taking of your property. Or to put it another way, the amount you're paid is supposed to place you in the same position that you were in before the condemnation, so that you suffer no loss. But there are so many exceptions to this rule that it really doesn't mean what it says.

As a basic proposition, you're entitled to be paid for two main items: the fair market value of what's taken, and for damage caused to the "remainder," or the part of the property that's not taken.

Market value is generally defined as the price that a willing seller and a willing buyer would agree on, in the open market, if both had full knowledge of the uses of the property. This isn't so simple to apply to a given case, though, since there's no common trading place for a piece of real estate, as there is for stocks, bonds, and other commodities. Entire books have been written on methods of determining market value, and various approaches are used. Two of them are the "cost approach" and the "income approach."

These are fairly technical processes, and are beyond the scope of this chapter.

The property is usually valued as a whole; that is, the land, the buildings, fixtures, crops, lumber and minerals, are all considered together, rather than as separate units.

Also, even though several people might have an interest in the property—such as tenants, or mortgagees—the value is determined as an entirety; then later, the various claims are decided (a tenant is usually entitled to some damages, unless the lease provides otherwise).

The key date for determining value is the date of the "taking" by the government. At times, even this can cause an argument. To illustrate, assume that your house is badly in need of an extra bedroom. You know that a road is being proposed, and that your property will be taken. But you don't know when. You're reluctant to put in money to add to the house, since the state will be tearing it down soon. Finally, after waiting several months, you spend five thousand dollars, adding the room. The next day, condemnation is filed by the state, and your house is taken. As of what date will your property be valued? The condemning authority will argue that since you knew about the road, you shouldn't be paid for improvements that you voluntarily made, after finding out. But you're safe. As long as you acted in good faith, you're entitled to be paid for the value of the property, as of the date of "taking"—which would include the new room.

Suppose though, the state announces it plans to take your property; but then it does nothing for several months. In the meantime, because of the premature announcement, your property might decline in value, since it's now unsuitable for sale or long-term lease. Any remedy? Yes, in a few states, notably New York, Michigan and Ohio. Recently the courts there have allowed damages to the owner.

What about business on your property? Are you entitled to be reimbursed for a loss when you're forced to close down? Generally, no. The courts have ruled that injury to a business isn't an appropriation of property that allows you to be paid. So in the average case, if you lose profits, or are inconvenienced by having to move to a new location, you're out of luck. Fortunately, in a number of states, either by statute or court ruling, a different result is followed, and some allowance is given under certain conditions. And a recent federal law provides payment for some of this loss if a federal-aid highway project is involved.

In addition to receiving the fair market value of property taken, you're also allowed compensation for "severance" damage—a loss caused to the rest of your property when only part of it is taken. Here's a typical case: you have a lot that's 200 feet deep; you built your house 100 feet from the front, far enough back so that traffic and noise won't bother you too much. Now the state decides to take the front 90 feet to widen the road. This leaves you only a hop-and-a-skip from the right-of-way, 10 feet back. What are your damages? There's no question about your right to be paid for the 90 feet that's taken. But how about the part you're left with? Instead of privacy, far from the road, the cars are almost on top of your front door, with dust, fumes, and screeching of tires. This is where severance damage comes in. You'd be permitted to show, by testimony, that the value of the rest of your property has now decreased substantially.

The severance damage to the balance of your property can be caused by a wide variety of situations. A few of them are:

1. Leaving the remainder in a distorted shape.
2. Allowing you too small a remainder for any practical use.
3. Cutting off access to a road or railroad.
4. Damaging the water supply of the remainder.
5. Causing an obstruction to view.
6. Increasing the danger to life and property.
7. Requiring fencing of the remainder.

How do you actually determine severance damage in dollars and cents? There are two methods most commonly used by appraisers:

1. The "before-and-after" rule. The expert decides on the value of the *entire* property before the taking, and the value afterwards. The difference between the two would represent "just compensation"—being the value of the part taken plus severance damages.

2. The "modified before-and-after" rule. Under this approach, only the *remainder* is valued before and after the taking. The difference between the two figures is then added to the value of the part taken.

Suppose that even though your remaining property is being damaged, you're also greatly benefited at the same time; for instance, by the state turning the old dirt road in front of your property into a well-paved highway. How far can these benefits be considered in determining fair compensation to you? Local rules differ on this point. In a few states, these benefits are immaterial, and can't be considered against you. But in other places, some of the benefits to you can be offset and deducted from the severance damages you're claiming. This doesn't mean, however, that all benefits can be set off. The courts distinguish between "general" benefits (those that improve the whole community or neighborhood) and "special" benefits (those that are particularly beneficial to *your* property). The prevailing rule is that only special benefits can be deducted from the damages you claim.

How can you tell the difference between the two kinds of benefits? If everybody in the area is getting approximately the same advantage—such as through paving, utility lines, or improved water supply—then it's a "general" benefit. But if the service or improvement is primarily helping *you*, or one or two of your neighbors, such as through facilities for entering and leaving your land, or special drainage or sanitation, then it's a "special" benefit.

F. What Can't You Claim?

Once the state takes your property, you'll be faced with various types of expenses and losses. Many of them, you'll find, aren't recoverable in most locales.

If your losses are uncertain, remote, or speculative, you'll have trouble claiming them anywhere. Take a case where you raise horses. The road department widens the highway, causing more traffic to travel in front of your property. You'd like to get damages because of the probability that your horses will be frightened by the cars. It won't hurt to try, but don't make any bets on your chances.

Neither can you make any claim for "sentiment." Some owners, when cross-examined about how they arrived at their valuation, are tricked into admitting that they considered sentimental value. This isn't a proper measure of damages.

Another expense that usually has been rejected is the cost of moving. In the past few years, a number of states have adopted rules permitting such expense, particularly when urban renewal occurs; and a recent federal law now provides "relocation expense" in some cases. Personal inconvenience, annoyance, and time you might lose from work are still nonrecoverable.

A common complaint by owners, especially in crowded cities, is that once they're forced to move, they're unable to find comparable houses or business sites. Many states have liberalized their rules on this type of damage, and the new federal law also gives considerable relief.

Can you claim damages if traffic is re-routed or diverted away from your property? As a rule, no. Although there are a few exceptions, the prevailing view is that this isn't a "taking," and that the government has the right to change the flow of vehicles as is necessary, and to establish one-way streets, center strips, and traffic control, as needed. If this sort of regulation causes a loss to you, you won't be able to recover, in the majority of jurisdictions where the point has been raised. The theory is that the state owes you no duty to see that the public travels past your door. A typical case arose in Georgia. A meat-packing plant, adjoining a highway, had a truck-loading platform attached to its building. The state highway department built a curb that prevented trucks from backing up to the platform. The court held that the installation was proper for traffic control, and that the owner wasn't entitled to damages.

In another case, a gas station owner argued that his business dropped because a new main highway was built a few blocks away. He lost.

Note, though, that if a street is completely closed, so that you can't even get in or out of your property at all, then you'll be allowed damages. Also, there are a few cases in some jurisdictions, that have adopted a minority view, and have held that even diminished traffic *can* be considered as an element of loss in measuring severance damages, when part of your property is taken.

G. Can You Get Your Attorney's Fees and Costs?

If you decide to challenge the amount that's offered to you for your property, it's likely you'll incur some costs, such as the expense of a survey, appraisal, and attorney's fees. Which of these can you get back?

Although it may not seem fair, the answer depends on which state you happen to be in. The courts are divided on the question of allowing recovery of such costs. In some states, like Florida, all of an owner's expenses, within reason, must be paid by the condemning authority. So you'd be reimbursed for a survey, the cost of an appraisal, and the appraiser's fee for testifying in court—all of which can run up into high numbers. On top of that, the court would order the state to pay a reasonable fee to your lawyer.

But very few states are that liberal. In several places, although the costs of the proceedings are not supposed to be charged against an owner, you'd have to pay the fees of any expert witnesses you call. And in the great majority of states, you'd have to take care of your own legal charges.

H. Should You Go to Court?

When all is said and done, you'll still need to decide the basic question: are they paying you the legitimate value of the property? Or to put it bluntly, are you getting a fair shake?

If you've had the property appraised, and know pretty well what it's worth, you're in a position to weigh whether you should go to court, or whatever other route is authorized in your state. In some cases, it's not worth fighting. If just a small strip is being taken, and you're not really damaged, you'll probably save a lot of headaches by accepting what's offered (usually a few hundred dollars). Don't give in, though, without at least one swing at trying to get them to raise the ante.

If your state doesn't allow fees or costs, then you'll need to decide how good your prospects are for getting substantially more than the offer. Let's say that the state tells you your house is worth $50,000, and your appraiser says $90,000. Then you have a good opportunity of getting a $70,000 verdict (juries are prone to "split the difference," in many cases). So even if you have to lay out several hundred dollars in costs in a situation such as this, it's worthwhile. But if your expert witness will testify the property's value is only $53,000, then it generally won't be practical to get wrapped up in long drawn-out litigation, especially if you're going to be hit with the costs. At the other end of the line, if you're in a state like Florida, where costs and legal fees are awarded to an owner, you'll almost always come out ahead by going to court. In effect, you can have your cake and eat it too. The state makes its offer, and usually sticks to that figure (except in rare cases of mistake). The jury then has to allow you *at least* that amount. And you have a strong possibility of coming out with considerably more, if the jury believes your evidence. Then too, you get your costs and legal fees.

So do some legwork (the simplest way is to call a lawyer) to find out if you can recover your costs and expenses, in your state. If you can, then you shouldn't hesitate in going to court.

If you can't get all the costs, see which ones you *are* allowed. If you'll have to absorb most of them, you'll need to carefully consider what your chances are of winning more than you're offered, based on the market value of the property and any severance damages (see Section E).

Even when you don't want to spend money for expert witnesses and appraisals, you might decide to just testify yourself, and give your own estimate of value (see Section D). It sometimes works out quite well. And like they say, you can't blame a guy for trying.

Form 1

APPRAISER'S CHECKLIST

Parcel No.   Type of Building
Owner's Name:
Address:

Quality of construction:
Age of Building: Condition: No. of Rooms:
No. of Bedrooms: No. of Baths:
Utilities Available:
Water .... Gas .... Electric .... Sewer ....
Type of Street: Land Drainage:

Foundation: Sills: Floor Joists:
Wall: Studs: Trim:
Rafters: Roofing: Condition:
Sub-Floors: Fin. Floors:
Painting: Inside: Outside:
Plumbing Fixtures:
Bath Finish:

Heating and cooling: Windows:
Type of cabinets: Closet Space:
Doors: Miscellaneous:
Privacy:
Wiring:

Other remarks:

Outbuildings: Porches:
Garage: Carport:
Walks: Drives:
Fences: Landscaping:

Other:

CHAPTER 10

So You're Having Work Done On Your House

PEOPLE ARE FUNNY. A WOMAN WILL CAREFULLY CHECK THE FOOD ads and shop at three different stores to save a few cents when she goes to buy her groceries. Or a man might drive ten miles out of his way if the filling station at the other end of town is having a gas war. In brief, everybody loves a bargain.

But when it comes to having some repairs or remodeling done to a house, the average homeowner suddenly loses all perspective, and acts as though he just "got off the boat." He forgets all the rules of prudent investment and money management, and is ripe for fleecing by one of the biggest and sleaziest gyps of them all— the home-repair racket.

In almost every part of the country, smooth-talking contractors and their salesmen have set up shop, usually operating just within the boundary of the law, but bilking the innocent and unsuspecting of millions of dollars each year. They make the rounds of the poorer neighborhoods, or use "bait" ads as a come-on to lure the gullible homeowner. Often they'll tell you that your house has been selected as a "model," for advertising purposes, and that you'll pay only a fraction of the cost of the work. Or they'll promise you a handsome rebate or commission for every prospect whose name you furnish them. But most of the time it turns out you're being charged far more than the value of the repairs or that when you're ready to collect the commission, the salesman is no longer with the company, or the company isn't even in business anymore.

You've been had.

Before you agree to anything, there are certain minimum safeguards you should *always* take. The most fundamental—and the one most often violated—is: never sign a paper of *any kind* until you know exactly what you're committing yourself to, and who it is you're dealing with.

A. Is the Contractor Reliable?

Once you decide you can use some remodeling of your house, or some major repairs, the first step is to pick a contractor. Certainly, not every home improvement company is unreliable or disreputable; but there are enough rotten apples in the barrel so that you better look carefully for the worm before you chew.

The best way to pick a contractor is through the recommendation of someone you can rely on. A neighbor or relative might have recently had some work done. Sometimes your banker or lawyer can give you the names of a few of the better builders.

But there are certain types of "contractors" you should avoid. Like vermin, they thrive in run-down neighborhoods, but they can also move into the better-class sections. Keep an eye out for the salesman who makes contact with you by phone, unsolicited. You can expect him to be glib and fast-talking (probably from making the same phony pitch so often), and tell you about their "specials," or "free offers," or once-a-year discounts. The reputable dealers have enough business so that they don't need to use this approach. But the shadier operators frequently use a "boiler room" technique, with half a dozen or more telephones set up in an office or hotel room for contacting "leads" and other prospects, to sell them a quick bill of goods. As a general rule, stay away from the phone-call offer, especially if it sounds too good to be true. If the caller says a salesman will be around to see you, tell him you're not interested. And hang up.

Closely related to the telephone gimmick is the door-to-door con artist. He rings your bell and tells you your house has been picked as a special advertising model, in a get-acquainted promotional campaign, and all you pay is "half the cost," or some other fictitious amount. A variation of this is to promise you a price reduction for any sales made to people who visit your house.

Occasionally you'll be offered a gift just for "letting me talk to you." Sometimes they'll use a direct approach and tell you they can save you money or repair costs if you act "now." Another technique is the phony claim that the salesman represents a famous national company (don't believe it; call their local office to find out). Still another scheme is the fake "inspector" who says he's checking for the "city"; he'll always find some defect, and then offer to have it fixed for you at a "good price."

More often than not, the salesman will be clean-cut and well-dressed. His sincerity and good manners are artfully contrived so that you'll lower your guard. But don't. If you haven't the willpower to close the door, then at least insist that he give you a list of other jobs he's done in the neighborhood. If he tells you that yours is the first they've selected, this is a sure tip-off. In case he does have a list of names, advise him that you'll think it over and let him know. Under no circumstances should you ever allow yourself to sign a "proposal" or any other papers, no matter how innocent-looking, without inquiring further. It can turn out to be a binding contract or mortgage.

Always find out the address of the contractor, and whether he's local. If he's operating out of another city, don't do business with him. You'll have an impossible time getting him to come back if you need any "touch-up" work, or if his repairs are defective. If he's from "just across the state line," then you're clearly asking for trouble if you deal with him. Also be suspicious of the guy who gives you only a post office address. If he's reputable, he should at least have an office, A post office box is fine for mail, but if you have a complaint or question, and need to take it up in person with him, you'll have a devil of a time tracking him down (quite often the ones with post office addresses also use telephone answering services, so they can conveniently forget to call you back if they don't want to bother with you after you've paid).

A favorite trick of the home improvement highbinder is to quote you a fantastically low price for the job. If a room addition would cost around $5,000, his price will be maybe $3,200. And he'll "guarantee" it. The temptation will be great. But resist it. He'll either use inferior materials, or he'll tell you later that the price didn't include labor. Or there'll be all kinds of necessary "extras." Or he'll have some other "out." It's true, of course, that even the prices of legitimate dealers will vary somewhat, and some will be lower than the others. And certainly there's nothing wrong with your trying to get the best price. But when the figure you're quoted is *too* far out of line, then you'll probably end up paying more in the long run.

Be sure you know how long the contractor has been in business. If he's only been around a few months, this is a danger sign. Naturally, everybody has to get started somewhere, but don't let him start with *you*. Ask him when he began business, and how long he's been licensed. It's not a bad idea, either, to check the licensing bureau to see if he's really authorized to do business. A great many fly-by-night operators are not.

In many communities, the local chamber of commerce or better business bureau keeps records of complaints and information on various businesses. Call there, and check on your prospective contractor. If there are a number of charges against him, stop right there. You can't afford to gamble with him.

If you've noticed extensive newspaper or mail advertising for a particular company, this isn't necessarily fatal. Many unsavory outfits go in for high budget campaigns, but apparently some of the reputable ones do also. But don't be taken in just because of the ads. Call their office and ask for references. Look over some of the jobs they've done. Talk to a few of their customers. Always try to get at least two other estimates.

More than half the battle is finding a reputable contractor. If it takes some time, it's worth it.

B. The Contract

Most home-improvement builders use a printed "form" contract. The agreement can be heavily weighted against you, and is designed to protect the contractor, not you. So you'll need to look it over carefully. A typical contract, used in many areas, is shown at the end of this chapter as Form 1.

If the contract has any blanks in it, don't sign it. Many salesmen are anxious to "close the deal" and will high-pressure you into signing an incomplete contract on their assurance that "it'll be typed in at the office." But there's no telling what'll be typed in: high interest rates, closing costs, and various other hidden charges. So just tell him politely to bring it back when it's ready for you to sign. And make sure you receive an exact copy of what you sign; that way, they can't add anything to their copy, later, so as to claim it was there all the time.

If you're paying all cash for the job, the ideal way to handle it is to provide in the contract that payment will be made only when the work is fully completed. If your credit is good, and the job is not more than a few thousand dollars, a reputable contractor might allow you to do this. But he might not. It isn't unusual for him to require "progress payments," or "draws," as the work moves along. Typically, he might ask for 25% when he starts; another 25% after he completes a stipulated phase of the work; and the balance as other parts of the job are finished. Be careful, though, about paying anything before the work actually starts. You might never see the salesman again. Also, a few states have rigid requirements that have to be met before you're safe in making the "downpayment." (In Florida, for example, the owner is supposed to file and post a "notice of commencement" before he can pay any money; if he doesn't, then he runs the risk that an unpaid laborer or supplier can file a lien against his property later. See page 300, for protective steps to take.) So it's a wise move to add a provision that no payments are to be made prior to the proper notice being filed and posted as required by law. A form of this type of notice, used in Florida, is shown as Form 2.

You'll also need to be cautious about making the final payment, unless you know that all materials and work have been paid for (see Section F, for what to do).

The contract should specify the total price you're paying for the job. Some builders use two figures: one is the so-called "cash price"; and the other is the "time price," which includes interest and other charges. You can get caught here, if you don't follow exactly what he's doing. If the work is supposed to be $1,800, he'll call this the cash price. But if you're planning to make monthly payments, he'll often add on a batch of other fees and expenses, including life insurance, recording charges, closing costs, plus a high interest rate; and you'll then have the "time price." This can be twice the amount of the cash figure. In the average case, if a homeowner questions it, the salesman produces a mysterious little book which "shows" the figures. Demand that you be given a complete breakdown: precisely how much you're paying for interest—and the rate—the cost of the insurance, and the recording fees. If the amounts are out of proportion, see if you can get financing through your bank (the insurance charge, in particular, is often much higher than you could get on your own). Many home repair jobs can be paid for through a loan insured by the Federal Housing Administration (called a Title I loan). So don't be stampeded into an inflated "time price," just because the salesman presents it to you. Also, you're entitled to a "3-day right of rescission" to cancel the contract, under federal law.

The agreement should also show the amount of your monthly payment, and how long it'll take to pay off. Some owners know they're to pay $60 a month, but have no idea how many years they'll be doing it. There's a particularly slimy practice, followed in a number of places, calling for deceptively low monthly payments, and then a large lump-sum at the end (called a "balloon payment"). The average owner doesn't understand this, and can end up losing his property. So keep your eyes open for the "balloon payment."

If the interest is pre-computed and added to the job price, as is quite common, there should be a provision allowing a rebate if you pay off the contract in advance. This method of "adding-on" interest is frequently used by contractors, but will sky-rocket your interest rate. It works like this. Say your contract is $1,800, and you plan to pay it off in five years. The contractor may tell you he's charging "only" five percent interest per year. But this is misleading. Since it'll take you five years, he tells you, he'll simply multiply five percent by five, which makes 25%. Then he'll figure 25% times the $1,800, and come out with an interest rate of $450. He adds this to the $1,800 contract price, making a neat total of $2,250, which he then divides by the monthly payments for five years (60 months). Result: $37.50 per month. What could be fairer? Anything wrong with it? Only that by using this clever device, he's charging you a true interest rate of about 10% a year, rather than 5%. How can this be? Because he's figuring interest on a constant, unchanging figure of $1,800, for the full five years. But each month you're paying back part of the $1,800, and your balance is being reduced continuously. For example, at the end of four years, you've repaid the majority of the $1,800. But Crafty Charlie, by his "add-on" system, is still charging you interest on the entire $1,800.

The point of the story is this: don't agree to "add-on" interest, unless it's the only possible way you can pay for the repairs. Keep in mind that with this form of interest, you'll actually be paying approximately twice the rate you're quoted (if you're told it's 6%, it'll be nearer to 12%). Instead, you should insist on so-called "simple" interest, which takes into account that as the balance is reduced, the amount of interest is reduced. This is sometimes spoken of as "amortizing" a loan. If you can't tell, from the contractor's figures, what kind of interest you're paying, or the rate, call your bank and talk to the installment loan department, before you sign any papers. They can generally tell you the true interest.

Congress, and several state legislatures, have recently passed legislation requiring fairer disclosures of interest rates and time charges. But there will continue to be abuses, and your best protection is to be aware of what the contractor is doing, and how he's figuring the charges and interest.

The contract should also set out, clearly, the work that's to be done. Too many of these agreements are vague. They'll indicate something like: "Fix porch and repair screens." This won't do you much good if there's any argument. How is the porch to be fixed? What kind of materials? Even worse, when a bigger job is to be done, the contract may read, simply: "Add 9′ × 12′ room on back of house, with panelled walls." But what are the specifications? Have you seen any plans? What type of panelling? This kind of broad language, used in countless home improvement contracts, may work out satisfactorily if you're dealing with a really trustworthy and honest contractor. But if you're not, then the contract is inadequate. You should ask the contractor to list exactly what he proposes to do, and attach a copy of the plans and specifications if remodeling or substantial repairs are being contemplated. If you decide to use an architect, he'll usually protect you on this. But in the ordinary case, you'll be on your own.

It's not a bad idea to have the contract provide that "All workmanship and materials shall be of good quality, and all materials shall be new." The law of your state may raise a presumption about the quality of the work, but it's safer to have it in the contract.

In most cases, the contractor will pay for building permits and licenses. But sometimes, after you've agreed on a price for repairs, a contractor may nonchalantly inform you that there's an extra charge for the permit. To be on the safe side, have the contract recite that he pays for all such documents and building requirements.

You'll also need a provision requiring the contractor to carry insurance. He should have liability coverage and workmen's compensation insurance, and the policy must be broad enough to cover you, as well. Otherwise, you might get stung if somebody is injured during the course of the work. Either have him furnish you a letter from his insurance company confirming the coverage, or a copy of the policy.

If your repairs are minor, you won't be too concerned with

"extras" or "change orders." But if you're remodeling a major part of your house, you'll be vulnerable to charges for extras anytime you make any alteration in the plans. It's advisable to put in the contract that all claims by the contractor for extra costs, or for additional work, must be made in writing, and signed by you. If any changes eliminate labor or materials, then you should be entitled to a credit on the contract price.

A reputable builder will come back and correct any defective work. But as a precaution, insist that this be covered in the contract. The following provision should be sufficient:

> "The contractor shall correct or remedy any work or materials not complying with the contract, and any defects in the construction or repairs, due to workmanship or materials furnished by him, his suppliers, or his subcontractors, which appear within one year from the completion of the work."

Now and then, you'll run into a contractor who starts the work, and then just doesn't finish—either because of financial problems or inefficiency, and sometimes even because of disagreements with your wife! How can you protect yourself? There's no fool-proof way, but it helps to put in the agreement:

> "If the contractor fails to proceed with the work, with reasonable diligence, or fails to perform any term of the contract, then the owner, after 7 days written notice to the contractor, may proceed himself with the work and may deduct the cost thereof from any payments due the contractor; or the owner may terminate the contract, take possession of all materials, tools and appliances, and complete the work. If the expense exceeds the unpaid balance, the contractor shall be liable for the difference."

It's advisable to also add a definite completion date, if this is important to you. If you have to be able to use the new room when the baby comes, then by all means specify a damage clause of a fixed amount per day (say $50) if the work isn't finished on time. Most contractors will not be happy with this type of restriction, so only use it when you really want a deadline.

A few home improvement contracts have a clause protecting the contractor if the owner defaults. This isn't necessarily objectionable, but sometimes it's slanted too heavily against you. One clause, used in certain parts of the country, requires the owner to pay a penalty of 20% of the contract price if he cancels the contract before any work begins. If a provision like this is used (although its validity may be open to question), you ought to be 100% certain you're ready to go ahead, and your financing is lined up, before you put your name on the papers. Some relief has been granted by Congress under a federal statute, passed a few years ago, allowing you three days to rescind any home improvement contract.

You should also know, in advance, what happens if a fire or other disaster destroys the work before it's finished. If you're building on to your existing house, then the regular fire insurance policy you have should be broad enough to cover you (but call your agent, to double-check). If you're adding a separate structure, such as a detached garage, there's a good likelihood you'll still be covered; but ask your agent.

The contract will also specify that when the work is completed you'll be protected from all liens and claims (see page 300).

A suggested form of home improvement contract is shown at the end of this chapter. This is intended for the average home remodeling job, rather than for new construction. For a new building, a commonly used form of contract is that prepared by the American Institute of Architects, reprinted with their permission, as Form 4, at the conclusion of this chapter. Many of the provisions in this kind of agreement are similar to the home repair contract, but there are more details. You'll notice that there are references in the contract to the use of an architect. An appropriate deletion can be made if no architect is employed. Note, also, that there is an optional provision for a bond (see discussion in Section D).

Keep in mind that if you're just having a three or four hundred dollar repair job, with no elaborate renovation, you obviously won't get involved with the type of contract proposed in this section. If you tried to suggest it, the contractor would probably tell you to forget the whole deal. But as the size of the work increases, and the cost goes up, then you need more protection than just a "handshake" or some oral understanding. Form 3 can be a helpful starting place for you, and can be adapted to most situations.

C. Some Things to Avoid

From time to time, you'll bump into a contractor who will try to do you a "favor," he'll say, by preparing a contract with a deliberately fictitious or inflated price. The idea is to mislead a lending institution into giving you more money. Consider a case where an owner would like to put up a $10,000 building or addition; but he knows that the bank will lend him only about 80% of the cost of construction, so that he'd have to lay out the other 20% himself. The contractor may therefore propose inflating the contract price to $12,500, so that now, even with an 80% loan, you'll get the whole $10,000. At best, this is risky and unethical. At worst, it's illegal in several states and can subject you to prosecution for fraud. So don't let yourself be talked into it by a "helpful" contractor.

You should also be careful about so-called "cost-plus" contracts. These are arrangements where the builder agrees to do the work for the cost of his labor and materials, plus a fixed amount—usually 10%—to cover his profit. This sounds good at first blush, but you can quickly drift in over your head. Unless you know, in advance, the actual cost of the labor and material (which is unlikely), it's easy for the contractor to run up a hefty amount of expense. There can also be disagreements about what's included in his "costs." Is insurance included? Overhead? Building permits? It's also not so simple to keep track of all the materials, to be positive they're being used in *your* house. A devious contractor can present bona fide bills to you, showing so many bricks or boards of lumber, but you can't always be certain where he's using them. If you feel you know enough about building materials, or have confidence in your contractor, to justify entering into a "cost-plus" contract, then you should at least have some ceiling on the total cost. Have the agreement provide that your aggregate expenditure won't exceed a certain set amount.

Another danger in building-contracts comes from oral agreements made after you sign the papers. You might have an iron-clad, 60-page written contract, covering every detail from the type of nails, to what happens if the foreman gets indigestion; but even a written contract can be modified or altered by verbal understandings made afterwards. Many an owner has been sued by an unhappy contractor who claimed the written agreement had been changed later. To protect yourself, don't agree to oral modifications, except as to minor and unimportant changes. Insist that there be a signed memorandum or letter, even if it's informal and handwritten. And you should see that the written contract requires all changes or additions to be in writing.

Suppose some "unforeseen conditions" arise during the work, and the contractor demands more money? This can easily happen if the cost of materials is raised drastically, or a labor strike occurs, or there are complications in the actual construction (the ground may be too swampy, the water supply is poor, etc.). Unless the contract makes specific provision for such unforeseen circumstances, the owner normally can't be made to pay any additional money. Sometimes, for the sake of fairness, you'll agree to adjust the price. But don't let the contractor hold you up, or bluff you into it with the threat that he'll walk off the job. Some unsavory contractors make a habit of finding two to three "unforeseen" contingencies on every job they do, and invariably chisel another $200 or $300 from the unsuspecting owner.

D. Should You Require a Bond?

In most large construction projects, it's customary—and some statutes require—that the contractor furnish the owner a surety bond, guaranteeing performance and payment of all bills. If there's a default, or somebody isn't paid, then the bonding company is required to step in and protect you.

Then why not require a bond in every case? Theoretically, you should. But in small repair jobs—the three or four hundred dollar variety—it's not practical or usual. There's also the expense of the bond. The prevailing charge is 1% of the contract price, but it can be much greater, depending on the construction and other circumstances. The contractor will ordinarily expect you to pay for the bond, or will add it to the contract price.

A more serious problem is that some small contractors are not "bondable." This means that either they don't have sufficient assets or collateral to justify such a bond, or they may have had financial reverses in the past. If they can't furnish a bond, this doesn't always mean you should refuse to deal with them. But it does mean you should be a little more cautious. It might be advisable, in such a case, to hold back the payment until the job is completed, and appropriate releases and affidavits are furnished (see Section F).

As a rule of thumb—unless you know that your contractor is financially responsible—it's desirable to require a bond for any repairs over $3,000. If the contract is greater than $10,000, then you shouldn't consider it at all without a bond. You might get by with it three out of four times, and have no difficulty, but you're taking a gamble the fourth time. Without a bond, if the contractor fails to complete the job (for any number of reasons: death, disability, bankruptcy, and so forth), you're wide open to liens, unpaid bills, and potentially a much greater cost if you need to bring in another contractor to finish the work.

Incidentally, when you're furnished with a bond, you better make a note to get the surety company's written consent to any substantial alteration or material modification of the contract. Otherwise, the surety will be released by law, in most places. Ask the surety if they'll require their consent to the changes; if they tell you no, request that they give you a letter to that effect.

Furthermore, if you have a bond, don't let the contractor talk you into making a payment to him before it comes due. In many states, a premature payment will release the surety on the bond.

E. How Can You Protect Yourself Against Liens?

By statute in almost all states, the law gives unpaid laborers, subcontractors, and suppliers the right to enforce payment of their bills by filing claims against the property. This type of claim is called a "mechanic's lien." The purpose is to give protection to people whose work or materials are used to benefit property. As an abstract legal principle, this is fair and equitable. But in actual practice, a naive owner can be socked with several liens even after he's finished paying the contract price.

The requirements for perfecting a mechanic's lien vary from place to place. But in many states, the owner can be trapped into paying twice, if he's not careful. In most jurisdictions, the claim of lien doesn't have to be filed until several days or even months after the work is finished. Where that rule prevails, it's quite possible that you, as the owner, might not even be aware of any unpaid bills when the job is done. You could innocently pay the contractor the full balance due, and still be vulnerable to a lien filed later. In addition, in a great many states, an unpaid supplier or laborer can file a lien even though the original contractor has defaulted or abandoned the job.

How can you protect yourself? One of the best ways, as mentioned earlier, is to require a bond. Equally as important is to deal with a reputable and financially responsible contractor (Section A). But if you haven't been furnished a bond, and you have any doubt about the solvency of the contractor, you should ask him to give you a notarized statement of the names and addresses of all the laborers, subcontractors and material suppliers, before he gets too far into the work. Then have him give you a "lien waiver" signed by all of them. If there are only three or four involved, he shouldn't have much of a strain doing this. A proposed form is shown at the end of this chapter (Form 5). If he objects, though, or tells you he can't do it, then ask him, as the job nears its completion, to give you the amounts owing to the various suppliers and workmen. You can verify these figures by telephone or letter. You should then make separate checks, payable jointly to the contractor and the suppliers for each bill. Many contractors won't be overjoyed with this proposal, and may even be insulted; but if they're planning to pay for the work and materials furnished, they shouldn't object.

In big commercial jobs, where payment is made in stages as the work progresses, it's fairly common to require an affidavit from the builder, at the time of each payment, listing all unpaid bills, and obtaining waivers of lien. But this usually isn't practical in a house remodeling job.

Another method is to specify in the original contract that no liens will be filed. Some states won't recognize this provision, but it won't hurt to insert it.

In a few localities, you can limit your liability to the amount of the contract price, if you record the contract. However, this is seldom done. It's advisable to ask a lawyer if your state has such a statute.

Regardless of what protective steps you take as the work is in progress, there should be no confusion of what you should do when the work is completed. You should always demand a waiver of lien, or release, from each of the suppliers and subcontractors, before you make final payment. (This would include, in the typical situation, the carpenter, electrician, plumber, plasterer, roofer, etc.) As a very minimum, in *every* case, you should require that the contractor give you his own affidavit of completion, as described in the next section.

F. Is a Paid Receipt Enough?

The average homeowner, when the work is completed, will usually pay the balance of the money to the contractor; get a receipt marked "paid in full"; and be content that all's well. However, don't go congratulating yourself yet. In a great many states, this isn't enough; if all you get is a paid receipt, you can be in deep trouble. Many legislatures, in trying to bend over backwards to protect the laborer and material supplier, have passed laws that unintentionally set an ambush for the unsophisticated owner. These statutes often require you to hold back a certain percentage of the final payment—sometimes ten to twenty percent—until the contractor gives you a *sworn* notarized statement that there are no unpaid bills (or, if he does owe money, he has to list who hasn't been paid). A form of contractor's affidavit of completion is reproduced as Form 6 at the end of this chapter.

What happens if you don't know about this law, and you pay the contractor without getting the affidavit? It's possible you can be forced to pay all the outstanding bills, and actually end up spending much more than the original agreed price. And by this time, your contractor has either flown the coop, or is out of business.

By getting the contractor's affidavit, you're legally protected, in most places. Make sure, though, that you have the affidavit *before* you make the last payment. Even if the contractor gives you a false statement, you'll be protected (and he can be prosecuted). If the affidavit shows some bills outstanding, verify the amounts with the person listed, and issue checks payable jointly to the contractor and the unpaid supplier or subcontractor.

G. What If a Lien Is Filed?

Even though you've carefully selected your contractor, entered into an air-tight agreement, and conscientiously watched the progress of the work, it's still possible that something can turn sour. The contractor can die or go bankrupt; some of the materials can be defective; a subcontractor might default.

And before you know it, a lien is filed against your property. Don't go to pieces. Remember, the lien is merely a formal claim that says the "lienor" (the one filing it) thinks he's entitled to some money. He still has to file a lawsuit to legally enforce the lien, and to prove the claim.

If the job is still in progress, you should immediately stop making any more payments to the contractor until the lien is released. It's possible there's some genuine dispute between the contractor and the lienor regarding the amount owing or the quality of the work performed; or it could be that the contractor has been slow in paying. In any case, it should be up to him to clear it quickly. If he can't, then you'll have to step in. Sometimes the money can be put in escrow with a bank, a lawyer, or a title insurance company, until the argument is settled. It's also possible to have a surety bond put up in court, to release the lien.

A much more troublesome situation arises when the contractor defaults or completely abandons the job. When that happens, it's not out of the ordinary for a number of subcontractors or material-men to be unpaid and to file liens. There's a conflict among the various laws; and in many states, the right to a lien depends on whether the owner owes anything to the contractor. You can't rely on this, though, in all sections of the country. Many courts allow a lienor to recover the full amount due him, even if nothing is owing to the contractor as a result of his default. If the contractor furnished you a surety bond (see Section D), you'll be safe. But if you're caught without a bond, you'll have to try to compromise and adjust the claims the best way you can. You could probably sue the contractor, but that can take several months.

If the contractor's default will make the job cost more money than the agreed price, make a formal demand that the contractor pay it. Then wait ten days. But don't be too optimistic that this will get you any results, since he may be out of business by that time. The best chance, then, is to offer a reduced cash settlement to the lienors. Most of them will accept, rather than go to court. You might have to wait as long as 90 days after the work stops to be sure you know about all the unpaid bills (since suppliers usually have that long to file liens). This is one of those times when a lawyer can be a good person to rescue you. Doing it yourself here can be dangerous when the liens start popping.

One small consolation is that on the typical home improvement job, there's a good likelihood that liens won't be filed, even when there's a default. This is because the subcontractors and workmen are usually slow-moving, and often wait too long to file the lien. In most states, there's a short statutory limitation period, ranging from 45 to 90 days.

One further thought: if somebody does file a lien, be careful about paying him directly, without notifying the contractor. Several statutes require you to give a written notice to the contractor (or get his signed consent) before you can pay any money straight to a supplier or subcontractor.

H. Arguments with the Contractor

A scrap with the contractor will usually begin over the quality of the work. There can be a multitude of additional problems: he's not doing the job fast enough; the materials are inferior; the workmen are second-rate; some of the agreed repairs have been left out; the supervision is inadequate or nonexistent; there's been a change from what he "promised" you. The list is endless.

About the most sympathetic comment that can be made is: you're in good company. Very few, if any, jobs are perfect. There's almost always some aggravation, or some detail that isn't the way you pictured it.

If the contractor is reputable, he'll try to correct the complaint. But even a conscientious builder resents cute remarks and sarcastic innuendoes. So don't insult him. Point out to him, courteously the problems. It's not improper to list the complaints in an informal letter or written memo. Go slow, though, on preparing legal-sounding correspondence at this early stage. If you get too formal, or if a lawyer writes the letter for you at this point, you're liable to end up in a courtroom. A suggested form of letter is at the end of this chapter (Form 7).

If your polite prodding gets no response, or if the contractor insists there's nothing wrong with the work, then this can be a sign of danger ahead. Try writing a second and firmer letter, as shown in Form 8. If a bonding company is involved, notify the agent in writing immediately.

If you're still having trouble after the second letter (and there's no bond), you'll probably need to invest in a lawyer's services. Find out approximately what he'll charge you; it'll usually be on a "time" basis for this type of case (see Chapter 11, page 324).

You have one advantage on your side, and it's a strong one. Because of the adverse publicity that the house remodelers have received in recent years, most judges and juries tend to favor the homeowner. If you wind up in court, you'll generally have the upper hand. Even without an expert witness testifying for you, you'll be permitted to explain in court the various defects and inadequacies in the work.

Be aware of this problem, though: if there are some substantial flaws right from the start, don't make any payments. The contractor might tell you he'll correct it "first thing tomorrow," or that it's the subcontractor's fault, and he'll "get after him right away." But if you make some partial payments on these assurances, before the work is corrected, a court might decide that you "waived" the defect and accepted it. If you feel you *must* make a payment, get a short written statement from the contractor, something like:

Date ....

The contractor acknowledges that the payment of $..............................
received today, is not a waiver or acceptance, by the owner, of the following claimed defects: (itemized below)

....

....

and the contractor agrees to correct these by ....(date).

Contractor:

....
Name of Contractor

By ....
Title

How should you react when the contractor refuses to do any more work unless he's paid? Don't let him blackjack you into paying him before the money is earned, or while there are still major defects not corrected. Many of the "here-today-gone-tomorrow" repairers will demand "pre-payments" before they go ahead with a promised stage of the improvements. Don't fall for it. You're likely to be left with an unfinished job on your hands, and no contractor.

You can also get into arguments over "extras" (see Section B). The unethical contractor will present you with a tidy little bill at the end of the job for "additional work" he claims to have done, not called for by the contract. If you object, he'll threaten to file a lien against your house. The surest way to cover yourself for this type of extortion is to insist, in the contract, that all extras be agreed upon in writing; then you have to practice self-control so as not to waver from that requirement.

If your agreement doesn't contain such a clause, or you haven't followed it, you'll need to negotiate the "extras" with him as best you can. Don't be afraid of the threat of a lien. In many states, if he files a fraudulent claim, he's subject to punitive damages. Even after filing a lien, he still has to sue you to collect; and the lien is discharged automatically, usually in a year, if he doesn't bring suit to enforce it (in fact, in some states, this period can be shortened considerably by filing a "notice of contest," disputing the lien). He might scream and cuss at you, but he'll be reluctant to go to court. And never forget, that he'd like to avoid lawyers as much as you would.

Form 1

PROPERTY IMPROVEMENT CONTRACT

Date _____19_____

Selling Dealer _____

Address _____

Purchaser's Name _____

Purchaser's Address _____

Description of Improvements and Material to be Used:

The Seller hereby agrees to and does sell and agrees to fabricate, manufacture and install in a workmanlike manner according to standard practices for _____herein referred to as Purchaser or as Maker, who hereby agrees to and does purchase the above described improvements and materials which are within a reasonable time to be installed on the premises situate in __ County, Florida, owned by the Purchaser and described as: _____

_____

Payment of said time balance shall be made in _____equal successive monthly installments of $_____ each, commencing on the _____ day of_____, 19_____, and continuing on the same day of each month thereafter until paid, except the final installment which shall be the balance due, and said obligation may be evidenced by a promissory note executed by the Purchaser which the Purchaser shall execute promptly upon request of the Seller (and when executed, such note and the obligation therein contained, shall become the sole obligation to pay in connection with this contract, sup-	Total Cash Price .... $_____ Less Down Payment_____ $_____ (Describe) Difference .... $_____ Add Official Fees _____ $_____ (Describe) Add Insurance _____ $_____ (Describe) Principal Balance .... $_____ Add Time Price Differential .... $_____ Time Balance .... $_____

planting the obligation herein set forth) and which note may contain all or any of the following provisions which are hereby made a part hereof and are agreed to by the Purchaser:

"If this instrument is referred to an attorney for collection or enforcement, the maker agrees to pay a reasonable attorney's fee, plus court costs. If the maker is delinquent for a period of ten (10) days in the payment of any installment hereunder, the holder hereof may collect, and the maker agrees to pay, a delinquency charge, such charge to be 5% of the amount of the installments delinquent."

"Any action to enforce payment hereof or any indulgences, arrangements, renewals or extensions granted the maker shall not be a waiver of or affect any rights of the holder."

"If any of said installment payments shall not be made promptly when due, the holder hereof may at the option of the holder, without notice or demand, declare the entire balance due hereunder to be immediately due and payable."

"As this contract may be assigned immediately, purchaser waives any cause of action against or defense to a cause of action by any such assignee in respect to any alleged defects in the material or services rendered hereunder, and purchaser agrees to settle all claims, defenses, set-offs and counterclaims it may have against seller and not set up any thereof against such assignee."

NOTICE TO BUYER

1. Do not sign this Contract before you read it or if it contains any blank spaces.

2. You are entitled to an exact copy of the Contract you sign.

3. You have the right to repay this Contract in full and, under certain conditions, receive a partial refund of the time price differential.

Executed in Triplicate, one copy of which was delivered to, and receipt is hereby acknowledged by Buyer, this _____day of _____, 19__.

Approved and Accepted:

_____(SEAL)   (X) _____(SEAL)
   (Dealer-Seller)   (Purchaser Sign here)

By _____   (X) _____(SEAL)
   (Title)   (Purchaser Sign Here)

The Purchaser understands and agrees that any provisions on the reverse side hereof are hereby incorporated by reference and constitute a part of this Contract.

ADDITIONAL PROVISIONS
ACKNOWLEDGMENT BY SELLER

STATE OF FLORIDA)
COUNTY OF DUVAL)

Before me, the undersigned authority, on this day personally appeared _____, (Seller) to me personally known and who acknowledged before me that he executed the foregoing property improvement contract as Seller, or as the duly authorized officer thereof, and said person is known to me to be the individual described in and who executed said conditional sale contract.

In Witness Whereof, I have hereunto set my hand and official seal this _____day of _____, 19_____.

_____
Notary Public, My commission expires: _____

ASSIGNMENT BY SELLER

FOR VALUE RECEIVED, the within contract and all right, title and interest of the undersigned Seller therein is hereby sold, assigned and transferred to _____, its successors and assigns, without recourse.

_____
                Seller

By _____

Form 2

NOTICE OF COMMENCEMENT
[Used in Florida]

Property to be improved: ....
....
General description of improvement: ....
....
Name and address of Owner:

Extent of Owner's interest in property: .... fee simple
.... other ....
Name and address of fee simple title holder if other than Owner:

(If ownership is other than fee simple, the name and address of the fee simple title holder must also be given)
Name and address of Contractor: ....
....
Name and address of surety on payment bond, if any, and amount of bond: .... Amount $...................................
Name and address, within the state, of a person other than the Owner signing this Notice, designated to receive service of notices and other documents: ....
Name and address of person to receive copy of Lienor's Notice (Optional) ....
   Dated this .... day of .... 19............

....
                                 Signature of Owner or authorized agent
Subscribed and sworn to before me this .... day of
.... 19............

....
                                 Notary Public. My commission expires:

(The previous notice is recorded with the Clerk of the Court of the County where the land is located, prior to commencement of improvements. A certified copy is posted at the site of the improvements)

Form 3

PROPERTY IMPROVEMENT CONTRACT

Date ....

Owner: ....

Contractor: ....

Property:

Legal Description, if known:

Street Address:

Owner and Contractor hereby agree that Contractor shall furnish and install the following improvements and materials for the above described property: (itemize in detail)

I. The cost of the improvements, materials and work shall be paid as follows: (Check applicable provisions.)

__1. Total cash price is $ ...., to be paid in the following manner: (Check applicable provisions.)

__A. When the work is fully completed and the Contractor furnishes Owner an affidavit showing completion and payment of all lien claimants (suppliers, subcontractors and laborers), and lien waivers or releases from all such lien claimants.

__B. Part payments as follows:

__(1) $ .... as a down payment, to be paid only after Contractor files and posts such notices and statements as may be specified or required by state law.

__(2) Payments as the work progresses, as follows: ....

__(3) Final payment of $ .... or ....% of the contract price, to be paid upon completion of the work and after Contractor furnishes Owner an affidavit showing completion and payment of all lien claimants (suppliers, subcontractors and laborers), and lien waivers or releases from all such lien claimants.

__2. If not paid in cash, the contract shall be paid as follows:

__A. $ .... as a down payment, to be paid only after Contractor files and posts such notices and statements as may be specified or required by state law.

__B. The balance to be payable after completion of the work and Contractor furnishing Owner an affidavit showing completion and payment of all lien claimants (suppliers, subcontractors and laborers), and lien waivers or releases from all such lien claimants. Payments shall be made by Owner executing and delivering to Contractor a promissory note with simple interest at ....% per year, payable $ .... per month, commencing 30 days after completion, for .... months, until the full amount of principal

and interest has been paid; and by execution and delivery of a mortgage on the said property, in the customary form used in the community, securing the note. Said note and mortgage shall contain provisions
for acceleration of payments, and payment of attorney's fees and court
costs, in the event of default. The note shall allow Owner the privilege
of prepayment without penalty.

__3. By proceeds from one of the following:

__A. F.H.A. Title I loan in the amount of $ ....

__B. A loan from a lending institution in the amount of
$ ....

This agreement is contingent upon Owner's qualifying for such loan.
If Owner is not approved for such loan, then:

__this agreement shall be void

__owner shall have the option of paying as set forth in paragraph
numbered 2, above.

II. The parties agree as follows: (Check applicable provision.)

__1. Contractor shall, prior to commencing the work, furnish Owner
a payment and performance bond from a reputable insurance company, licensed to do business in the state, such bond to be conditioned
upon satisfactory completion of the contract by Contractor, and payment of all subcontractors, suppliers, materialmen, laborers, and lienors.

__2. No surety bond shall be furnished.

III. All workmanship and materials shall be of good quality, and all
materials shall be new.

IV. Contractor shall pay for and furnish all permits, licenses, and
other documents required by any governmental agency or department.

V. Contractor shall carry workmen's compensation insurance, and
liability insurance protecting Owner and Contractor from all claims because of bodily injury or death, and property damage, arising out of the
improvements or repairs, whether such improvements or repairs are by
the Contractor, a supplier, subcontractor or anyone directly or indirectly
employed by any of them. Such liability insurance shall be in an amount
not less than what is commonly spoken of as "100,000/300,000/5,000."
A copy of such policies, or a certificate from the insurer, verifying coverage, shall be furnished Owner before commencement of the work.

VI. All claims by Contractor for extra costs, alterations, or additional
work, must be in writing and signed by Owner. If any alterations cause
labor or materials to be eliminated, Owner shall be entitled to a credit
on the contract price.

VII. The Contractor shall correct or remedy any work or materials not
complying with the contract, and any defects in the construction or
repairs, due to workmanship or materials furnished by him, his suppliers, or his subcontractors, which appear within one year from the
completion of the work.

VIII. If the Contractor fails to proceed with the work, with reasonable diligence, or fails to perform any term of the contract, then the Owner, after 7 days written notice to the Contractor, may proceed himself with the work and may deduct the cost thereof from any payments due the Contractor; or the Owner may terminate the contract, take possession of all materials, tools, and appliances, and complete the work. If the expense exceeds the unpaid balance, the Contractor shall be liable for the difference.

IX. Contractor shall: (Check applicable provision.)

__1. Use due diligence to complete the work within a reasonable time.

__2. Complete the work no later than ....

__3. If the work is not completed by ...., Contractor shall pay Owner as follows (insert provisions for damages) ....

X. Upon payment of the balance due under the contract, Contractor agrees that no liens shall be filed; that not withstanding the foregoing, Contractor shall promptly pay and discharge any liens or claims arising out of this contract or the work and improvements, and shall hold Owner harmless from loss or damage resulting from a failure to do so.

XI. Contractor warrants and represents that all governmental ordinances, laws and requirements shall be complied with.

XII. Owner shall have the right to withhold any payments as a result of: defective work not corrected by Contractor; liens filed; damage caused by Contractor; or failure of Contractor to pay for materials and labor. Owner shall have the option to make checks payable jointly to Contractor and subcontractors and suppliers.

XIII. This contract contains the entire agreement of the parties, and neither party shall be bound by any statement or representation not contained herein, unless made in writing, and signed by the parties.

XIV. Other provisions:

OWNER:

Witnesses:

.... (SEAL)

....
Signature

....

.... (SEAL)
Signature

CONTRACTOR:

.... (SEAL)
Name of Contractor

By ....
Title

Form 4

THE STANDARD FORM OF AGREEMENT
BETWEEN OWNER AND CONTRACTOR
THE AIA SHORT FORM CONTRACT FOR
SMALL CONSTRUCTION CONTRACTS
WHERE THE BASIS OF PAYMENTS IS A
STIPULATED SUM

For other contracts the AIA issues the standard forms of owner-contractor agreements and the standard general conditions for the construction of buildings for use in connection therewith.

THIS AGREEMENT

made the   day of   in the year Nineteen Hundred and

BY AND BETWEEN

hereinafter called the Owner, and

hereinafter called the Contractor.

WITNESSETH,

That the Owner and the Contractor, for the considerations hereinafter named agree as follows:

ARTICLE 1. SCOPE OF THE WORK—
The Contractor shall furnish all of the material and perform all of the work for

as shown on the Drawings and described in the Specifications entitled

prepared by

all in accordance with the terms of the Contract Documents.

ARTICLE 2. TIME OF COMPLETION—The work shall be commenced and completed as follows:

ARTICLE 3. CONTRACT SUM—The Owner shall pay the Contractor for the performance of the Contract subject to the additions and deductions provided therein in current funds, the sum of

dollars ($)

ARTICLE 4. PROGRESS PAYMENTS—The Owner shall make payments on account of the contract, upon requisition by the Contractor, as follows:

ARTICLE 5. ACCEPTANCE AND FINAL PAYMENT—Final payment shall

be due _____ days after completion of the work, provided the contract be then fully performed, subject to the provisions of Article 16 of the General Conditions.

ARTICLE 6. CONTRACT DOCUMENTS—Contract Documents are as noted in Article 1 of the General Conditions. The following is an enumeration of the drawings and specifications:

GENERAL CONDITIONS

ARTICLE 1. CONTRACT DOCUMENTS

The contract includes the Agreement and its General Conditions, the Drawing, and the Specifications. Two or more copies of each, as required, shall be signed by both parties and one signed copy of each retained by each party.

The intent of these documents is to include all labor, materials, appliances and services of every kind necessary for the proper execution of the work, and the terms and conditions of payment thereof.

The documents are to be considered as one, and whatever is called for by any one of the documents shall be as binding as if called for by all.

ARTICLE 2. SAMPLES

The Contractor shall furnish for approval all samples as directed. The work shall be in accordance with approved samples.

ARTICLE 3. MATERIALS, APPLIANCES, EMPLOYEES

Except as otherwise noted, the Contractor shall provide and pay for all materials, labor, tools, water, power and other items necessary to complete the work.

Unless otherwise specified, all materials shall be new, and both workmanship and materials shall be of good quality.

All workmen and sub-contractors shall be skilled in their trades.

ARTICLE 4. ROYALTIES AND PATENTS

The Contractor shall pay all royalties and license fees. He shall defend all suits or claims for infringement of any patent rights and shall save the Owner harmless from loss on account thereof.

ARTICLE 5. SURVEYS, PERMITS, AND REGULATIONS

The Owner shall furnish all surveys unless otherwise specified. Permits and licenses necessary for the prosecution of the work shall be secured and paid for by the Contractor. Easements for permanent structures or permanent changes in existing facilities shall be secured and paid for by the Owner, unless otherwise specified. The Contractor shall comply with all laws and regulations bearing on the conduct of the work and shall notify the Owner if the drawings and specifications are at variance therewith.

ARTICLE 6. PROTECTION OF WORK, PROPERTY, AND PERSONS

The Contractor shall adequately protect the work, adjacent property and the public and shall be responsible for any damage or injury due to his act or neglect.

ARTICLE 7. ACCESS TO WORK

The Contractor shall permit and facilitate observation of the work by the Owner and his agents and public authorities at all times.

ARTICLE 8. CHANGES IN THE WORK

The Owner may order changes in the work, the Contract Sum being adjusted accordingly. All such orders and adjustments shall be in writing. Claims by the Contractor for extra cost must be made in writing before executing the work involved.

ARTICLE 9. CORRECTION OF WORK

The Contractor shall re-execute any work that fails to conform to the requirements of the contract and that appears during the progress of the work, and shall remedy any defects due to faulty materials or workmanship which appear within a period of one year from the date of completion of the contract. The provisions of this article apply to work done by subcontractors as well as to work done by direct employees of the Contractor.

ARTICLE 10. OWNER'S RIGHT TO TERMINATE THE CONTRACT

Should the Contractor neglect to prosecute the work properly, or fail to perform any provision of the contract, the Owner, after seven days' written notice to the Contractor, and his surety if any may, without prejudice to any other remedy he may have, make good the deficiencies and may deduct the cost thereof from the payment then or thereafter due the Contractor or, at his option, may terminate the contract and take possession of all materials, tools, and appliances and finish the work by such means as he sees fit, and if the unpaid balance of the contract price exceeds the expense of finishing the work, such excess shall be paid to the Contractor, but if such expense exceeds such unpaid balance, the Contractor shall pay the difference to the Owner.

ARTICLE 11. CONTRACTOR'S RIGHT TO TERMINATE CONTRACT

Should the work be stopped by any public authority for a period of thirty days or more, through no fault of the Contractor, or should the work be stopped through act or neglect of the Owner for a period of seven days, or should the Owner fail to pay the Contractor any payment within seven days after it is due, then the Contractor upon seven days' written notice to the Owner, may stop work or terminate the contract and recover from the Owner payment for all work executed and any loss sustained and reasonable profit and damages.

ARTICLE 12. PAYMENTS

Payments shall be made as provided in the Agreement. The making and acceptance of the final payment shall constitute a waiver of all claims by the Owner, other than those arising from unsettled liens or from faulty work appearing thereafter, as provided for in Article 9, and of all claims by the Contractor except any previously made and still unsettled. Payments otherwise due may be withheld on account of defective work not remedied, liens filed, damage by the Contractor to others not adjusted, or failure to make payments properly to subcontractors or for material or labor.

ARTICLE 13. CONTRACTOR'S LIABILITY INSURANCE

The Contractor shall maintain such insurance as will protect him from claims under workmen's compensation acts and other employee benefits acts, from claims for damages because of bodily injury, including death, and from claims for damages to property which may arise both out of and during operations under this contract, whether such operations be by himself or by any subcontractor or anyone directly or indirectly employed by either of them. This insurance shall be written for not less than any limits of liability specified as part of this contract. Certificates of such insurance shall be filed with the Owner and architect.

ARTICLE 14. OWNER'S LIABILITY INSURANCE

The Owner shall be responsible for and at his option may maintain such insurance as will protect him from his contingent liability to others for damages because of bodily injury, including death, which may arise from operations under this contract, and any other liability for damages which the Contractor is required to insure under any provision of this contract.

ARTICLE 15. FIRE INSURANCE WITH EXTENDED COVERAGE

The Owner shall effect and maintain fire insurance with extended coverage upon the entire structure on which the work of this contract is to be done to one hundred per cent of the insurable value thereof, including items of labor and materials connected therewith whether in or adjacent to the structure insured, materials in place or to be used as part of the permanent construction including surplus materials, shanties, protective fences, bridges, temporary structures, miscellaneous materials and supplies incident to the work, and such scaffoldings, stagings, towers, forms, and equipment as are not owned or rented by the contractor, the cost of which is included in the cost of the work. EXCLUSIONS: The insurance does not cover any tools owned by mechanics, any tools, equipment, scaffolding, staging, towers, and forms owned or rented by the contractor, the capital value of which is not included in the cost of the work, or any cook shanties, bunk houses or other structures erected for housing the workmen. The loss, if any, is to be made adjustable with and payable to the Owner as Trustee for the insured and contractors and subcontractors as their interests may appear, except in such cases as may require payment of all or a proportion of said insurance to be made to a mortgagee as his interests may appear.

Certificates of such insurance shall be filed with the Contractor if he so requires. If the Owner fails to effect or maintain insurance as above and so notifies the Contractor, the Contractor may insure his own interests and that of the subcontractors and charge the cost thereof to the Owner. If the Contractor is damaged by failure of the Owner to maintain such insurance or to so notify the Contractor, he may recover as stipulated in the contract for recovery of damages. If other special insurance not herein provided for is required by the Contractor, the Owner shall effect such insurance at the Contractor's expense by appropriate riders to his fire insurance policy. The Owner, Contractor, and all subcontractors waive all rights, each against the others, for damages caused by fire or other perils covered by insurance provided for under the terms of this article except such rights as they may have to the proceeds of insurance held by the Owner as Trustee.

The Owner shall be responsible for and at his option may insure against loss of use of his existing property, due to fire or otherwise, however caused.

If required in writing by any party in interest, the Owner as Trustee shall, upon the occurrence of loss, give bond for the proper performance of his duties. He shall deposit any money received from insurance in an account separate from all his other funds and he shall distribute it in accordance with such agreement as the parties in interest may reach or under an award of arbitrators appointed, one by the Owner, another by joint action of the other parties in interest, all other procedure being as provided elsewhere in the contract for arbitration. If after loss no special agreement is made, replacement of injured work shall be ordered and executed as provided for changes in the work.

The Trustee shall have power to adjust and settle any loss with the insurers unless one of the Contractors interested shall object in writing within three working days of the occurrence of loss, and thereupon arbitrators shall be chosen as above. The Trustee shall in that case make settlement with the insurers in accordance with the directions of such arbitrators, who shall also, if distribution by arbitration is required, direct such distribution.

ARTICLE 16. LIENS

The final payment shall not be due until the Contractor has delivered to the Owner a complete release of all liens arising out of this contract, or receipts in full covering all labor and materials for which a lien could be filed, or a bond satisfactory to the Owner indemnifying him against any lien.

ARTICLE 17. SEPARATE CONTRACTS

The Owner has the right to let other contracts in connection with the work and the Contractor shall properly cooperate with any such other contractors.

ARTICLE 18. THE ARCHITECT'S STATUS

The Architect shall be the Owner's representative during the construction period. He has authority to stop the work if necessary to insure its proper execution. He shall certify to the Owner when payments under the contract are due and the amounts to be paid. He shall make decisions on all claims of the Owner or Contractor. All his decisions are subject to arbitration.

ARTICLE 19. ARBITRATION

Any disagreement arising out of this contract or from the breach thereof shall be submitted to arbitration, and judgment upon the award rendered may be entered in the court of the forum, state or federal, having jurisdiction. It is mutually agreed that the decision of the arbitrators shall be a condition precedent to any right of legal action that either party may have against the other. The arbitration shall be held under the Standard Form of Arbitration Procedure of The American Institute of Architects or under the Rules of the American Arbitration Association.

ARTICLE 20. CLEANING UP

The Contractor shall keep the premises free from accumulation of waste material and rubbish and at the completion of the work he shall remove from the premises all rubbish, implements and surplus materials and leave the building broom-clean.

IN WITNESS WHEREOF the parties hereto executed this Agreement, the day and year first above written.

Owner

....

Contractor

....

Form 5

LIEN WAIVER

For value received, we, the undersigned, having furnished the following services, labor or material, namely:

....
                    (description of services, labor or material)
for the property located at ....
owned by ....
do hereby waive and release all right that we have now or hereafter to a lien upon the above property.

   We warrant that we have the right to execute this waiver and that we have not assigned our claim for payment or our right of lien; that all laborers and suppliers employed by us, or dealing with us, have been paid, and have no claims against the property or materials.

                              ....
                              By ....
                              Sworn to and subscribed before
                              me this .... day of ....
                              19............

                              ....
                              Notary Public, State of ....
                              County of ....
                              My commission expires: ....

Form 6

CONTRACTOR'S AFFIDAVIT OF COMPLETION

State of ....
County of ....
   Before me, the undersigned notary public, personally appeared ...., who, being first duly sworn, says:

   1. On or about ..., the Contractor, ..., entered into
                                        Name of Contractor
an agreement with the Owner ...., for improvements
                                        Name of Owner
to the following property located at ....

   2. The undersigned is either the owner or a principal officer of the Contractor, and has personally supervised the performance of the contract.

   3. The improvements and work have been fully completed and the agreement fully performed. All persons, firms and corporations dealing with the Contractor as subcontractors, laborers, suppliers of material, and otherwise, in connection with said improvements, have been fully

paid and their releases are hereto attached, with the exception of the following:

NAME OF LIEN CLAIMANT AMT. DUE SERVICES OR MATERIALS

4. The Contractor has in no way assigned, pledged or transferred said contract, or any amounts due or to become due thereunder.

5. In consideration of the balance due, the Contractor hereby agrees to pay and discharge, promptly, any liens or claims arising during the statutory period for filing such liens or claims, and shall hold the Owner harmless from loss or damage resulting or arising from a failure to do so.

....
Name of Contractor

By ....
Title

Sworn to and subscribed before
me this .... day of ....
19............

....
Notary Public, State and County
Aforesaid. My commission
expires: ....

RECEIVED from the Owner this .... day of ....
19............, $................................, as balance in full of all amounts due and to become due in connection with the said contract and improvements.

....
Name of Contractor

By ....
Title

Form 7

FORM LETTER TO CONTRACTOR OUTLINING COMPLAINTS

16 Squirrel Street
New York, N.Y.

Date _____

Atomic Contractors
123 Main Street
New York, N.Y.

Gentlemen:

I'd appreciate very much your taking care of the following items, in connection with the work you're doing on our house:

1. The window in the den is hard to open.
2. The door doesn't lock properly.
3. The vinyl tile has cracks in it.
4. The paint on the bedroom wall is caked and streaked.
Thank you for your prompt attention.

Sincerely yours,

_____

Form 8

SECOND LETTER TO CONTRACTOR

16 Squirrel Street
New York, N.Y.
Date _____

Atomic Contractors
123 Main Street
New York, N.Y.

Gentlemen:

I've previously called your attention to a number of complaints we have with the work you're doing on our house.

I'm quite disappointed that you haven't corrected them by now, and I'm unable to understand why it's taken so long for you to begin fixing them.

I ask that you take immediate steps to correct these items, no later than _____, so that we can avoid the unpleasantness of having to take this up with our attorney.

We feel sure that you'll give this matter your promptest consideration. Thank you.

Sincerely yours,

_____

CHAPTER 11

Do You Really Need A Lawyer?

LAWERS, OR THEIR PREDECESSORS, HAVE BEEN WITH US SINCE THE dawn of recorded history. In fact, if you believe a story that made the rounds a few years ago, the practice of law is the oldest profession of all. The tale has to do with an argument between a doctor, an attorney, and an engineer, as to which of their callings had been in existence the longest.

"Everyone knows," said the physician, "that the practice of medicine is the oldest profession. Why, when God created Eve from Adam's rib, He performed an act of surgery. So medicine is the oldest profession."

"Not so," protested the engineer. "even before Adam, God created the earth and the heavens. And anybody can tell you that this act of creation was a feat of planning and engineering. So engineering is the oldest profession," he added proudly. "Why, before that, there was nothing but chaos and confusion."

"Aha," beamed the lawyer, "but who caused the chaos and confusion!"

A. When Can You Get By On Your Own?

There are certain legal matters where it's obvious you should have a lawyer. If you're charged with a crime; if you have a complicated and technical claim for damages, such as a slander action or a patent infringement suit; where you're merging one corporation with another business; when you're foreclosing a mortgage—

321

these are all situations that are far too complex and cumbersome for the average layman or businessman to handle. There are many more, of course—times when an attorney's special training will be indispensable to you; and times when it's apparent (and has often been said) that if you tried to act as your *own* lawyer, you'd have a fool for a client.

But nevertheless, there are occasions when you can legitimately "do-it-yourself." We've analyzed some of these in the previous chapters. If you don't have the patience or the time to tackle them without an attorney, then at the very least, you should know some of the ground rules and requirements that have been explained in these pages, before you see a lawyer.

B. How to Pick One If You Need Him

If you have never used a lawyer, you may be somewhat in the dark about picking one. It's not true that "they're all alike"; and it's important that you use care in choosing one. The best way is to talk to your friends, relatives, or business acquaintances who deal with attorneys. Find out who they use as their lawyer; what kind of cases he handles; his ability; something about him. Try to get more than one opinion, if you can.

Your bank, or its trust department, can recommend a lawyer to you. The bank should be especially helpful if you're looking for a lawyer who handles estates and wills. If you're working for a business, you might consider using the company attorney.

Very often you can find out the name of a good lawyer from your accountant or bookkeeper. They deal with attorneys on various financial and tax matters, and can usually direct you to a competent one.

The telephone directory might not be much help in certain places, since lawyers have generally not been permitted to cite their special field as doctors do; but this is now changing, and in many states attorneys have been "certified" to practice a specialty, and can list it in the phone book and elsewhere.

Several companies publish law directories of attorneys that practice in the various states. The most complete listing is a multi-volume set distributed by Martindale-Hubbell, Inc. of Summit, New Jersey. It lists all the lawyers in the United States, and in many foreign countries, and then rates them by their ability and reputation. It's not practical to try to buy this directory (unless you're a lawyer). But you can usually find a copy of the directory in the public library or in your county law library, and in some banks. Not every attorney is ranked, so don't draw any adverse conclusion if a lawyer has no rating at all. Many leaders of the bar, for one reason or another, sometimes aren't rated (occasionally they fail to submit background information). Martindale-Hubbell, in addition, summarizes the types of cases that many of the attorneys handle.

In the last few years, lawyers have been allowed to advertise for the first time. The ad can give you some idea of the fees charged and the types of cases handled, but you still won't know too much about the attorney's ability or experience.

You can also call your local bar association for the name of a lawyer, although it's rare that they'll specifically recommend any-one by name. Many communities or bar associations have a "law-yer reference service," and will give you the name of an attorney to call. Technically, though, they won't be "recommending" the lawyer. They merely have an alphabetical list of licensed attorneys who have signed up for the program, and they'll refer you to the next name on the list. Unfortunately, a large number of experienced lawyers don't put their names on the referral list. Those that do usually indicate the type of cases they prefer to take (divorce, real estate, accidents, and so forth), so you'll ordinarily be referred to someone who's at least interested in your type of problem. This is, naturally, better than the hit-or-miss approach of just picking a name out of the phone book, but it's still not the ideal method. If the other techniques fail, though, you might try it. In the typical situation, you'll be charged a prearranged nominal fee for a con-sultation (the reference service will advise how much it is, in ad-vance), and if further legal work is needed, the lawyer will estimate his charges, and tell you what his fee will probably run.

If you can't afford a lawyer at all, then you should call the legal aid association in your locality. Under various federal and state programs, a lawyer's services can be made available, if you don't have the money. Many of these legal aid associations have set up neighborhood law centers to give advice and help to the needy, without charge.

C. The "Specialist"

In keeping pace with the problems of the modern age, a large segment of the legal profession has begun to "specialize." You now can deal with "labor lawyers," "accident specialists," "collection attorneys," "tax experts," and "criminal lawyers," to name a few. Unfortunately, in many states, lawyers are still not permitted by their ethics to officially hold themselves out as specialists. There have been strong efforts, in recent years, by the American Bar Association and by state legal groups, to formally recognize specialties, either by requiring a lawyer to practice in a certain field for a minimum period of time, or to have him take prescribed courses or tests.

At present, you can't always be sure that a lawyer is trained in the area of law you're looking for. Often, you won't find a specialty listed on his door or on his business card, or in the phone directory (but more and more attorneys are advertising). The best way to find out is through word-of-mouth from someone who knows him, or has dealt with him. Or you might take your problem to a general practitioner; if he feels he's not qualified to handle your case, he'll refer you to a specialist, or suggest one to you.

D. Fees and Expenses

In earlier chapters, there have been references to fees that are fairly typical in certain cases. But how does a lawyer decide on his charges?

Several factors are commonly considered. The American Bar Association, in its code of ethics, mentions the following as guides, although none, in itself, is necessarily controlling:

1. The time and labor required, the novelty and difficulty of the questions involved, and the skill needed.

2. Whether handling the matter will keep the lawyer from taking on other cases.

3. The customary charge made by other lawyers.

4. The amount involved, and the results obtained.

5. The time limitations imposed by the client or the circumstances.

6. The experience, reputation, and ability of the lawyer.

7. Whether the fee is fixed or contingent.

8. Whether the work is a "one-time" piece of business, or for a regular client.

In general, a lawyer calculates his charges on three main criteria:

1. Time spent.
2. Value involved.
3. Contingency.

If your legal matter consists of work in the lawyer's office, involving a few hours of conferences, preparing routine documents, or simple contracts or leases, he'll often charge on the basis of the time he spends. The average lawyer, particularly in metropolitan areas, charges from $100 to $200 an hour, although you might find lower rates in the "legal clinics" springing up around the country.

But if the case is more complicated, or involves trial preparation, research, negotiations, collection of a claim, or extensive consultations, then the attorney will probably consider the amount of money at stake. You might feel that he shouldn't "penalize" you with a larger fee just because there's more money at issue. But the lawyer's responsibility and legal exposure are proportionately greater in such a case, and you can expect to be charged more.

The third most common type of charge is the contingent fee, used primarily in the accident or personal injury claim (see Chapter 1, page 17). Damages in these cases are generally uncertain, and it's not always easy to estimate, ahead of time, what a fair charge would be. In addition, many injured claimants can't afford to pay a lawyer, other than from the moneys collected. Whatever the reason, though, it's become fairly standard practice for a lawyer to handle such cases on a contingent basis, and to charge a fixed percentage of the recovery.

Never expect a lawyer to give you "free advice." It'll probably be worth what you're paying for it. If you call an attorney on the phone and ask him for a legal opinion or for information, you should be prepared to pay for it. Some people are shocked when the lawyer sends them a bill for twenty or twenty-five dollars, marked "telephone consultation." Remember, you're taking up his time, and he's rendering a service to you, just as if you came to his office. It's not a good policy, though, to get in the habit of getting advice by phone. Too often, important items are overlooked; and if you're asking for information about a legal document, you should let the lawyer at least look at it—not rely on a quick reading over the telephone.

Monthly or yearly "retainers" are often used by large corporations, but are not as popular as they once were. Retainers are fees, paid on a regular basis, for a lawyers' advice and services. Characteristically, you might pay $100 a month, or other agreed figure, and be entitled to unlimited telephone and office consultations, general legal advice, review of documents, and correspondence. Sometimes the retainer won't cover litigation or unusual problems, requiring detailed study or research; you'd be charged extra for those.

The retainer will be based on the estimated time required, the complexity of the cases, and the amounts involved. By custom, the fee is subject to adjustment, if it turns out the amount of work you have is out of proportion to the charge. The retainer has some advantages; you know how much your ordinary services will cost; you're not hesitant about calling your lawyer for day-to-day problems; and you're more likely to be kept informed of changes in the law. But there can be disadvantages, too. Often either the client or the lawyer will feel he's on the short end of it, and not getting his money's worth.

The term "retainer" is often used in a different context, to refer to the "down payment" or "temporary fee" that a lawyer will ask for, at the beginning of a case. For example, if you ask him to represent you in a divorce case, he may tell you his fee will be $750, and that he'd like to have a "retainer" of $300 when he starts the case. You would then "retain" him with the fee.

In the past, many attorneys have used minimum fees suggested by the state or local bar associations. It's unfortunate, however, that these weren't usually made public, and were primarily for lawyers' use; so you had difficulty knowing the amounts. More recently, though, governmental agencies and consumer groups challenged the concept of minimum bar fees, claiming they're a form of price-fixing. These challenges have been generally successful, and now the minimum fee concept has been pretty well discarded. At best, though, there was a great variation in these fees, and past studies by the American Bar Association of minimum fees adopted in various parts of the country showed a remarkably wide difference.

When you talk to a lawyer about his fees, and if you're wondering why he charges what he does, don't forget his fees also include his overhead (secretary, rent, telephone, books, etc.). So if you can't understand how he can charge say, $100 an hour, remember that he has a bundle of bills and expenses to pay out, to maintain his office.

E. The Substitute: the Realtor, the Insurance Agent, the Accountant

Hovering around the fringe of the practice of law, and often stepping over the line, are several other professions. Sometimes you'll need the services of one or more of them. But don't make the mistake of relying on them to give you legal advice.

For instance, the Realtor can be a great help to you in buying or selling property (see Chapter 3, page 78). And he's permitted in most places to draw up a contract for the sale of real estate. But many of them will go further, and also prepare the deed, the mortgage, affidavits, and do a handful of other legal services. Step cautiously if this happens. The Realtor is not a substitute for a lawyer.

The insurance agent, in recent years, has been instrumental in encouraging buy-and-sell agreements in businesses (see Chapter 6), and in helping establish sound estate planning programs. Many of these agents are quite knowledgeable, and can make some excellent suggestions. Don't sell them short. But don't let them prepare any forms for you, or talk you into some way-out insurance arrangements when you don't know or understand what it's all about.

The accountant also works closely with the lawyer; and in many cases, is better equipped to handle tax problems. He usually knows about new rulings from the Internal Revenue Service, as well as recent tax regulations, and can make valuable proposals for handling your financial affairs. But if he says he can also prepare your will or trust instrument, then he's going too far, and is straying into a lawyer's field. Unless he happens to be a licensed attorney (and even then, there's a serious question about whether he's allowed to ethically do both at the same time), he's not supposed to prepare legal documents.

In some sections of the country, you'll see notaries that act as substitutes for attorneys, and serve as a "poor man's lawyer." You're asking for a king-sized lawsuit if you consistently rely on a notary for legal services. Very few of them are properly trained to prepare a deed or other document but some will eagerly jump at the chance if you let them. Don't do it.

F. Lawyers' Ethics

You've probably heard or read about the lawyers' code of ethics. Despite the "shyster" image often portrayed in fiction, the lawyer has the strictest and most exacting rules of conduct of any profession. The lawyer is required to uphold these rules, and a violation can cause him to be disbarred from the practice of law. Some of the more important of the attorney's canons of ethics include the following:

1. A lawyer is not permitted to represent conflicting interests (unless everybody consents).
2. He's not allowed to communicate with an opposing party who has a lawyer (he can only talk to the party's attorney).
3. He's not supposed to testify as a witness for his client (there are exceptions here—for purely formal matters, such as the attesting of a legal paper, and where it's essential to the ends of justice).
4. He isn't permitted to knowingly deceive the Court.
5. He's not allowed to "stir" up litigation or volunteer advice to bring a suit (except in unusual cases, such as with relatives).
6. He's not required to accept every case he's offered; he has the right to turn it down.
7. He isn't permitted to take a case when he's convinced it's solely to harass or injure the opposite party.
8. He's under a rigid duty to preserve his client's confidences and communications, and not to disclose them.

G. What You Should Expect

Like all human flesh, lawyers have their faults. And some, no doubt, have more than others. They're accused of "being in it only for the money," of "getting guilty people off," of being "ambulance chasers," and a multitude of other assorted sins. Sad to say, some attorneys are guilty of these charges.

But don't condemn all of them. If the situation arises when you really need a lawyer, and you can't handle it yourself, don't be afraid that you'll be cheated or taken advantage of. The vast majority of them—notwithstanding the occasional "crooked lawyer" image of the movies—are honest, reputable and fair.

You have the right to expect courteous treatment, to have your case or problem handled promptly, to be kept informed of what's going on, and to be charged a reasonable fee. Let's face it, not every lawyer will pass these tests. But a good one will.

Remember these suggestions when you deal with a lawyer:

1. Tell him the truth. If you exaggerate or hold back pertinent information, or feel you can't trust him, then you have no business hiring him.

2. Discuss fees with him. But don't insist that he tell you exactly, to the penny, what he'll charge. All he can do is estimate (see page 117).

3. Don't be afraid of him; relax.

4. Don't waste his time with jokes and stories; his time is valuable. Get to the point and leave when you're through.

5. If you know you're going to have to use a lawyer, go to him *before* you sign a contract or legal paper, not afterwards.

6. If you go to him for advice, then be sure that you *take* his advice. Too many people pay for a lawyer's time, and then don't do what they're advised.

And above all, remember that the best way to avoid legal entanglements and to stay out of courts is to condition yourself so that you won't put off seeing an attorney when you really need him. It's hoped, then, that with the information and advice in the previous chapters, you'll be in a better position to recognize some of those situations, and to know and understand when—and how—to avoid lawyers.

INDEX

ABOUT THE AUTHOR

Edward Siegel—an experienced Florida lawyer—graduated from the University of Florida College of Law with high honors, and was Executive Editor of the University of Florida Law Review. He occupied the post of Special Assistant Attorney General of Florida and was a Legal Officer in the United States Air Force. Since 1957 Mr. Siegel has been practicing law in Jacksonville, Florida, as a partner in the firm of Adams, Rothstein & Siegel. He is a member of Phi Beta Kappa, the American Bar Association, the Association of Trial Lawyers of America, and both the Florida and Jacksonville Bar Associations.